New Directions
in American Humor

New Directions
in American Humor

Edited by
David E. E. Sloane

The University of Alabama Press
Tuscaloosa and London

∞
The paper on which this book is printed meets the minimum
requirements of American National Standard for
Information Science-Permanence of Paper
for Printed Library Materials,
ANSI Z39.48-1984.

Library of Congress Cataloging-in-Publication Data

New directions in American humor / edited by David E. E. Sloane.
p. cm.
Includes bibliographical references and index.
ISBN 0-8173-0910-1 (alk. paper)
1. American wit and humor—20th century—History and criticism.
I. Sloane, David E. E., 1943- .
PS438.N49 1998
817´.509—dc21
97-45387

British Library Cataloguing-in-Publication Data available

For Bonnie, Rachel, David, and Sarah

Contents

Acknowledgments

We are grateful to the following for their generous help and assistance: Alfred Bendixen and the American Literature Association, original sponsors of the conference organized by the American Humor Studies Association and the Mark Twain Circle in Cancun, Mexico, in 1994, which brought about this project; and Paula Pini, Marion Sachdeva, and June Cheng of the University of New Haven Peterson Library; Terri Reccia of the University of New Haven English Department.

We are grateful to the following sources for permission to reprint articles, excerpts, speeches, or other material:

Mark Twain Collection (#6314-Q), Clifton Waller Barrett Library, Special Collections Department, University of Virginia Library, for permission to quote the letter from Mark Twain to Sarah McClean in the chapter "'Quite unclassifiable': Crossing Genres, Crossing Genders in Twain and Greene," by Karen Kilcup.

Studies in American Humor for permission to reprint here the article by Thomas Grant from *Studies in American Humor,* ser. 3, vol. 3 (1996).

©Tribune Media Services, Inc. All rights reserved. Reprinted with permission are four lines from "Casey at the Bank," by Jeff MacNelly, in "The Mark Twain of Baseball?: A Proposal for Humor Research of Turn-of-the-Century American Sportswriting," by David Lott.

Michael Weiner, for permission to quote him—from an interview of 5 December 1994—in "The Mark Twain of Baseball?: A Proposal for Humor Research of Turn-of-the-Century American Sportswriting," by David Lott.

New Directions
in American Humor

Introduction

David E. E. Sloane

Is there an *American* humor? Plainly, humor is a crucial aspect of our culture. In what other country but this—the (at least for now) most powerful nation in the world—could a head of state begin an eight-year tenure in office with a joke, as Ronald Reagan did in his State of the Union message. Reagan told the story of two small boys, one a pessimist, the other an optimist, confronted by two closed rooms. When the first room was opened for the young pessimist, it was filled with toys, but the child descended into gloom, saying, "Aw, they'll all be broken pretty soon." When the young optimist was presented with a room filled with horse manure, he leaped into the pile and started throwing it against the walls. After the psychologists pulled him out, he told them, "With all that horse poop, there's got to be a pony in here somewhere!" Would a prime minister of Japan begun his career thus? Would Helmut Kohl of Germany present his outlook on the status of German culture in such a metaphor? For Reagan, the speech was one of many triumphs that led to his title "The Great Communicator." The joke itself will serve as the apologia for much of contemporary American life, popular and academic, and with befitting humility we will also adopt it as our motto here.

Whether or not American humor is different qualitatively from other nations' humor is a vexed and vexing question, considered by three scholars here. Germany's Baron Munchausen represents the tall tale as fully as Babe the Blue Ox, Paul Bunyan, or Mike Fink, king of the river—all held up as American icons by Constance Rourke in her search for a unique American humor of the frontier. *The Good Soldier Svejk* of the Czech Republic is certainly close enough to Bill Mauldin's G. I. Joe, of World War II fame, to suggest that the democratic humor of the common man cuts across international boundaries. One still hears the (possibly apocryphal) story of American GIs who, in their push toward the German fatherland, overrun a German intelligence bunker and find a Mauldin cartoon posted for analysis on a bulletin board. The cartoon showed G. I. Joe and the wide-eyed "Raw Recruit" looking into a gigantic bomb crater. G. I. Joe is saying one word, "Mice." Underneath the cartoon a German analyst had scrawled, "But it was *not* mice! It was *a bomb*!" The disjunction between reality and skeptical irony defeated the German, who didn't see its profound rejection of the fear of death when reduced to a single incident. Artemus Ward had joked during the Civil War, taking as his text the Copperhead insistence that the country be restored with slavery intact, "I'm in favor of the Union as it was; and, if we can't have that, I'm in favor of the Union as it wasn't, but the Union anyhow." Hierarchies of idealism replace each other as Ward climbs the ladder of conception to its highest premise. His greatest successor took the same art to a higher level than Ward could ever have hoped, offering, in *Adventures of Huckleberry Finn,* what must be America's most visionary statement of democratic idealism: "I'm going to head out for the Territory ahead of the rest. Aunt Sally says she's going to sivilize me, and I can't stand it. I've been there before." What does a U.S. Marine say when pinned down on a beachhead by twenty submachine gunners? "Charge." As our humor tells us, we are moral risk-takers and frontiersmen—or at least we wish to see ourselves that way.

New Directions in American Humor does not argue line by line and author by author that American humor is unique. Overlap might be found between France's *Figaro* and American humor magazines, between *Krokidil* and Paul Krasner's *The Realist,* between Juvenal and the pessimistic humorists of the Vietnam era. At the beginning of the twentieth century, for instance, infuriated Japanese intelligentsia transported the format of the comic magazine *Puck* to Tokyo to create a *Tokyo Puck* that attacked American racism. The purpose of this book is to show the breadth of a tradition central in our culture and perhaps crucial to the way Americans—pragmatic, quirky, highly individualistic—approach problems and seek solutions. From the beginning, Americans have attempted to come to grips with the materials that confronted them: the frontier setting that departed from the traditional concepts of geographic sublimity; the urban frontier that came into shape in the Northeast as early as the 1820s and 1830s and is now reemerging as a race frontier in humorists such as Richard Pryor. American culture is an expansive force supported by seemingly infinite resources for growth and powered by capitalist enterprise and an ever-loosening but never fully abandoned Christian ethical center. Tracing this culture through its comic artifacts reveals an incredibly colorful crazy quilt of cultural dynamism. This dynamic comic discourse shows no signs of decreasing, even as television challenges print media and as issues of egalitarian ethics bring about transformations in the roles of women and ethnic minorities and changes in the criminal justice system. Nor has this discourse been diminished by recent changes in sexual mores in the face of AIDS, a modern medical catastrophe that has seemed to have the potential of equaling the bubonic plague.

American humor denies the control of life to any agency or reality, although male-created humor and female-created humor, according to the authors included here, may take different positions on how or whether this freedom can be fully gained. The sarcasm in American humor derives from the conflict between reality and idealism, but unlike Voltaire's *Candide,* American humor typically does not accept hoeing a garden as a natural outcome. More typical is the picture, late in Ken Kesey's *One Flew Over the Cuckoo's Nest,* of McMurphy: although brain-dead he triumphs by not lifting the impossibly heavy machine to set free Chief Bromden, making Bromden sane so he could head out for the territories ahead of the rest. Cervantes might have Don Quixote tilt at windmills, but a more pragmatic realist, Little Big Man, accepts an Indian "squaw" for a wife, listens to his horse before a great battle—"The hell with what you say," he tells disbelieving readers, jumping across the line of fictional verisimilitude into a far broader realm of intellectual verisimilitude—and escapes with his life when his cohorts, the Cheyenne "human beings," perish. The ultimate Platonism of the American position is to escape all boundaries into a pure formalism of experiential reconstruction—"Consider the mummy, he ain't had no fun in 4000 years," argued Bill Barlow of *Sagebrush Philosophy* in 1904, as he considered the skull of a pioneer sitting on his desk. When Mark Twain finally ran hard up against the reality of death—a reality that haunted his canon throughout his life but only broke through as he outlived those he loved—it brought him to his ultimate universal despair. Yet when Woody Allen starts with such despair as a premise, he ends by seeing a Napoleonic battle as a football game.

Readers of this book, then, should be able to start at nearly any point and discover an alignment of writers, comic metaphors and symbols, and issues that place American humor in a social and historical context and allow, or at least suggest, ways of viewing humor that lead to further inquiries. Those inquiries might lead back to the canons of major American humorists, or they might point forward, toward the significance of humor in developing social, ethical, and cultural premises in arenas such as race, feminism, vulgarity, sex, and politics. Questions raised here might relate humor directly to historical chains of events and their outcomes, such as Thomas Nast's devastating cartoon war on Tammany corruption, one of many such cartoon wars in New York journalistic history that marked the reformist comic periodicals of the nineteenth century. Or one might, indeed, be lead to the broadest issues of philosophical belief, national versus international cultural identity and self-definition. Certainly these facets of American humor have been noted by past critics who found in the wild exaggeration of American humor some sort of arresting phenomenon that urged them toward deeper study and recognition of it as a cultural denominator.

   New Directions in American Humor brings together seventeen essays loosely configured in five groupings: Popular Culture, Popular Humor in Print, Gender Issues, Dimensions of Major Authors as Humorists, and Foreign Language and American Humor. These groupings are rounded out with a bibliographical survey of the field and an afterword in which I suggest that it is the divergent components of American humor that make monolithic analysis a problematic undertaking at best. The idea of this book grew out of the American Humor/Mark Twain Conference sponsored by the American Literature Association, the American Humor Studies Association, and the Mark Twain Circle in Cancun, Mexico, in December 1994. The purpose of that conference was to bring together specialists to explore developments and to pursue inquiries that would propel our field of study forward in the twenty-first century. The essays presented here do just that. They cover issues of televised literature, race, gender, cartooning, high and low letters, reportage—athletic and political, and historical/theoretical. This book provides a helpful spectrum of work under way and work still to be done in the field. More yet will be said, and rather than attempt to say everything here, it would be better to outline the various segments of the book and allow readers to find their own way into the material in detail.

   In "Popular Culture," four essays take up dimensions of popular humor that is nonliterary in its origins and intent. Doug Sun's essay on *Beavis and Butt-head* argues that the TV series should be seen as satire rather than as a component, through its reputed breeding of pathological violence in underage viewers, of the decline of Western civilization. Is the series a nihilistic glamorization of stupidity, as Gregg Camfield argues, or genuine satire that laughs to scorn our obvious cultural degeneracy? Is satirizing bad taste, or is bad taste necessary, as Sun finds in Mike Judge's representation of the sexual exploitation and juvenility of rock culture? Could the same effect be achieved in abstract discourse? Camfield suggests that not only the comedy but also its envelope—its environment—plays a role in its effect. If he is correct, then a pervasive malaise may indeed infect popular humor. Siva Vaidhyanathan's chapter on Richard Pryor, however, argues that an eruption of previously suppressed racial humor is part of a natural ongoing development of culture. Pryor reinvented himself to succeed as a black humorist in a general cultural market. Yet his daring is hardly nihilistic, for he offers whites a privileged glimpse of African-American society beyond the race barrier. The comic Texan, Don Graham's topic, is both a visual image and a rhetorical type that Graham traces from Davy Crockett to our own time. The image also defines an expansive worldview that rules out responsibility in favor of exaggerated expression—a technique best and most unsettlingly seen in the images from *Dr. Strangelove*. The more the American psyche is truly "Texan," the more troubling the image becomes, although another side of the image might have a more redeeming aspect.

The next section, "Popular Humor in Print," deals with mainstream topics occupying an area of ephemeral literature—primarily the periodical press—that seldom receives full attention by academics involved in literary study, although Frank L. Mott's work on American periodicals is an exception. First is an essay by Thomas Grant on P. J. O'Rourke, the manqué Mencken. Avowedly and openly conservative, O'Rourke is a *Rolling Stone* debunker occupying the conservative bleachers of American life, lobbing bombs of "white man's humor," with all its fears and resentments, into the multiethnic, multigendered camps of his enemies. O'Rourke, like Pryor, seems to be the outgrowth of traditions built in the twentieth century; yet whereas Pryor is revelatory of a submerged attitude, O'Rourke uses trenchant attacks on easy and superficial targets. "The Mark Twain of Baseball," David Lott's chapter on Charles Dryden, one of the best and most humorous sportswriters in the early twentieth century, elevates him to a place beside Grantland Rice, Damon Runyan, and Red Smith. Here, the medium of humor occurs within and elevates another journalistic medium, reminding us once again that humor is, finally, a tool for a varied menu of social discourse. Steven Gale's "Humor High and Low" assesses the levels at which humor operates, from pratfall to eyebrow raiser. His survey of the persistent mixing of levels of humor shows that this very mixing itself is one of American humor's chief characteristics.

"Gender Issues" features essays by Nancy Walker on modern feminist cartoonists, Judy Sneller on Stuart's local color figures, and Karen Kilcup on the varied nature of gender viewpoints projected through humor. Walker looks at popular visual projections of women—who no longer, as characters, populate strips drawn by men—and asks, "Are a cigarette-smoking, beer-drinking, no-nonsense writer, a thirty-something career woman riddled with anxieties, and a beleaguered wife and mother improvements over the bimbo and the bitch?" Indeed, she answers, the real answer lies elsewhere, in the testing of reality rather than fantasy—a breakthrough of the medium in feminist hands into contemporary conversation and away from adventure romance. Here the concerns of earlier chapters spill over into this section.

Asking a similar question, Judy Sneller drops us back a century to Ruth McEnery Stuart's wily "widders" and "old maids." To Sneller, the "Old South" social agenda is a weight around Stuart's conceptualization that compromises her portraiture of women. Her discussion suggests rich ground for future studies. Karen Kilcup's study of Sarah Pratt McLean Greene, who became prominent with *Cape Cod Folks* in 1881, finds valuable contrasts with Twain's method, however unlikely the pairing might at first appear. To Kilcup, the multiple perspectives of Greene baffle monist interpretations and vary significantly from Twain's perspectives on bad boys like Huck Finn. Humor can, in Greene, be both satire and sentiment, relying on changes in perspective and shadow narratives to inculcate women's viewpoints. Kilcup notes this characteristic—an important one, available especially to humor projected through gender issues—even in the Judith Loftus segment of Twain's novel. Major writers are often capable of this effect.

Edith Wharton's work, here discussed by Michele Ware in the first chapter of the "Dimensions of Major Authors as Humorists" section, reflects similar qualities in its sensitivity to characters. Major authors are regularly treated in studies on the author as a humorist: for instance, Twain, in a massive critical canon; and Melville, in various studies, most recently John Bryant's *Melville and Repose* (1993). The four chapters in this section represent what is, in fact, a subgenre of critical studies on American writers whose work possess substantial comic components. Ware takes up the irony of Wharton's tragicomic short story "The Legend." John Pellerin, the Henry James–like central figure of the story, is not seen from a feminist perspective, but his complexity and interior strength plays out in a context of love and possession. Lawrence Berkove, in his contribution, does not consider Twain himself but rather the comic milieu of lying that characterized the literary environment of the mining camps where his journalistic capabilities as a humorist began to take final form. The importance of journalism as a comic inspirator, proposed as well in David Lott's chapter on Dryden, is now reinforced by its connection to a major author. Louis Budd's discussion of *Pudd'nhead Wilson* shows how an important writer's work can be assessed as an artifact: the application of critical theories become themselves part of the apparatus by which the work can be understood. All students of humor in the coming century will need to master such a delicate balancing of literary perception with perceived critical realities. David Tomlinson's essay on Poe lays out in bibliographic terms Poe's standing as a humorist and notes Dennis Edding's compilation of fifteen essays on the subject in *The Naiad Voice: Essays on Poe's Satiric Hoaxing.* Poe's capabilities, as listed at the end of the essay, once again impress on one how far humor in the hands of a master can get from "thigh slappers" and still be humor.

"Foreign Language and American Humor," the subject of the final group of essays, is a category that should expand significantly in the next several decades, assuming that America consciously develops the language capacities that go with its presumed role as a world leader. Holger Kersten's study of Twain and German, which notes the extensive commitment of the Twain family to that language, suggests that language uses a variety of modes to amuse, and play revolves around even sound likenesses that lead to scatological considerations. Yet, it is as an expression of deep feeling that humor can have its deepest effect, when intended, just as *Adventures of Huckleberry Finn* may lose some of its effect in inept translations. James Papp's study of difficulties associated with translating *Adventures of Huckleberry Finn* into Slovak reinforces the obvious problem of how local village dialect is perceived in the global village. If dialect is crucial—Huck's 204 uses of the word "nigger" have made the book a current lightning rod for racial censorship in the United States—studying the impact of language in humor is more than just a scholarly foible. The connections made between language and moral force are in fact crucial considerations. Alita Kelley, in her chapter on translating Bryce Echenique's Lima humor, makes two important points. First, she reminds us that there is more to America than merely North America, and we would do well to reach beyond our literal borders for contrast and comparison with those whom Walt Whitman identified as the "Americans of all nations." Cervantes, after all, an author whose humor is sometimes viewed as compromising his dignity, is not appreciated as a humorist by critics in his own language nearly as much as he is appreciated in other cultures. Second, Kelley's introduction to the complexities of translating humor into English is an important contribution to another area of concern that needs to be enlarged as we consider both the exporting of American humor and the relationship between Hispanic and Anglo cultures and language. Her close analysis of the first line of Echenique's Lima novel further cautions us as language consumers that where context is unknown, due to either distance, social experience, geography, or language change, the loss of comic nuance and crucial meaning becomes more likely. The interplay of these three essays on humor and foreign language educates us on the importance of language context in literature generally and humor particularly.

The two concluding chapters cover bibliography and metatheory. First, Donald Stauffer surveys the field of American humor publishing in relation to course texts in American humor. Offering a useful way to identify the influences of book sales and marketing on the humor canon, he provides both an index to current humorists and cartoonists and a useful general bibliography. And finally, my afterword discusses the conceptual processing of language in relation to American humor and emphasizes the complexities of assessing a medium where formalist effects rather than ideological milieus provide some of the parameters for discussion.

Much in the study of American humor is negotiable. As this book suggests, the flourishing field of American humor studies is now beginning an important period, one in which new topics, new names, and new ideas will be brought forth in the hope of adding levels of understanding to one of American culture's most important mediums of intellectual exchange.

Popular Culture

"Change It! This Sucks!": Beavis and Butt-head, Idiot Savants of Cultural Criticism

Douglas Sun

Several years into its run, *MTV's Beavis and Butt-head* is no longer a source of much overt controversy. Jeremiahs in the mainstream press have largely given up bashing the show, either directly or by using it as a metonymy for a range of cultural woes. No domestic atrocities have been blamed on it for quite a while. One can find Beavis and Butt-head in the home video bin at large chain stores, and the show has become a successful merchandising vehicle for MTV. In fact, with the motion picture *Beavis and Butt-head Do America* released in time for the 1996 Christmas season, one can say that Mike Judge, the show's creator, has taken his two teenage dimwits from "Sick and Twisted Animation," the annual animation festival where Judge's "Frog Baseball" (yes, it's as sick as it sounds) was showcased and later picked up by MTV for its now defunct *Liquid Television* series to citywide release—from the margins to Main Street—within a handful of years.

The show itself has changed somewhat, reflecting both market pressures and the inherent limitations of the material itself. Episodes produced since early 1994 have repressed, among other formerly salient features, both Beavis's love of fire and scenes portraying the execution of grasshoppers with chainsaws to strains of Judas Priest's "Breaking the Law"—all in response to concern over the effect of cartoon characters on impressionable children. One also notices a subtle change in the characters themselves. The dialogue that overlays the videos has become more elaborate, less provocatively guttural. This makes Beavis and Butt-head seem more recognizably human, less the primitive beings that provoked such fear and loathing. Such personality changes may be a commercial move on the

11

part of Judge and his writers; more likely, the changes reflect the limits of the material he has chosen to work with. One can only produce so many useful variations from characters the essence of whose being it is to say, "Huh-h . . . You said 'member'" over and over again; after a while it becomes necessary to alter the theme.

Given its present character, it is hard to recall how *Beavis and Butt-head* became the anti-Christ of American television on its debut in March 1993. That was no mean feat, for there was (and still is) much competition. The demonization of the show started at the very beginning when *Variety* reviewer Drew Soros greeted its premiere by writing, "The decline of Western civilization continues with MTV's animated series, 'Beavis and Butt-head.'"[1] The expression was hardly original, but the sentiment would prove characteristic. Almost a year later, James Wolcott, a lukewarm admirer, would note in the *New Yorker* that the show's protagonists had been chosen by publications as diverse as the *Nation* and *Playboy* as "the official pet rocks of the New Stupidity."[2] The nadir of its public reputation came in October 1993 when an Ohio woman blamed Beavis for inspiring her five-year-old son to set fire to their mobile home with a cigarette lighter, killing his two-year-old sister (the question of why a child that young had access to a cigarette lighter was largely ignored). Immediately, *Beavis and Butt-head* entered the killing zones of children's television advocates and others concerned over violence on TV. One child psychologist went on record in the *Los Angeles Times* demanding that MTV cancel the show altogether.[3]

Negative reaction to *Beavis and Butt-head*—and there was quite a lot early in its run—derived from two basic misperceptions of the show. One was that its creator, Mike Judge, intended to valorize his protagonists, glamorizing their stupidity and antisocial behavior. The other was that the show represented a threat to our culture by being as low as lowbrow gets. It was an ironic state of affairs for a show that has always been, in fact, the opposite of what its most strident detractors have assumed. *Beavis and Butt-head* is an ongoing act of cultural satire. From the moment of its premier it has delivered the most devastating critique of American mass culture of any program on television. Unlike its oft-cited cognate *The Simpsons,* which often evades the ugliest implications of its satiric viewpoint, *Beavis and Butt-head* leaves us with no comforting illusions that things will be all right at the end of the day, that everyone and everything is ultimately redeemable. If Mike Judge ran into problems in those early episodes, it was because he had devised a satiric rhetoric so subtle and so dependent on his audience's knowledge of cultural context that many viewers not already aligned with the show's ironic perspective either never got the point or lost patience and changed the channel. The show is brilliant, vicious satire layered with generational and experiential barriers. It even pronounces a pox on, among other things, MTV itself, but mainly for the benefit of those who already watch MTV and can understand the design of the jokes.

Because Judge's rhetoric is so easily misinterpreted, one can easily understand how casual and uniformed viewers could be misled by the surface texture of the show. Parents and educators probably squirm at its portrayal of authority figures; whether it is the drunken school principal McVicker, the fatuous hippie schoolteacher Van Driessen, the perpetually clueless neighbor Tom Anderson, or even the somewhat disconnected President Clinton, who appears in the episode "Citizen Butt-head"—adults always seem flawed and ridiculous. The only character who consistently escapes ridicule from the show's implied perspective or humiliation at the hands of the plot is Daria Morgendorfer, the honors student who plays the familiar role of the lone, long-suffering smart kid in a public high school and who acts as Nemesis to Beavis and Butt-head. However, she appears in only a minority of episodes, and so the show often unfolds itself without a viable moral center. This can prove disorienting in a work of satire.

The brunt of the show's satire really does fall on its protagonists, a point that becomes clear if we put *Beavis and Butt-head* in its proper generic context. It is occasionally remembered in connection with the show that our popular entertainments have been spotlighting male adolescent dim-wittedness for at least the past decade. Bill and Ted of the *Bill and Ted's Excellent Adventure* movies, Wayne and Garth of *Wayne's World,* and even Doug and Bob MacKenzie of *SCTV* are made of much the same material as Beavis and Butt-head. Yet what comparisons have been made rarely point out that these earlier characters differ from Beavis and Butt-head in the essential likability their creators granted them. For all their stupidity and bad taste, we always understood that they were nice kids underneath it all. Bill and Ted, and Wayne as well, even had beautiful girlfriends. With Beavis and Butt-head, by contrast, it remains clear, episode after episode, that beneath their veneer of stupidity and bad taste lies only more stupidity and bad taste. Girlfriends? Girls will not even enter their airspace, to borrow a popular colloquialism, and we in the audience don't blame them. What explains the difference? The most obvious answer is that Mike Judge refuses to retreat from his own satire. He holds firmly to his creation of Beavis and Butt-head as we see them: unredeemable.

This seems a relatively simple point to make; however, more complex and difficult to answer is the matter of the vulgar, adolescent humor that the show embodies through its crude, adolescent protagonists. The show's detractors assume an absolute correspondence between its implied perspective and its protagonists' senses of humor—hence the perception that the show is itself the product of a lowbrow sensibility. I believe, however, that the reverse is true: *Beavis and Butt-head* assumes a sophisticated audience that can maintain an ironic distance from the main characters and can also shift gears so as to empathize with these characters when they are used to subvert a broad range of social and cultural phenomena. The humor in the show has a double edge to it, one that not only cuts Beavis and Butt-head themselves but also cuts outward, at the world that both shapes and is tormented by them. *Beavis and Butt-head* is not a show for simpletons; it is written for an educated, adult audience that has outgrown teenage mores but that can still take sheepish pleasure in dumb teenage humor for a worthy satiric cause.

No doubt this double edge to the show's humor presents cognitive problems for many who might otherwise endorse its point of view. Being in tune with *Beavis and Butt-head* seems to come most easily to the generational cohort of twenty- and thirty-somethings, all of whom say, "I knew guys like that in high school" (or even, "I dated guys like that in high school"). The shock of recognition plays an important role in appreciating the show.[4] Still, the show incorporates moments of obvious cultural and social satire—such as the montages of film or television spoofs that open many episodes—moments that reveal a strong satiric vision at work.[5] In "Blackout," for instance, Beavis and Butt-head are watching a movie called *Asbestos in Obstetrics,* "starring Melissa Gilbert, Robert Urich and Lou Ferrigno," on a channel called *The Crap Network,* when the lights go out. Many cable viewers will immediately recognize the show the protagonists are watching as a dig at the *Lifetime* channel, which has a habit of retreading mediocre made-for-TV melodramas during prime time, passing them off as "women's television." *Lifetime* is to a certain extent a triumph of marketing over substance—a phenomenon that is as old as commercial television itself and has bred in many of Mike Judge's generation, raised as they were on a steady diet of cathode rays, cynicism about the process of selling entertainment.

But the larger satiric set pieces invariably involve Beavis and Butt-head mucking up someone else's business, and this is where the humor gets complicated, for it requires viewers to understand that Judge has more than one target in his sights at any given moment. Excellent examples occur in the episodes "Canoe" and "Politically Correct," which take aim at the men's movement and the recovery movement. In the latter episode, Mr. Van Driessen dragoons Beavis and Butt-head into running for class treasurer, and in an effort to make them more sensitive to the electorate, hands them a stack of recovery movement self-help books. The boys actually read them, and the running joke of the episode has them using the lingo, obviously without understanding or endorsing any of it. At one point, a student asks them a question about managing class funds. Butt-head, stuck for a real answer, responds:

> BUTT-HEAD: Uhh . . . huh-huh . . . I respect your
> boundaries.
> BEAVIS: Yeah. Go with your anger.
> BUTT-HEAD: Uhh, can I have a hug?
> BEAVIS: Aah! Don't touch me, asswipe! I'll wound
> your inner child. Then I'll kick your ass.

On the one hand, the joke here is on Beavis and Butt-head. This exchange contains several of the standard elements of character that make them ridiculous to us: adolescent homosexual panic, the impulse to violence, crude language and the manipulation of concepts they obviously don't understand. But on the other hand, their appropriation of this trendy psychobabble is also subversive of the psychobabble itself: they show how easily this mush can be substituted for genuine discussion. Furthermore, the meaning Beavis imparts to the concept of wounding the inner child is somehow more real, more tangible than the "proper" sense as used by its true believers. His follow up, "Then I'll kick your ass," only emphasizes his own crude incomprehension. Now he will wound the inner child in a behavioral action. This exchange reveals Beavis and Butt-head as idiots, but their idiocy also highlights the ridiculous in a contemporary American social phenomenon.

The double-edged quality of Judge's satiric vision becomes an even more delicate rhetorical strategy in the show's use of music videos, particularly in the earlier episodes. Although this use of videos forms the most important aspect of *MTV's Beavis and Butt-head,* it is rarely discussed. Viewers need a fairly substantial knowledge of contemporary popular music to get the jokes, and it is here that much of the audience—especially older viewers—can fail to grasp the context and comprehend the humor. Judge expects us to bring to his material not only significant knowledge of pop culture that tends to be generation specific but also a certain attitude toward that knowledge, an attitude that assumes a definite set of tastes and, if not a certain level of education, at least enough intelligence and self-awareness to understand the ways in which the commercial forces that drive our popular culture function. Yet Judge has chosen to let videos carry so much of the show's satiric load that viewers who don't fully understand the references and how the videos are being used can easily misinterpret his message.

Part of the satiric content communicated through the videos is fairly straightforward. Most of the groups that get Beavis and Butt-head charged up either appeal primarily to adolescent sex/power/rebellion fantasies—Gwar,

AC/DC, Metallica—or substitute screaming and banging for actual musical talent—Pantera, The Beastie Boys, Biohazard. Taken together, enthusiasm for these bands implicates the protagonists in a brand of stupidity most characteristic of teenage boys. Nevertheless, it would help to have some contextualizing knowledge of the music. The boys themselves give us periodic hints with exclamations like, "Yelling is cool!"[6] But the early episodes tended to rely on fragments of videos, cutting quickly between them to simulate the effects of remote controls and thirty-second attention spans on television viewing. If the audience has seen these videos before and knows the featured artists, the full impact of how Judge uses these videos is apparent because the fragment can stand in for a larger whole. But if the audience has no idea who these strangely dressed people are and why they're behaving in such ways, the fragments can be mystifying, overlaid as they are with commentary like, "Yes! Pantera kicks everybody's ass!"[7]

Judge relies on eliciting the shock of recognition in his audience through his choice of videos. He seeks the reaction of viewers for whom most variants of heavy metal (as well as the urban white boy rap shtick of The Beastie Boys) have always been—for want of better phrasing—the kind of music favored by the "losers" in everybody's high school class. Such viewers would also be familiar with this body of music through passive listening or viewing of music television; these viewers would not seek out heavy metal, but songs belonging to the genre would come up on the MTV playlist before they could change stations or punch up PBS on the remote. Such viewers might well have cultivated a talent for making fun of metalheads through crude imitation of their speech and mannerisms. The irony would be lost on a true metalhead, who would not immediately see the music as open to satire; the irony would also be lost on viewers who lack the frame of reference to understand heavy metal in its cultural context—to associate it with a certain, inherently ridiculous body of listeners, or to fix it in popular music's current hierarchy of genres. Those viewers possessing the body of knowledge and attitudes that Judge assumes would make the connection immediately: "Yes, of course; Beavis and Butt-head are exactly the sort of dim bulbs who would be into Gwar and take it seriously."

The same satiric dynamic is at work when the show's implied perspective makes fun of Beavis and Butt-head for their appalling lack of cultural memory. They say things that are really stupid, but their lack of memory isn't nearly as appalling or funny if viewers don't know the larger context in which the joke unfolds. Uninformed viewers would not recognize an Elvis impersonator when they see one, and jokes are usually more sophisticated than that. For instance, the protagonists discuss the video for Led Zeppelin's "Over the Hills and Far Away," in the episode "Kidnapped:"

BUTT-HEAD: These guys have all done it.
BEAVIS: Yeah. Huh-huh.
BUTT-HEAD: I bet these guys have done it more than once?
BEAVIS: Yeah. Huh-huh. That's when you're really
                    cool.

If Butt-head really knew what he was talking about here he wouldn't phrase that as a question. Butt-head seems ridiculous to us because what he's just said is a gross understatement and because he's said it in a knowing fashion, without realizing what an understatement it is. But in order for us to laugh at Butt-head, we must come to the joke with knowledge of Led Zeppelin's fearsomely Dionysian reputation, a knowledge the character obviously doesn't have, but one that gives us yet another layer to the joke.

When Judge throws in the double-edged quality he so often gives the show's satiric riffs, the rhetoric of his use of music videos becomes even more complex. One of the most potentially off-putting aspects of the show has to be Beavis and Butt-head's crudely enthusiastic reaction to the sexual content in videos, an aspect most cogently summarized by the moment in "Baby Makes, Uh, Three" when Judge cuts away from the flesh-filled video for Aerosmith's "Rag Doll" to show us Butt-head rubbing himself underneath his shorts. A superficial viewing would dismiss this as a moment of appalling bad taste—which indeed it is. But it also makes vivid, as a more subtle gesture would not, the sort of base instinctual response that MTV and video auteurs beg when they resort to the lowest common denominator. Butt-head understands what this video is about; he simply demonstrates that understanding in a way that most of us would find socially unacceptable. Equally on target but only marginally less uncouth are the boys' comments on the video for "Alright" by rapper Doug E. Fresh, featured in "Let's Clean It Up":

BUTT-HEAD: Rap videos are cool because they don't mess
                    around with a lot of crap that you don't want
                    to see?
BEAVIS: Yeah. Bouncing boobs.

Their reaction to the close-ups of jiggling female body parts suggests that, more than anything else, the video for "Alright" taps into a sexual impulse that is immature and narcissistic. That Beavis and Butt-head are prone to such impulses is borne out by their frequent, varied, and enthusiastic use of synonyms for erection and masturbation. It's a disturbing conception of sexuality that sees the human form not as an expression of humanity but as a

mere collection of parts. This conception of sex, although characteristic of
Beavis and Butt-head, is by no means unique to them. Rather, it is part of
the potential worst in all of us; Beavis and Butt-head simply display what the
rest of us have succeeded in relegating to the backs of our minds.

Given their obsession with—and idiot-savant understanding of—sex
in music videos, it is only right that Beavis and Butt-head should comment
on Madonna, as they do over the cover to her video *Fever,* in "Beavis and
Butt-head Meet God." Madonna's antics always seem to slide by on code-
word adjectives like "provocative" or "outrageous," used by an entertainment
press that is either too polite or too invested in her to analyze the basis of
her appeal with any depth or rigor. But Beavis and Butt-head, as we know,
are anything but polite when seeing a female body in a state of undress:

> BUTT-HEAD: Look at her thingies.
> BEAVIS: Yeah. Yeah. Huh-huh. I like it when they're
>   pushed together really close.
> BUTT-HEAD: Yeah. Huh-huh. That's pretty cool.

If Madonna is going to allow herself to be dressed (or rather, undressed), as
she is in that video, she will give the impression that she's trying to show off
her "thingies." Then, the boys drift off into a characteristically degraded
discussion of the Woody Allen/Soon-Yi Previn scandal, including a predictable discourse on the name "Woody," returning their attention to the video
only when Madonna reappears wearing nothing but three strategically placed
bits of costume. Butt-head exclaims: "Whoa! She's almost naked. That gives
me a special feeling on my Woody Allen." Madonna has blatantly exploited
prurient adolescent sexuality in her career; she has even enjoyed a vogue
among scholars of popular culture. But Beavis and Butt-head show an understanding of her appeal more profound than any academic commentary
has proposed. The show's implied perspective argues persuasively here that
when a performer relies on shock value as much as Madonna has, her
reputation is going to get the strongest rise ("Huh-huh. Huh-huh. He said
. . . ") from repulsive, dirty-minded teenage boys like Beavis and Butt-head.
The satire is double-edged; it hits Madonna and her video without absolving
Beavis and Butt-head for their repulsiveness. Fortunately, readers of my
essay are so debased, so the humor is a strictly academic issue for them.

Judge's method of satire-by-inanity reveals basic truths about the
trashiest music videos, but it also works with videos that highlight artists at
the opposite end of the spectrum, those who are more notable for their pre-
tentiousness. For instance, the boys encounter orange-haired John Lydon—
who became a punk icon under the alias Johnny Rotten—in their episode

"Rabies Scare," through the video for "The Body," a song recorded with his post–Sex Pistols group Public Image Ltd. The video is set in a nightmarish rendering of a hospital. Over a shot of Lydon kneeling on a gurney in surgical scrubs, our interlocutors say,

> BUTT-HEAD: Huh-huh. That guy has a disease.
> BEAVIS: Yeah. Huh-huh. Huh-huh. He's got wussy-itis.
> BUTT-HEAD: Yeah. First it causes your hair to turn red.
>   Then your butt falls off.

No one could ever call the punk movement dignified. Yet, like most poses of rebellion, it had a self-seriousness to it that all but begged ridicule. The boys' reaction to the video, unmeditated though it may be, renders Lydon ineffectual (especially the part about his butt falling off). To make fun of John Lydon for his spiky orange hair (in "Customers Suck," Beavis remarks over the video to PIL's "Rise," "He's got a hair stiffy") and call him a "wuss" is to misunderstand him; but it is also to *understand* him, and in a way that is different from how Lydon appears to understand himself.

The same satiric dynamic comes into play when Beavis and Butt-head meet one of rock music's more recent angry young men: the leader of Nine-Inch Nails, Trent Reznor. On the one hand, the boys approve of Nine-Inch Nails musically—a cutaway from the video for "March of the Pigs," which appears in the episode "Figure Drawing," shows them thrashing (which is a sign of enthusiasm). On the other hand, they cannot overlook Reznor's pouty refusal to stand up straight and look at the camera. No doubt Reznor's affected on-camera attitude is a deliberate gesture of revolt against the conventions of musical performance, which are rendered meaningless when a performer is merely lip-synching on a video. In that sense Reznor's deconstruction of the artifices of music videos is interesting, heady stuff. Nevertheless, it looks weird, as Butt-head points out:

> BUTT-HEAD: This guy keeps, like, stumbling around and
>   stuff.
> BEAVIS: Yeah. I don't think he's having a very good
>   day.
> BUTT-HEAD: I think he's just drunk off his ass.

Butt-head identifies a visual reality here: Reznor, lurching about the set, does look like he is falling-down drunk. Whether or not viewers want to attribute to Butt-head any sophisticated satiric intent here (and I would hesitate to do so), his commentary reduces Reznor to the absurdity that dispassionate analysts would see. The Beavis viewpoint refuses to accept Reznor on his own terms, but it describes him in a way that inspires laughter of recognition because it nonetheless *looks* like it might be accurate. Again, Judge's satiric sensibility has a double edge: Beavis and Butt-head demonstrate, with characteristic crudeness, that they don't get the point, but at the same time their alternate "reading" leaves us with a residual thought that maybe they do, after all.

Beavis and Butt-head's adolescent crudeness, with its gutter-level diction and with their willingness to say things that more mature people are too polite to say, seems to discourage sustained viewing and to screen some viewers out entirely. Whereas some viewers don't mind jokes about erections, others do. Even when Beavis and Butt-head make inoffensive remarks, their humor never rises above the sophomoric. And yet, that crudeness acts as a screen behind which Judge and his writers comment on a popular culture that provides Beavis and Butt-head with entertainment—a culture that itself can achieve an awfulness verging on the sublime. In "The Crush," the boys watch the video for rapper Biz Markie's single "Just a Friend," in which Markie tries to sing the chorus but does so in a howl so strident that it is capable of causing physical pain. Beavis and Butt-head take turns mocking him through imitation—Butt-head in a throaty yell, Beavis in a piercing, avian screech. Anyone who observes teenagers (or remembers being one) knows that mockery through imitation is a common adolescent form of humor that adolescents typically outgrow. Yet, their imitations are uncannily accurate. If Beavis and Butt-head were to enact the same sequence in response to Frank Sinatra or Tony Bennett, the difference in vocal ability between them and their objects of imitation would be painfully obvious. No such difference is apparent when they imitate Biz Markie—which suggests, conversely, that Biz Markie has somehow carved out a career as a pop vocalist with a voice no better than those of Beavis and Butt-head. Judge's satiric insight here implies that if Western civilization is declining, as Drew Soros remarked in his review, "MTV's Beavis and Butt-head Show," the popularity of the cartoon dramatization is less symptomatic of that decline than the fact that Biz Markie was able to get a contract from a major recording company (Warner Brothers) with such a complete lack of talent.

Of course, even if viewers are willing to accept Beavis and Butt-head as idiot-savant oracles of cultural criticism, the satire for which they are vehicles almost inevitably doubles back, making them satiric objects once again. One of the most piercing observations the show makes through them occurs in the episode "Naked Colony" during Stone Temple Pilots' video *Plush.* The first hit single gets this reaction:

BUTT-HEAD: I heard these guys, like, came first, and Pearl
                     Jam ripped them off.
BEAVIS: No way, Butt-head. Pearl Jam came first.
BUTT-HEAD: Uhh, well, they both suck.
BEAVIS: Hey, Butt-head. Pearl Jam doesn't suck;
                     they're from Seattle.
BUTT-HEAD: Oh yeah.

At the time this episode was written, Pearl Jam and Stone Temple Pilots were both much touted, new "alternative" bands, mainstays of the Lolla-palooza tour, the annual event first organized in the early 1990s by Perry Farrell, rock impressario and lead singer of Porno for Pyros, to promote alternative rock. MTV, not least of all, had helped establish their success. But Beavis and Butt-head's reaction to this video suggests that there is less to both than meets the ear, that despite their "alternative" status, they are less distinctive than their advertising would indicate. Perhaps, Judge is telling us, they are even (gulp) mediocre.

The satire doubles back again when Beavis points out that Pearl Jam can't possibly "suck" because the band is from Seattle, and Butt-head agrees. Two satiric points exist here; one is more cultural commentary: Seattle is cool in their imagination because it is the spawning ground of the Grunge movement. The logic of Beavis's appraisal doesn't flow from the music to the city that produced it but from the existing reputation of the city to the music. So how do they know that Seattle is cool? Because the idea is established in the cultural ether of this milieu, placed there by marketers (especially MTV) who use it to package bands like Nirvana, Pearl Jam, and Soundgarden and sell them to the public under the Grunge banner. The Grunge movement has a certain self-impor-tance to it: its refusal to sit up straight, get a haircut, and put on decent clothes is put forward as an anomic form of youthful rebellion. Beavis's reaction suggests that Grunge is as much a trick of marketing as an authen-tic cultural expression, its status a product of advertising more than genuine collective experience. But the joke is also on Beavis and Butt-head them-selves, because this moment catches them in one of the most pathetic and ridiculous traps of adolescence: the desire to conform to what is "cool"—in other words, ideas that are drawn from the cultural ether and that never grow from individual taste or experience. Beavis and Butt-head have never been to Seattle; we even guess that it was MTV itself that convinced them Seattle is "cool."

The same boomeranging dynamic is visible in the episode "Held Back," which uses two videos that provide the show an opportunity to comment on violence in music videos. At one point the video for "Breaking Up" by Violent Femmes shows the group's lead singer, baseball bat on his shoulder, standing behind a wedding cake. The implied spectacle to come sends Beavis into paroxysms, which draws this reaction from Butt-head: "Settle down, Beavis. Huh-huh. . . . This is a video. Any time you see a cake and a baseball bat in the same video, the cake is going to get its ass kicked." Butt-head is right—the cake does get smashed—and his comment, whether he intends it as such or not, points to the fact that violence has become a convention in music videos, a shock tactic to be used when the creators can find no other means to keep the audience's attention. That a video featuring Violent Femmes should rely on such a base, conventionalized appeal is ironic, for the band has always been most popular on the college rock circuit, popular music's most self-consciously intellectual spawning ground. Later in that same episode, Beavis and Butt-head watch the video for "Grudge" by a group inappropriately named "The Dylans," and Beavis displays an almost sensual excitement over a series of soft-focus shots of appliances being wrecked: "Hey, maybe they'll break it! . . . Ooh, yeah." Later Butt-head comments,

> BUTT-HEAD: This song, it's like, it sounds like everything
>   else sounds like right now?
> BEAVIS: Yeah, it's like, there's a bizillion bands that
>   sound exactly like this right now.
> BUTT-HEAD: Yeah.
> BEAVIS: At least they're breaking stuff.

Actually, they're merely breaking stuff. Beavis and Butt-head judge that The Dylans are a mediocre band, no different from a "bizillion" others—and they're right. But the joke rebounds on them at the very end, returning to their repulsive love of gratuitous violence even as it points out how video directors often resort to that violence (as they resort to using sex) to cover up either the essential mediocrity of the music or their own lack of imagination.

The only moments at which Beavis and Butt-head rise above the drivel that flashes before them on the TV screen and achieve something approaching genuine cleverness come when Judge has them ridicule inept heavy metal groups. Of course, one could argue that all heavy metal is inherently ridiculous, and trying to isolate gradations of quality within the genre is pointless. It is one thing to draw the scorn of an uninformed outsider; it is another, and a much stronger and more genuine insult, to be scorned by someone who understands what you are trying to do and knows you do it ineptly. In "Laughing," Beavis and Butt-head encounter the video for "Rock You Like a Hurricane" by the band Scorpions. At the sight of the 1980s German metal band's balding lead singer, Butt-head quips, "Huh-huh. I'm not just a Hair Club member. I'm the president." By travestying the hook line from an unrelated advertisement selling miracle hair-growth lotions to gullible viewers, he forces the clichés to comment on each other through his sarcasm. Cheap commercial fraud is made to be the aesthetic of the group. Heavy metal, even more than most other forms of rock, relies on projecting an image of unlimited youth and raw male sexuality. It swims in testosterone so as to appeal to its target audience, because that audience needs to see a fantasized image of itself in the performers. But it is more than a little ridiculous to try to project that image to sixteen-year-old boys when the lead singer is partially bald. Butt-head's allusion to Cy Sperling's now famous TV commercial renders the Scorpions heavy metal pose ineffectual by associating the band with the loss of virility and the sad need on the part of some men to deny the aging process.

Scorpions, however, might merit at least a little respect for having achieved a measure of commercial success. An entirely obscure band like Accept is a different matter, and Butt-head harshly criticizes them while viewing the video for "Balls to the Wall" in the episode "Tornado." Of the band's gnomelike lead singer, Butt-head says, "Who's this? What's this buttmunch doing on stage? . . . [mimicking a security guard] 'You got a backstage pass, sir?'" Heavy metal, at least as much as other forms of rock music, relies for its appeal on the charisma of its performers, especially a band's lead singer or lead guitarist. Without that superhuman aura, a band can easily appear to be pathetic or ludicrous, as does Accept. As Butt-head's remark brings out, the lead singer so lacks the requisite star quality that he could easily be mistaken for an ordinary schmo. That possibility, in turn, raises a question: How could these guys possibly think they'd make a passable heavy metal band? Near the end of the song, the video splices in a shot of underweight, long-haired postadolescent extras in motorcycle jackets wandering, zombielike, over a field of rubble. Butt-head administers the coup de grâce: "Check this out. It's Krokus coming to kick their asses. . . . It's the Night of the Living Bands That Suck."

The rhetoric of the videos in *Beavis and Butt-head* is complex. No doubt the show lost many viewers early in its run simply because they didn't follow popular music closely enough to understand the references. A further portion of the show's potential audience could not or would not penetrate the deadpan veneer of adolescent humor and see that as part of the joke. Beavis and Butt-head themselves are sometimes the objects of satire and at other times its vehicles; at still other times they play both roles simultaneously. Those who stayed with the show discovered some of the most trenchant satire on American pop culture to be found anywhere. The show spares least of all its official patron. As a colleague of mine once remarked, it is ironic that MTV should air—and even take possession of, through the act of naming—*MTV's Beavis and Butt-head,* for the show is so harshly critical of the network's bread and butter and the role it plays in shaping our popular culture.

Beavis and Butt-head are genuinely appalling characters, but they are also products of a world that refuses to make such individuals better than they are. The world that suffers from Beavis and Butt-head in turn gives them a collapsing social fabric (notice how their parents are completely absent, as if the boys had been left to raise each other), weak and unreliable authority figures, cynical entertainments that pander to the worst in all of us, and a youth culture that discourages the intellect and encourages disrespect for others. The double edge of Mike Judge's satiric vision encompasses the failure both of individuals within our society to make something of themselves and the larger cultural forces that guide them. That the show had such a difficult time in its early days making its point to a substantial number of viewers is unfortunate, but perhaps understandable. In February 1994, a New Jersey boy dropped a bowling ball from a highway overpass, killing an infant girl when it smashed through the roof of her family's car. As Jon Katz noted in *Rolling Stone* one month later, media watchdogs and reporters covering the case drew a connection between the incident and "Ball Breakers," an episode in which Beavis and Butt-head drop Mr. Anderson's bowling ball off of a tall building with willful disregard for people standing below.[8] The hysteria subsided only after it was discovered that the culprit did not have access to cable TV and had never seen the show. Postmodern wisdom notwithstanding, the old axiom that art should hold a mirror to life is still valid. The truth that *MTV's Beavis and Butt-head* reveals about ourselves and the times in which we live has, apparently, been too unpleasant for many commentators to comprehend.

Notes

1. Drew Soros, "Beavis and Butt-head Show," *Variety* (15 March 1993), 67.

2. James Wolcott, "Everyone's a Critic," *New Yorker* 70:2 (28 February 1994), 96–98.

3. Jane Hall, "'Beavis' Move Not Enough, Its Critics Say," *Los Angeles Times,* 20 October 1993, part F, p. 1, col. 4.

4. Judge himself is in his early to mid-thirties, as are at least two of his current corps of writers, Chris Marcil and Sam Johnson, both of whom were college classmates of mine. As undergraduates (long before Judge conceived of *Beavis and Butt-head*) Marcil and Johnson wrote a satiric piece about a fictitious heavy-metal theme park, which they called, "Shitloads o' Fun." The piece was eventually published in the *National Lampoon* in February 1991. Subsequently, Marcil and Johnson began working with a set of characters whom Marcil called "the Idiot Teens" (see Sam Johnson and Chris Marcil, "Road Trip to Glory," *National Lampoon* [August 1991]), based on kids he and Johnson knew growing up in Troy, New York, and Omaha, Nebraska, respectively.

5. Unfortunately, this device has been largely absent from episodes produced since early 1995, perhaps because MTV began to capitalize on the show's notoriety by commissioning new episodes at a faster rate, thus forcing greater reliance on simpler plot/joke formulas.

6. Spoken by Butt-head over a video by D.R.I., "Acid Rain," in an untitled episode about Billy Bob's heart attack.

7. Spoken by Butt-head over a video by Pantera, "Mouth for War," in the episode "Sperm Bank."

8. Jon Katz, "Animated Arguments: Why the Show's Critics Just Don't Get It," *Rolling Stone* (24 March 1994), 45.

How MTV "Re-Butts" the Satiric Argument of *Beavis and Butt-head*

Gregg Camfield

Television is, on the whole, nihilistic. I do not mean to suggest that network executives harbor an anarchic plan to substitute the pleasure of destruction for the pleasure of creativity; they are not brainwashing viewers into becoming storm troopers of mass destruction. Rather, I see television's task as supporting advertisers' needs to sell us illusions of redemption packaged in products. It is not easy to sell a healthy-minded person a hamburger as anything but a meal. It takes a spiritually or emotionally hungry person to buy a hamburger as a ticket to heaven, or even as a "happy meal." Television's job is to create that hunger through an unending assault on humane values and on the integrity of individuals as agents of their own emotional destinies. Television trivializes the best aspects of human life and exaggerates fear and pain, thereby creating a void of positive meaning under the assault of negativity. It generates a psycho-dynamic similar to that of Calvinism—induced self-loathing generates a passive pain that only grace can salve. Television rarely really "brainwashes" consumers into believing the claims of commercial messages; instead it works so insistently on breaking down any faith in the efficacy of any kind of activity besides criticism that it leaves audiences hungry enough to try, or buy, anything as an alternative. It creates a moral vacuum that dirt abhors. The sophistication of the viewer matters not a bit, because TV programming's cynical assault on value plays as easily into the hands of a sophisticated viewer who is critical of television's putative values as it does into the hands of the unsophisticated viewer who accepts the imagery without question. The point is to induce discomfort in the viewer, a discomfort that makes the viewer unwilling to act in his or her own behalf, captivated either by television's negativity or by the viewer's own attempt to criticize the critic in an escalating cycle of cynicism.

If this is true of television as a whole, it is especially true of MTV and its flagship show, *Beavis and Butt-head,* or at least so I concluded in mid-1994 when I saw my first episode. *Beavis and Butt-head* struck me

26

during that first viewing as perhaps the most extravagant fare on television's menu of despair. Of course, since I consider myself among the sophisticated viewers, I have to acknowledge that perhaps I approached *Beavis and Butt-head* from the point of view of a defeated cynic, unable to find positive values in the show. Douglas Sun's fine chapter on satire in *Beavis and Butt-head* certainly encourages me to think so. His point is cogently argued, impressively documented, and alive with an insider's knowledge of the culture under scrutiny. When I learned that Sun knows the show's creator, Mike Judge, and has discussed Judge's intentions with him, I grew closer to agreement. But my initial impressions would not go away, nor was I willing to dismiss them as the result of mere prejudice or cynicism. So, I asked a friend to record six hours of MTV programming, including three hours of *Beavis and Butt-head.* After viewing (too) much of this material, I'm now convinced that my first impression was right, although Sun, too, is correct. *Beavis and Butt-head* is certainly satiric, but there is more than one kind of satire. The show's inability to discriminate between Horatian satire—that is, satire built on an ironic gap between an audience's held values and the values promoted by naive speakers—and Juvenalian satire—that is, the satire of sarcastic railing—is one reason that its satiric message destroys itself. Regardless of authorial intention, the satire of *Beavis and Butt-head* is at best weak because it is overly veiled in setting its standards of moral judgment and inconsistent in signaling the viewer how to read the ironies. Satire this weak is in danger of failing, and MTV makes sure it does; MTV has robbed *Beavis and Butt-head* of any potential satire, no matter how crude, by disrupting the conditions necessary for it to work.

The least important of the ways *Beavis and Butt-head* fails as satire lies in authorial obscurity. Assuming that all satire is Horatian, Sun acknowledges the obscurity of the satiric messages, pointing out how subtly and rarely the show's creator establishes positive moral values to undercut the authority of the boys. Subtlety is often a virtue of satire, as long as three conditions are met. Sun speaks of the first of these when he notes that satire of MTV requires an extensive and sophisticated grasp of the culture of MTV itself, and many of us, not possessing this knowledge, miss the point. Cultural competence is not enough, though. Not only must one be primed with the information that enables ironic vision, but one must also know how Horatian satire works. One must be alive to the implied criticism in an ironic gap between a representation and an ideal. Finally, to find that implied criticism, one must also recognize cues signaling how to read the irony appropriately. One problem with *Beavis and Butt-head* is that its writers do not give us clear cues; instead they overshadow any Horatian satire against Beavis and Butt-head with the Juvenalian satire in which the characters themselves indulge.

Juvenalian satire, the satire of railing, uses the crudest, most basic form of irony—that of tone, of pure sarcasm. Such satire requires virtually no sophistication; it is accessible to any viewer who can comprehend emotion in tone of voice. Beavis and Butt-head's contempt for the world, then, can be understood by children so young that they cannot even understand the minimal conceptual content of the show. For most viewers, Juvenalian railing is the dominant satire of the cartoon. Two self-appointed judges criticize freely; in the most base terms, using puerile sarcasm, they scorn everything, even those things they profess to value. Their sarcastic tone professes to invest them with superiority even over the objects of their desire, such as sexually attractive women. While a sophisticated viewer can read their sarcasm as a defensive mechanism against the anxiety of ignorance and thus turn the boys' satire against them, MTV's typical early teen viewer is unlikely to have the experiential base from which to break out of the circle of sarcastic self-defense. On the contrary, the pure invective of Juvenalian satire of *Beavis and Butt-head* tends to overwhelm the more sophisticated irony beneath, both because it is easier to understand, closer to the frame of reference of the show's target audience, and because it is given a disproportionately large amount of each show's time.

Perhaps, too, the Juvenalian mode is simply more powerful when presented through images and live voice rather than through print. It is, after all, primarily the satire of tone, whereas the more sophisticated Horatian satire is the satire of stance. In print, the reader must use imagination to invest a speaker with any of these aspects of rhetorical ethos. In person, or in the electronic imitation of personal immediacy, attributes of tone are immediately apparent, both in literal tone of voice and—in the case of video —in physical gestures. Look at the popularity of Rush Limbaugh, whose heavy-handed sarcasm lacks the subtlety of what habitual readers consider irony. Image and attitude overwhelm ideas without the cool distance of print.

Thus, in *Beavis and Butt-head*, the defensive egotism of saying no to everything, the transparent power grab of a two- or a twelve-year-old in a struggle for self-definition through negation, has tremendous power in its immediacy. An adult viewer with a taste for irony and an identity based on positive values can laugh at the boys by filling in the blanks behind their nihilism, but by what rhetorical cues are even the most sophisticated of viewers supposed to discount one satiric mode for another? Perhaps Sun is right in claiming that a viewer more steeped in MTV culture would pick up the cues that Mike Judge has planted, but it seems unlikely that such a viewer would have the skills as a reader of satire to choose to follow the subtler cues instead of the more overt ones. It is, I suppose, possible that young viewers of the show, the kind who buy the *Beavis and Butt-head* merchandising spin-offs, are more sophisticated than I give them credit for. Cool (in the subjunctive).

Regardless of the audience's sophistication, the internal conflicts between satiric modes alone make the satire of *Beavis and Butt-head* weak and confusing. However, even if the satire were clear, consistent, accessible, and devastatingly powerful, the context of MTV itself would draw the satire's teeth. Commercial television is intrinsically antithetical to satire, and MTV, a network self-consciously and admittedly contemptuous of both its programming and its audience, has taken the art of moral nihilism to such an extreme that no satire is possible on it.

The first part of that context, television itself, goes beyond the simple immediacy of voice and gesture to exploit the seductive power of images themselves. In concentrating on viewing objects of desire, even while attacking them as immoral, inaccessible, or frightening, television encourages deep ambivalence, an ambivalence that is always part of satire but that does not allow satire's resolution. This partly explains why MTV as a medium is so antithetical to satire. The image's power to attract is too great for moral commentary to offset, thus allowing humor's fundamental, and paralyzing, ambivalence to have full unending play.

This is where I believe Sun's faith in rationality prevents him from seeing what MTV does. While he acknowledges that only the habitual MTV viewer can read the deeper satire of the show, he downplays the implications of his own observations—that is, that satire stems from simultaneous attraction and revulsion. Who spends hours watching a medium for which he or she has complete and utter contempt?[1] Perhaps someone who enjoys the exercise of contempt itself. Either way, there *is* joy in watching MTV, be it the joy of contempt itself or be it a deeper visceral pleasure of seeing and hearing things that spark, at many psychological levels, desires common to us all. The point of *Beavis and Butt-head*'s satire, according to Sun, is to get us to acknowledge our "baser" aspects so that, in self-knowledge, we can change. That is the traditional justification of satire; it holds up a mirror in which we see our vices, and then, in ridiculing us, encourages us to reform.

Thus, satire is affirmation through negation. In *Beavis and Butt-head* we affirm brains by ridiculing stupidity. It's an easy pleasure, the facile superiority of the normal person over such numskulls, and we need to ask how honestly challenging of our own complacency such an easy superiority could be. More important, we need to recognize that affirming one trait by negating its ostensible opposite is a dangerous game psychologically and ethically, for it allows a vicarious indulgence in vice from the moral high ground of judgment. Satire does have its value when it allows one to move beyond nay-saying in making choices. After all, the moral life is the life of choice, and free choice of virtue is impossible without a knowledge of the possibility of vice. Danger is implicit in moral choice, and satire is a technique by which many of us try to manage the attraction of vice by sealing our decision to behave virtuously. But for satire to work requires an awareness of the difficulty of choice and a requirement that made choices move the chooser beyond satire itself. Satire fails when all it does is encourage continuing satire. Then it is merely the vortex that Kierkegaard describes in *The Concept of Irony*; it becomes "Infinite absolute negativity, . . . the secret trap door through which one is suddenly hurled downward . . . into the infinite nothingness of irony."[2]

Sun, in his altogether admirable optimism, does not fully acknowledge the fundamental ambivalence of satire and so misses how MTV short-circuits the movement toward moral resolution, toward positive judgment. He does not see how MTV, in exaggerating irony, amplifies ambivalence in a way that is finally destructive of virtually all social value.

Of course, my assertion about the ambivalence of satire makes no sense if one forgets that satire begins in humor and that humor has no moral valence. It is merely an openness to different interpretations of meaning and value. It is essentially a time-out from seriousness, a willingness to look at and enjoy alternatives. It is a willingness to enjoy any possibility in prospect and as such militates against making choices. Humor is, I believe, a healthy and positive attribute of mind, and while I do not have space here to develop fully what I see as the psychophysiological basis of humor, I do think that its attributes of passivity as well as aesthetic and intellectual openness are a fundamental part of human freedom.[3] Without some leverage against seriousness, we would be locked into what paths we have chosen, whether they remain worthwhile or not. Humor usually stems from perception of incongruity, from sudden recognition that the world is not as we expected it to be. Incongruous dislocations, when they cause no immediate pain, when distant enough to be safe, force us into laughter, into a suspension of action in favor of aesthetic contemplation. In such a state of suspended activity we are alive to new possibilities, alive to alternative modes of thought that could entail alternative modes of action.

But humor implies no action of its own. It is part of a dialectic between choices and choosing. Made choices require repression of alternatives in order to suspend incessant recrimination. Humor provides a way to second-guess without consequence, to wallow in alternatives without recrimination. Perpetual humor would entail perpetual passivity, just as humorlessness would entail dogmatically inflexible pursuit of goals. The problem for the human mind is how to move from the openness of humor to the directed behavior of seriousness. Satire is one resolution.

Satire begins with the simultaneous attraction and revulsion of humor, but moves to choice in negating one possibility. Satire is a directed mode of comedy in which a moral center challenges the purposeless conceptual wandering of humor. Satire requires that the viewer recognize two possible constructions of reality, see one as virtuous and one as vicious, and while enjoying both through the passive openness of humor, choose the virtuous. Usually, the viewer does so because the satirist raises the fear of scorn, threatening the viewer with ostracism if he or she remains passive in his voyeuristic indulgence of fantasy vice. Thus, by bringing into play additional emotions, rather than residing in the passive pleasure of humor, the satirist transforms appreciation into moral reformation, encouraging viewers to take the next step toward virtuous action, that step being to choose among possible paths of action. If, however, satire is contextualized in a way that strips it of its moral center, or alternatively that encourages either the humorous passivity at its root or criticism as an end in itself, then satire loses its power as a bridge toward moral activity.

Modern commercial television usually does all these things. I saw recently on a regular broadcast station, during one of those strange mixes of happy talk and lurid sensation that the networks call "news," an advertisement for Mercedes Benz that used as its soundtrack Janis Joplin's haunting satire against American materialism, the song that begins "Lord, won't you buy me a Mercedes Benz." Here is an example of how television appeals not to the moral telos of satire but to the ambivalence behind it: by showing the automobile as an icon of desire, the judgment against it is ironized, suspended, made moot in an inverted negation. Words seem microscopic next to the image, or rather they become mere ornamentation, the resistance of desire that merely whets the appetite. Moral values still stand but seem trivial and weak by comparison to augmented desire. Satire in such an environment is, if not dead, nothing more than a still small voice in a culture of stridencies.

MTV takes the cake in depriving any irony of satiric force, and indeed, it is precisely this kind of recontextualizing of satire that robs MTV's commercial presentation of *Beavis and Butt-head* of any moral meaning the show might latently contain. To understand the medium's power to shape the message, it is important to recognize the social conditions specific to MTV. MTV's target audience is between ages twelve and twenty-five.[4] Thus the network counts on two kinds of discontinuity. One, its viewers have no historical perspective, viewing their own moment as a fairly substantial representation of the human experience. Two, its viewers resist the continuity of narratives, of shows. The brief history of MTV itself shows a move away from narrative videos with musical background to more assertively postmodern videos in which the cult of personality dominates over story line and outrageous outtakes insistently vie for attention. The point is to grab attention out of a discontinuous viewing experience. Arguably, the development of shows like *Beavis and Butt-head* indicates the network's desire to have a narrative vehicle that will command attention for a longer stretch of time than that elusive wave that the channel surfer catches on any station at any time.

But in striving for that audience captivity, the network relies on its usual mode of discontinuity as a form of tease—in the case of *Beavis and Butt-head,* a comic-strip tease. I timed a typical half-hour program, which contained two episodes, "Stewart Moves Away" and "Walking Erect." Each episode contains about six minutes of minimalist story, but even so, we do not get the story in one sitting. Each is broken into *four* pieces, with two Beavis and Butt-head video "reviews" and one block of advertisements disrupting each story. In the programs I timed, each block of advertisements—that is one block smack in the middle of each episode—lasted about four minutes, and two of the ads were repeated from one block to the next. Fragmented repetition. The essence of television.

Although we have long since grown accustomed to advertisements breaking the narrative flow in any television program, *Beavis and Butt-head* takes fragmentation two steps further by first breaking a half-hour show into two episodes and then breaking each episode twice for video reviews that are completely discontinuous with the plot. No matter where the boys might be for the story, they are always in the same position on the same couch for their video reviews.

These video reviews occupy about one-third of the total time of a *Beavis and Butt-head* show and are the most coherent section of any show in that they alone are not broken into pieces. Of course the videos they review are usually themselves highly fragmented, so viewers are not looking at islands of continuity in a sea of discontinuities. But the relative coherence gives these sections a dominant position in the show. What, then, does the show primarily offer? The criticism of fools. Not only do the ostensible reviews "dis" the videos under review, but they also burlesque the entire idea of art criticism. The first of many vortices of value that lead to judgmental paralysis occurs here. Even if the videos themselves have no artistic value, and even if the viewers are shown to be worthless, the exercise of criticism itself is mocked. Cynical passivity creeps into the void.

Vying with this cynicism is a world not of narrative or satire but of commercial advertisements, each of which promises a kind of heaven but implies a malaise that needs the compensatory relief of a purchased pleasure, of purchased "coolness." In MTV's case, the advertisers are so convinced of the malaise of viewers that they can be quite blunt in their promises. An ad for a video game called *Virtual Guitar,* for example, pitches its virtue with the slogan "More fun than just sitting there." Such ads overwhelm the show, and the discontinuities of the show itself merely reinforce the dominance of the ads. Of course, the paid advertisements that promote products are the reason the network exists; the programming is merely window dressing for the real product. Indeed, when MTV was born, video promotions for record albums constituted its entire programming. The earliest music videos were not designed as programming at all but were in fact nothing more than commercial "spots."[5] The success of MTV itself created a new genre of programming in the made-for-TV music video, but such videos never moved too far from their roots as advertisements.

Of course the irony of commercial television is that the audience itself is the crucial product, the product the network sells to its primary customers, the advertisers. And in order to sell its audience to the advertisers, it first has to sell itself to its audience. Thus, the most telling of MTV's commercials are the advertisements in which it sells itself. The entire content of the programming could be seen as this form of advertising, but there is another kind as well, the kind that "educates" its audience, that teaches its viewers how to be the ideal viewers of MTV. Not only does this kind of advertisement inform its audience members what to view and when, but it also tells them how to view. In one way MTV uses *Beavis and Butt-head* as precisely this kind of ad, telling viewers how not only to ignore any programming that might encourage judgment based on positive attributes of a civic community but also to scorn everything that does not relate to satisfying basic desires. *Beavis and Butt-head* as Juvenalian satire does that.

MTV is not, however, afraid of more sophisticated irony. MTV mocks self-consciousness, daring the viewer to come to the same nihilistic end through the more complicated avenue of sophisticated irony. So while it is, as Sun points out, "ironic that MTV should air—and even take possession of, through the act of naming—'MTV's Beavis and Butt-head' because the show is so harshly critical of the network's bread and butter and the role that it plays in shaping our popular culture," the irony keeps turning until it turns not on MTV, but on the "sophisticated" viewer with so much taste for irony that they keep watching anyway. Ironic commentary on both the medium and its viewers is not new to MTV with *Beavis and Butt-head.* On the contrary, the spots that promote its own programming have long relied on a sophisticated irony that enchants and demoralizes the viewer able to stand above the imperatives of the screen.

Obviously, if this evaluation is even partially accurate, the MTV self-promotional spot is nothing like the kind of hype we all know and loathe from the old broadcast networks, the self-adulation and congratulation over the endless production of tripe that make self-reflective viewers gag with disgust or guffaw with glee over unconscious self-parody. MTV's ads occupy an intellectual galaxy light-years beyond such spots in sophistication, robbing the viewer of any possibility of judgment by beating him or her to the punch with glib self-parody, as two of my favorite spots from 1991 suggest.

The first of these, a brief parody of MTV's "history," advertises a 1991 retrospective program of MTV's first ten years. The ad divides itself in two parts, the first done completely in sepia-toned black and white, the second in full color. The first half is a quick series of images, but the voice-over and music background give it a semblance of continuity at odds with the network's characteristic style and purpose. The spot begins with soft, sad violin music sounding simultaneously with the appearance of the MTV logo in black and white, followed by a date, 1981–1991, as if it were for an epitaph, above the words "A Strange and Frightening New World." Thus, viewers are to hear a story, a story as much of a life, a world, that has come to an end as of one that has just been born.

Then the narrative begins, telling a story not of order and meaning but of confusion and discouragement. A voice says gently, softly, articulately, in deep-pitched, somber tones, "My dearest Sarah, it is hard to describe the feelings here." The image shifts to a shot of a moon landing, still black and white. The voice continues: "We are as babes born into a strange and frightening new world." New shots appear in quick succession, some from "rock art," some photos of music video stars, all suggestive of extreme emotion, either manic or depressive. The one exception in the series, and the most startling in the entire ad, is an image of the MTV logo in three-dimensional perspective perched on a dias constructed out of a classical column (ionic fluting, no capital). Providing the backdrop of this MTV logo-as-altar is a drawing of Michelangelo's Sistine Chapel finger-touch between God and man.

This image alone, flashing so quickly across the screen that the details can't be absorbed on one viewing, is a monumentally entertaining parody. It collapses distinctions between religion and television, between high art and popular art. It can be read satirically as an attack on high art in favor of popular forms or as an attack on the sacrilegious stupidity of the television viewers who see gross commercialism as an adequate replacement for faith. But viewers have no certain cues about how to read the image; indeed, if they want to try, they will have to stay glued to MTV until it comes around again (or do as I did and study it on the freeze frame feature of the VCR). And those who *do* want to try will find themselves caught in a vortex of unresolvable irony. All this in one image from one self-promotional MTV spot.

As the spot continues, against the backdrop of images and persistent violin music, the voice-over delivers its mock somber message. In my transcription here, I mark with a slash (/) the appearance of each new image:

> It is sad / to see the populace so transformed / the women brazen / the men merely strange. / And those who lead the charge, / dear wife, an odder lot I have never encountered. / If I make little sense it is because this thing they call MTV is like nothing / I have ever experienced. I can only pray that someday / I may relive these days and / at last, perhaps, make sense of it all.

The violin music ends. Several sharp drum beats introduce rock music. The accompanying visual transition consists of a screen filled with splotches of bright color, especially blues and oranges, diagonally dancing over the screen, followed by a color shot of a Titan rocket carrying an Apollo space capsule, breaking free of a gantry at liftoff. A new voice—hard, gritty, aggressively masculine—takes over. This new voice's patter is accompanied by another quick succession of images, but these are all in color. We see a brief color shot of a moon walk followed by a picture of an explosion that blows the screen clear, with debris apparently flowing toward viewers, followed by a color screen of the MTV logo over the words "Reunion Weekend." The word "Reunion," inscribed in Art Deco lettering, forms an arch over black, newspaper headline–like lettering in the word "Weekend." These words stand out over an orange-pink background that on close scrutiny reveals a collage of faces of video performers.

The new voice says: "That day is here. / History comes alive during MTV's reunion weekend." Then the video portion turns into a series of clips from early videos while the voice-over intones in sentence fragments, "Great videos and specials from the early years." The screen is again blotted with a blue-orange motion pattern, followed by a color action clip of original MTV video jockeys. The voice continues its fragmentary report: "The five original vee-jays' homecoming." Then, over another shot of the reunion weekend logo, this time over a more colorful, predominantly blue background, the voice growls, "Reunion weekend." The video fragmentation has been accelerating throughout the piece; now it shifts into overdrive, rapidly flickering many video clips, color splashes, and so forth. The growling announcer then states and restates the main pitch: "Next weekend on MTV, and nowhere else. MTV and nowhere else."

This is an extraordinarily sophisticated promo, incorporating and deconstructing not only a series of iconic symbols of Western civilization—from the ceiling fresco of the Sistine chapel, to the pillar of classical art, to a primary instrument of classical music—but also the idea of history itself, mocked in the blandness of sepia-toned black and white. Postmodern television often uses "film-noirish" deeply shadowed black and white to suggest grittiness, but in this "spot," by coloring the black-and-white images with a sallow sepia and by softening the corners, the videographers suggest that history itself is a wash, a dull, piss-colored wash.

Against this backdrop, MTV celebrates its own "history," turning ten years—ten years that completely postdate the Apollo space program that is so much a part of their own symbolic blastoff—into a culture-founding mythological eternity. But the mockery of history itself plays into MTV's own resistance to temporality. Its history is one of discontinuity, of complete weirdness. Its history is one of sex role distinctions blurred to destroy traditional stories of desire and fulfillment, turning femininity in its "brazen"-ness into a object of simultaneous fantasy and fear, while condensing traditional masculine purpose into the diminutive sobriquet "merely strange." Here, the entire history of feminism as co-opted by commercial culture is latent, with fear and desire encouraging passivity, the passivity of a "conventional" voice saying he is paralyzed into numbness by the strange new world he wants to "re-live," which of course in television terms means merely to review. The very concept of living is redefined, and strangeness, the fragmentation of meaning, becomes the preferred goal of communication itself.

This spot entails a steady and sophisticated assault on the meaning of meaning, and while its full import requires a sophisticated audience, it is glitzy enough to carry its energy to those unable or unwilling to indulge in critical analysis. This ad, then, is an act of self-derision that preempts viewers' own reactions. Worse, it forces contempt back on viewers, for it suggests that if the medium is aware of its own emptiness, the truly strange are those on the other side of the tube.

If watching the empty programming, as opposed to the self-promotional spots, frightens or bores, one has the option of turning the channel off, which I admit I did in 1991 when I canceled my cable subscription. Most MTV viewers rise to the bait of this dare, demonstrating their courage by saying it is no big deal to live in this strange and frightening new world. One's guts are tested by one's staying power in the face of such disgusting fare, but let's face it, the adolescent audience to which MTV caters loves to take dares.

Perhaps the most delightful and disgusting self-promotional piece I have seen on MTV also comes from 1991. It is a much simpler spot, mixing a repetitive voice with a repetitive image, the rhythm and intensity of which both rise to a climax. The voice-over says, quite simply, "BLAH, BLAH, BLAH," in a deep voice and in syncopated rhythms that caricature the patterns of normal speech. The screen fills repeatedly with nothing but block lettered words, at first a direct transcription of the voice-over. Initially, the word "BLAH" dances all over the screen, jumping around in different sizes, almost always white against a black background, with occasional traces of yellow and orange. Quickly, in very small letters, slipped between "BLAHS," are small words in brightly colored letters. These words, supposedly representing subliminal advertisements, are not echoed by the voice-over; they appear on their own.

The first of these colorful words is "product," followed by "lie" in orange, which disappears and then quickly returns as part of the word "believe," with the "lie" at the center of "believe" still in orange, but the rest of the word in blue. Later, the screen flashes a similar treatment of "promise" followed by "compromise." Other words inserted between the "BLAHS" include "phallic symbol" in orange and "product name" in blue. The interpolations grow larger and come faster, including such words as "new," "different," "better," "sexy," "big," "bigger," "better," "faster," and so on, until they increase in size, filling the screen and moving too fast to be legible. Indiscriminate sound—a carefully orchestrated cacophony created to sound quasi-industrial—rises in the background, replaces the voice-over, reaches a climax, and then cuts to a hollow silence. The MTV logo appears against a black screen, with the "M" of "MTV" filled with a picture of a green-colored human eye and "TV" scripted in blue. A new voice-over in a slightly sharper voice, baritone instead of bass, says "M T blah, blah blah teleblah."

Now, as satire this is devastating, accurately stating that television programming is tediously predictable, less interesting than the advertising, and that the advertising makes untenable promises in underhanded ways. The spot further suggests that the course of true seduction never did run smooth, needing to compete against itself in ever larger, ever blunter, ever cruder and more transparently deceitful ways. But since this satire is not only directed at but promulgated by MTV itself, it again has the effect of preempting any strike that any outsider could make. MTV has an energetic habit of indulging in mea culpas with a comic panache that not only disarms its critics but also keeps them coming back for more. Again, the real purpose of this ad is to be so entertaining that viewers will watch the network to see it take itself apart, to allow viewers to indulge in the pleasures of criticism without consequence. The more important effects of this preemptive strike, it seems to me, are to convey MTV's contempt for its audience and to get its audience to register and accept that contempt as legitimate—after all, if they can get you to buy while honestly telling you that you are buying dreck, you've been conned with your eyes open, and if there is anything more humiliating than being a sucker, it's knowing it while you're being suckered.

In this context, viewers of MTV's *Beavis and Butt-head* expect nothing more than self-conscious self-parody, intended not to get viewers to turn the tube off but to tease viewers to stay tuned, all the while assaulting their integrity. The entire context of MTV's programming wallows in satire but turns it not into a tool of moral reform but instead into an excuse for indulging vicariously in vice. It seems to say, "If you are still watching, even though we have told you our programming is at best value-free, then what are you doing but seeking your own degradation in your most repugnant fantasies? OK, we'll help you, but don't say we didn't warn you. And after we've abused you for watching junk not only by showing you two couch potatoes whom you should recognize as your own caricatured selves but also by mocking the very videos that captivate you even though we all know that they are garbage, we offer you, cynically, your salvation in products, such as the plastic sled called the 'Downhill Screamer,' the slogan of which is 'slide around on your butt.' Yes, you, too, self-loathing couch potato, can buy activity, surcease of sorrows, but in this case you'll need a snow job. Tune into the weather channel for that."

MTV, "blah, blah, teleblah," sells the blahs, that is, emptiness, acedia, the knowledge that you who watch are vacuous. Perhaps it should rename itself NTV—Nihilism Television. Even the redundancy of this moniker is appropriate to a medium in which the heartbeat is repetition and in which the only real vitality is contempt. The point is not, as Doug Sun puts it, that *Beavis and Butt-head* "is brilliant, vicious satire [that] . . . pronounces a pox on . . . MTV" (though his use of the term "vicious" may be more revealing than he intends) but that, as Sun also states, it is an attack designed "mainly for people who already watch MTV." MTV's owners don't care if the only reason you watch is to see MTV flagellated; all they care is that you watch. And if you watch knowing that MTV is worth flagellation, then who is the joke ultimately on?

I've risen to the passion of jeremiad, but I must stress that I don't see MTV as the end of Western Civilization, as much as its own iconography wants to suggest. No, its promoters—or should I call them negators?—merely want to encourage the mindlessly materialistic side of Western culture by discouraging any mental effort that is capable of promoting positive values or of encouraging active and creative work *for* something. Instead they occupy our minds with the pleasures of criticism, with the endlessly repeatable but ultimately empty pleasure of saying no. They have no intention, I suspect, of encouraging active evil, and not merely because they wish to avoid lawsuits. When that now famous Ohio child set fire to his home in October 1993 in emulation (my wife says "immolation") of his heroes Beavis and Butt-head, I suspect that the executives of MTV were just as appalled as the rest of us. It was proof, after all, that the child was neither in front of the tube watching the show nor in the mall buying the products. Any active evil promoted by MTV is merely a sign of rhetorical failure, something even the moral nihilists of cable would be loathe to embrace.

Notes

1. It is worth digressing here to note that satire usually attacks the vices of a culture to which the satirist and his or her audience have no choice but to belong. Their attraction and revulsion, then, are natural consequences of the conflict between their insiders' knowledge and their idealistic vision of the culture. Television's "culture" is voluntary. Doesn't this change the moral basis of any satire that attacks television from an insider's point of view?

2. Søren Kierkegaard, *The Concept of Irony,* trans. Lee M. Capel (Bloomington: Indiana University Press, 1965), 63–64.

3. I address this issue extensively in chapter 6, "Humorneutics," of my book *Necessary Madness* (New York: Oxford University Press, 1997).

4. Robert M. Ogles, "Music Television (MTV)," in Robert G. Picard, ed., *The Cable Networks Handbook* (Riverside, CA: Carpelan, 1993), 139. While the network has been enormously popular virtually since its inception in 1981, it has only recently become profitable because, for its first ten years, its programming encouraged channel surfing. As early as 1986 the network began to develop shows designed to prolong audience attention. *Beavis and Butt-head* is the most successful of these, turning MTV into Viacom corporation's cash cow. See Ogles, 139; Bill Carter, "Cable Networks See Dimmer Future," *New York Times,* vol. 140, no. 48669, 22 July 1991, p. D1, col. 6; and Viacom's annual reports for 1993 and 1994.

5. Ogles, 137.

Now's the Time:
The Richard Pryor Phenomenon
and the Triumph of Black Culture

Siva Vaidhyanathan

"Times were so hard back then, they didn't even have a
name for them. They just called them 'Hard Times.'"
—Mudbone, a Richard Pryor character

From a nation torn by racial strife—one that elected Richard Nixon
twice, showed strong support for George Wallace, and insisted that in order
to succeed, African Americans had to dress, talk, and act as unthreatening
as possible—emerged Richard Pryor. With a swaggering attitude that challenged the American racial status quo only slightly less than did his chosen
vocabulary, Richard Pryor became more than the most influential black
stand-up comic in a generation: he was arguably the most successful comedian in America during the 1970s. This was the "Richard Pryor phenomenon," and it deserves a full exploration and explanation. How did a young
black man who started out a timid clone of the acceptable Bill Cosby re-
invent himself and burst through the color line to emerge as the most
bankable act in Hollywood?

Pryor rose from a bit actor and unreliable nightclub act to become
the most dominant comic force of the 1970s. He wrote the best bits for Mel
Brooks's *Blazing Saddles,* won an Emmy award for writing for the Lily Tom-
lin comedy special in 1973, and hosted *Saturday Night Live* in its first season.
He starred in a series of cinematic hits in which even his small parts stole
the show—*Car Wash* (1976), *Silver Streak* (1976), *The Bingo Long Traveling
All Stars and Motor Kings* (1976), *The Muppet Movie* (1979), and *The Lady
Sings The Blues* (1972), among them. He appeared on the cover of *Newsweek*
magazine in 1982. Two Pryor stand-up albums from the mid-1970s, *That
Nigger's Crazy* (1974) and . . . *Is It Something I Said?* (1975), went gold and
won Grammy awards.[1]

There are three possible explanations for the Richard Pryor phenomenon. The first asserts that Pryor was the last and loudest of a series of black comics who had been trying to get over the racial wall in American entertainment, and so he represents the culmination of years of effort and a well-defined tradition. The second explanation has been put forth by Pryor's friend Ishmael Reed. According to Reed, the wall never really came down. Pryor simply leapt it on the strength of his comic genius. Once stranded on the other side of the wall, as Reed sees it, Pryor sunk to creative lows under the influence of Hollywood and its various social and creative pressures.[2]

The best explanation, however, is that the cultural wall was never that formidable to begin with. According to this model, which I call "the triumph of African-American culture," American culture has benefited from an undeniable fascination with its African-American elements, and these expressions have in the past thirty years emerged as dominant voices in the cultural dialogue. America was never as culturally segregated as it was legally segregated. As a result, the wholesale desegregation of the past fifty years has created a nearly open competitive market for cultural expression. In many areas—such as comedy, popular music, and sports—black culture has established the greatest market share. In others, such as literature and film, African-American expression is just beginning to show its might. Richard Pryor was among the most recognizable African Americans to take advantage of the triumph of black culture in the last half of the twentieth century. We must count him with Lena Horne, Jackie Robinson, Chuck Berry, Julius Erving, and most recently, Toni Morrison as champions of the triumph. None of their battles were easy, but their victories made possible future triumphs by later artists. Clearly, to understand the rise of Richard Pryor, one must entertain all three explanations.[3]

Two recent books trace Pryor's success with detail and context: *If I Stop I'll Die,* by John and Dennis Williams; and Mel Watkins's *On the Real Side,* an invaluable history of African-American humor. Watkins's work is the most encyclopedic resource for examining where Richard Pryor stands in the historical context of African-American expression. It is, as most initial histories are, a "great man" epic. *On the Real Side* traces modern African-American humor from its African roots through the chain of creative talents who have chipped away at the barriers that segregated African-American from mainstream American humor. Watkins describes a cultural wall that sealed African-American humor from its mainstream counterpart. Some artists, like Lenny Bruce, were able to borrow from the other side of the wall. But for the most part, it was not until the irresistible crossover appeal of Dick Gregory, Flip Wilson, and Bill Cosby emerged in the 1960s that black comics were taken seriously by the entertainment industry. As Watkins sees it, Richard Pryor launched himself from his immediate predecessors' shoulders and busted down the cultural wall. Once Pryor and his contemporaries crumbled the wall, they could offer the rest of America the purest form possible of African-American comic styles and substance.

Pryor's personal rise is an amazing story, but his stylistic triumph is even more impressive. Pryor did not succeed by sugarcoating his act or his personality. He was one of the first major black comedians who did not have to develop two acts—one for white audiences and one for blacks. Pryor showed the same African-American experiential groundings regardless of his audience. He spoofed misguided liberals as well as dangerous rednecks, even though his audience was often filled with white liberals. Pryor riddled all authority figures with the full arsenal of his comic tools: parody, tricksterism, hyperbole, double-edged vernacular, and rapid-fire revelations of hypocrisy. Pryor generally employed two methods in his stand-up routines: the autobiographical anecdote and the character sketch. Within both methods Pryor's strength was his voice characterization. He could skewer whining whites with a dead-on imitation or transform himself into a wise wino. Some voices came from his childhood in Peoria, Illinois. Some came from Hollywood parties.

Pryor's subject matter was even more threatening to whites than his styles were. In his act and in interviews, Pryor described having sex with prostitutes while growing up in Peoria, where his grandmother ran a brothel. He often used anecdotes about his sexual conquests, both interracial and extramarital. He boasted of his drug use in ways that equally addicted comics, such as John Belushi, dared not for fear of marring their marketability. Pryor was in a sense freer to paint a negative and dangerous picture of himself because his growing audience loved his unpredictability and daring. In addition, Pryor subversively used racist assumptions about the proclivity of sexual promiscuity and drug use in his act. Yes, he was bad, but no one else was any better. Pryor's stylistic and substantive experiments touched nerves in an increasingly nervous nation. Some might surmise that a growing desire for racial justice and equality contributed to Pryor's rise. This hypothesis may apply more to the success of Gregory, Cosby, and Wilson. But Pryor was often well beyond the tolerance level of nervous liberals. For these reasons, Watkins rightfully labels the Pryor phenomenon "nothing short of revolutionary."[4]

How did this revolution arise? What sparked it, or at least made it possible? How did Richard Pryor go from a struggling young comic with no sense of personal stage presence to a figure about whom white and black comics of three generations sing his praises? How could this bold and often frightening black man achieve so much commercially and artistically in a nation that still shows its racially sensitive underbelly every other first Tuesday in November? Ishmael Reed—the noted novelist, scholar, and professor of writing at the University of California at Berkeley—says Pryor sparked his own revolution. "Richard's a genius," says Reed; "just outrageous." For Reed, the Richard Pryor phenomenon was the classic story of a hungry genius who struggled, succeeded, and sold out. The fact that Pryor had that wall of stylistic segregation to either destroy or hurdle is a sign, for Reed, of how much more of a genius Pryor had to be than his white contemporaries, for instance, George Carlin or David Brenner.[5]

Reed first saw Pryor perform in a coffee shop in Greenwich Village around 1965 or 1966. Reed's wife was performing in an art troupe that included Yoko Ono, and Pryor opened for them. Pryor immensely impressed Reed because in that setting Pryor, facing a crowd yearning for experimentation, was free to say or do anything. "The talent was there," Reed said of the early Pryor. "The style was different," meaning it was yet to be defined and refined. Reed was among those who helped Pryor define himself in 1969 and 1970. Reed and Pryor grew intellectually close in those years while Pryor was woodshedding in Berkeley. The term "woodshedding" is of special significance here because of its roots in a black culture to which Pryor was closely connected; jazz musicians use the word to describe the gestational process of mastering an instrument and its stylistic canon. For instance, after playing in several mediocre bands around Kansas City in the early 1930s, Charlie Parker took a stack of Lester Young recordings to the Ozarks and mastered all of the older man's licks. When he returned, Parker had found his own voice as well as the technical mastery required to play along with Young.[6] Among their circle of friends were novelists and playwrights such as Claude Brown, Cecil Brown, Al Young, and David Henderson. "[Pryor] was a scholar of comedy" before he got to Berkeley, Reed said. "We just gave him extra materials. We had some long discussions. He was a very experimental comedian, even early on. But even then, he said he wanted to 'get over,'" to be rich and successful in the mainstream world. This was the time of black power and the black arts movement. Reed asserts that the movement's attempts to valorize and isolate the blackness of African-American expression did not really affect Pryor in those days:

> Black arts was confined to Harlem. It frightened people, so
> it got all the attention. But I don't think black arts had that
> much significance out here to Richard. He was into El-

dridge Cleaver, Richard Wright, Mort Saul, and Lenny
Bruce and the people who loosened up things in the 1950s.
In Berkeley, we had free speech—taking language perfor-
mance to an art.

Before 1969, Pryor—especially on television—was doing what Pryor
called "that Cosby shit." His material, mostly innocuous stories with some
racial tinge, was generally reheated, "safe" material. When Pryor returned to
Los Angeles from Berkeley in 1970, he was angry, he was sexual, he was
scary, and he was almost instantly successful. Yet to Reed, he was still pure
Pryor—immensely talented but flawed by ambition: "Richard should have
stayed in Berkeley. Free speech was invented in Berkeley. I don't think Hollywood served him too well. The circle he was running around with here was
very positive to him. Hollywood just ruined him. What was that thing he did
with Jackie Gleason? *The Toy*? What was that shit? Two geniuses . . ."

If we accept Reed's hypothesis as complete and definitive, then the
Pryor phenomenon is explainable because Pryor was a flawed genius willing
to mug for the cameras. But we are left with the question of how Pryor was
allowed to get away with so much angry and scary material for so long. Six
years before Pryor embarrassed himself in *The Toy* (1982), he ad-libbed his
lines for a scene in which he convinced Gene Wilder to sport blackface in
Silver Streak, a scene Williams and Williams describe as a very subversive
improvisation. In addition, Pryor's greatest artistic and commercial triumphs
were his solo concert films, which were undeniably sexual and daring.[7]

To explain these elements of the Pryor phenomenon, we must look
to something much bigger and grander that occurred in the United States
during the twenty years or so before Pryor went woodshedding in Berkeley:
the culture was deeply and irrevocably Africanized. At the dawn of the
twentieth century, W. E. B. Du Bois began an intellectual war against the
prevailing racial situation. He set the color line as a battleground on which
America might well live up to its promise. Significantly, Du Bois—Napoleon's
lessons notwithstanding—declared a two-front war, one political and cultural.
The political conflagration rages on, with some significant victories behind
it, but the cultural war is nearly over. African-American culture has always
been—as described by Ralph Ellison—a major "tributary" of American culture.
Several influential scholars have agreed with Ellison and have produced
books that support the claim for the interdependence of black and white
expression. These works of literary history and criticisms show fairly
conclusively that from the birth of American letters, both white and black
authors have been listening to both white and black voices. The two literary
traditions have been engaged in a dialogue of differences and have borrowed

style and substance from each other.[8] As Toni Morrison wrote in *Playing in the Dark*, "There seems to be a more or less tacit agreement among literary scholars that, because American literature has been clearly the preserve of white male views, genius, and power, those views, genius, and power are without relationship to and removed from the overwhelming pressure of black people in the United States. . . . the contemplation of this black presence is central to any understanding of our national literature and should not be permitted to hover at the margins of the literary imagination."[9]

In 1903, W. E. B. Du Bois asked, "Would America have been America without her Negro people?"[10] Ralph Ellison answered Du Bois in a 1970 *Time* magazine essay, "What America Would Be Like Without Blacks": "If we can resist for a moment the temptation to view everything having to do with Negro Americans in terms of racially imposed status, we become aware of the fact that for all the harsh reality of the social and economic injustices visited upon them, these injustices have failed to keep Negroes clear of the cultural mainstream; Negro Americans are in fact one of its major tributaries."[11]

Ellison's description did not go deep enough for 1970. By that time, as Richard Pryor was emerging, that tributary had swollen over its banks, supplying much of what American culture thirsted for: rebelliousness, courage, creativity, and soul. Deep blues had once again shaken the whitewashed world of American rock and roll. Motown had pushed urban rhythm and blues up the white pop charts. A black Muslim was the heavyweight champion of the world. A black pitcher, Bob Gibson, had paralyzed the Detroit Tigers in the 1968 World Series with his intense, angry stare and unhittable fastball. Earl "the Pearl" Monroe and Walt "Clyde" Frazier were about to dazzle the National Basketball Association with their improvisational skills on the hardwood. Neither Richard Pryor nor any of these other figures burst down any cultural walls or dams. The strength of and demand for black cultural expression simply overflowed the levies that white America had futilely built after Reconstruction.

Two authors—both journalists—have described this triumph of black cultural expression. One is Nelson George, whose *Elevating the Game: Black Men and Basketball* tells the story of how black athletes took over the game in less than fifty years.[12] The other is W. T. Lhamon, who declares in his 1990 book *Deliberate Speed: The Origins of a Cultural Style in the American 1950s* that American youth grew to equate black expressions with youthful, forward-looking style. Black and white youths in the 1950s identified with each other through the works of Vladimir Nabokov, Thelonius Monk, Chuck Berry, Jackson Pollock, Jack Kerouac, and Martin Luther King, Jr.[13]

If, by 1970, black expressions had crowded out non-black forms and had become the dominant voice in some sectors of American culture, how did Richard Pryor fit in? Why was comedy one of these sectors? What did white audiences want from African-American humor generally and Richard Pryor specifically? It is important to remember that—as in literature and music—a constant dialogue between black and white storytelling traditions has existed for nearly as long as there have been black and white storytellers on this continent. Although no one has yet traced the interdependence of black and white humor through American history, there are clearly similarities in function, if not structure, between these black and white comic traditions.

One convenient location from which to begin tracing the interdependence of these two traditions of humor is Hannibal, Missouri. Mark Twain—as Shelley Fisher Fishkin shows in *Was Huck Black?*—was enchanted by African-American comic storytelling styles. Twain showed a deep respect for African-American humor, seeing it as much more than just quaint folk expression. Much like Pryor would do for white voices, Twain spent years trying to master the spoken inflections of African-American dialects so he could employ them during his lucrative speaking engagements, which were the nineteenth-century version of the stand-up circuit. Twain, like Elvis, made a good living out of selling black expressions to a white audience who would never think of paying for the real thing. In his book *Mark Twain and the Art of the Tall Tale,* Henry Wonham shows how Twain tapped into the deep American oral tradition of yarn spinning. In his description of the function of the tall tale among a "community of knowers," Wonham provides a clue as to how Pryor's appeal translated itself to white audiences as well as black. Wonham explains that the American pragmatic tradition, as defined by Charles Sanders Peirce and William James, recognized that the truth of a statement depended on its ability to generate consensus among a community. In other words, in America truth is a matter of agreement. Conversely, the community of knowers marks anyone who accepts as "true" a notion they do not accept as outside the community and thus the object of ridicule. Wonham describes the function of tall humor in the United States: "For the group that shares the yarn spinner's privileged point of view, the inflated story of cruelty and suffering—by making those things laughable—may signal a dual victory over both condescending outsiders and the very conditions of life that inspire the tale." In other words, tall tales involve the teller feigning sincerity, stretching credulity, and tricking the outsiders for the bemusement of the insiders.[14]

This feigning, or lying, is certainly made easier by the use of a mask, a cold poker face, an innocent-looking simpleton or a jester in minstrel makeup. Only those who know the authentic identity of the performer would feel included in the joke. As Ralph Ellison wrote, in words that invoke some of the same themes that Wonham explores,

> For the ex-colonials, the declaration of an American identity meant the assumption of a mask, and it imposed not only the discipline of national self-consciousness, it gave Americans an ironic awareness of the joke that always lies between appearance and reality, between the discontinuity of social tradition and that sense of the past which clings to the mind. And perhaps even an awareness of the joke that society is man's creation, not God's. Americans began their revolt from the English fatherland when they dumped the tea into the Boston Harbor, masked as Indians, and the mobility of the society created in this limitless space has encouraged the use of the mask for good and evil ever since. . . . Masking is a play upon possibility and ours is a society in which possibilities are many. When American life is most American it is apt to be most theatrical.[15]

Richard Pryor was a master of the tall tale. He could pose, don a mask, and exaggerate with the best of them. These were skills he observed in elders as a child in Peoria and then rediscovered in Berkeley. For example, Pryor's character Mudbone, the wise street wino, relates a tall tale common in African-American humor:

> Ah, that nigger could tell lies. That's how we became friends, see. He tell a lie, I tell a lie, see, and we compliment each other's lies. He make me laugh all day long, bless his soul. He told me this lie one time, told me 'bout the niggers with the big dicks, see. Y'all ever heard it? The niggers had the biggest dicks in the world, and they were trying to find a place where they could have their contest, see. And they wasn't no freaks, didn't want anybody lookin'. . . . They was walking around lookin' for a secret place. So they walked across the Golden Gate Bridge and the nigger seen that water and it make him want to piss, see. Boy say, "Man, I got to take a leak." He pulled out his thing and was pissing. The other nigger pulled his out, took a piss. One nigger say, "Goddamn! This water cold." The other nigger say, "Yeah, and it's deep, too."[16]

Certainly, no outsider would fall for this tall tale. It does not, unlike some of Pryor's jokes, unite a community of knowers and exclude outsiders. But it remains an effective humorous device because it tests the teller of the tale to strike a convincing pose successfully. The delivery is more important than the tale itself. For white audiences in the 1970s, this glimpse into African-American humor through Richard Pryor made them feel they were being accepted uneasily into the community of knowers. From the time of Mailer's "White Negroes," the Hipsters, and the beats, white audiences have been trying to buy a seat in the community of knowers and have been borrowing vocabulary as badges of membership. If white audience members got more than half the jokes at a Pryor concert, they could feel included. They could then try to learn what Pryor meant by those jokes they did not get. Pryor mastered this playful inclusion and exclusion of his audience throughout the early 1970s and continued it into the early 1980s, when he stopped making concert films and records. White America desired an avenue into black oral tradition, and Pryor offered it on a large scale at their local theaters. In this way, Pryor masterfully exploited the triumph of black cultural expression.

Notes

1. For the chronology of Richard Pryor's career, see John A. and Dennis A. Williams, *If I Stop I'll Die: The Comedy and Tragedy of Richard Pryor* (New York: Thunder's Mouth Press, 1991). For a view of Pryor in historical context, see Mel Watkins, *On the Real Side: Laughing, Lying and Signifying; The Underground Tradition of African-American Humor That Transformed American Culture, from Slavery to Richard Pryor* (New York: Simon and Schuster, 1994).

2. Siva Vaidhyanathan, personal interview with Ishmael Reed (6 December 1994).

3. This notion will be the subject of future work of mine on these and other cultural figures.

4. Watkins, 562.

5. Vaidhyanathan, interview with Reed. For a detailed account of Pryor's hiatus in Berkeley, see Williams and Williams, and Watkins.

6. Significantly, Pryor was supposed to star in a film adaptation of Ross Russell's 1973 biography of Parker, *Bird Lives!* It was never made.

7. Williams and Williams, 84–86.

8. For an exploration of the intermingling of African and African-American influences in American culture, see Eric Sundquist, *To Wake the Nations: Race in the Making of American Literature* (Cambridge: Harvard

University Press, 1993). See also Shelley Fisher Fishkin, *Was Huck Black?: Mark Twain and African American Voices* (New York: Oxford University Press, 1993); Werner Sollors, *Beyond Ethnicity: Consent and Descent in American Culture* (New York: Oxford University Press, 1986); Paul Gilroy, *The Black Atlantic: Modernity and Double Consciousness* (Cambridge: Harvard University Press, 1993); Michael North, *The Dialect of Modernism: Race, Language and Twentieth Century Literature* (New York: Oxford University Press, 1994); and Henry B. Wonham, ed., *Criticism on the Color Line: Race and Revisionism in American Literary Studies* (New Brunswick: Rutgers University Press, 1995).

    9. Toni Morrison, *Playing in the Dark: Whiteness and the Literary Imagination* (Cambridge: Harvard University Press, 1992), 5.

    10. W. E. B. Du Bois, *The Souls of Black Folk* (New York: Penguin Classics, 1989), 215.

    11. Ralph Ellison, "What America Would Be Like Without Blacks," *Going to the Territory* (New York: Random House, 1987), 108.

    12. See Nelson George, *Elevating the Game: Black Men and Basketball* (New York: Harper Collins, 1992).

    13. W. T. Lhamon, Jr., *Deliberate Speed: The Origins of a Cultural Style in the American 1950s* (Washington, D.C.: Smithsonian Institution Press, 1990), xiii.

    14. Henry B. Wonham, *Mark Twain and the Art of the Tall Tale* (New York: Oxford University Press, 1993), 18.

    15. Ralph Ellison, "Change the Joke and Slip the Yoke," *Shadow & Act* (New York: Signet, 1964), 68.

    16. Pryor, as quoted in Watkins, 550–51.

Selected Works

Du Bois, W. E. B. *The Souls of Black Folk.* New York: Penguin Classics, 1989.

Ellison, Ralph. "Change the Joke and Slip the Yoke." *Partisan Review* (1958). Reprint, *Shadow & Act,* New York: Signet, 1964, 61–73.

———. "What America Would Be Like Without Blacks." *Going to the Territory.* New York: Random House, 1987, 104–12.

Fishkin, Shelley Fisher. *Was Huck Black?: Mark Twain and African American Voices.* New York: Oxford University Press, 1993.

George, Nelson. *Elevating the Game: Black Men and Basketball.* New York: Harper Collins, 1992.

Gilroy, Paul. *The Black Atlantic: Modernity and Double Consciousness.* Cambridge: Harvard University Press, 1993.

Lhamon, W. T., Jr. *Deliberate Speed: The Origins of a Cultural Style in the American 1950s.* Washington, D.C.: Smithsonian Institution Press, 1990.

Morrison, Toni. *Playing in the Dark: Whiteness and the Literary Imagination.* Cambridge: Harvard University Press, 1992.

North, Michael. *The Dialect of Modernism: Race, Language and Twentieth Century Literature.* New York: Oxford University Press, 1994.

Russell, Ross. *Bird Lives!* New York: Charter House Publishers, 1973; reprint, New York: Da Capo Press, 1966.

Sollors, Werner. *Beyond Ethnicity: Consent and Descent in American Culture.* New York: Oxford University Press, 1986.

Sundquist, Eric. *To Wake the Nations: Race in the Making of American Literature.* Cambridge: Harvard University Press, 1993.

Watkins, Mel. *On the Real Side: Laughing, Lying and Signifying; The Underground Tradition of African-American Humor That Transformed American Culture, from Slavery to Richard Pryor.* New York: Simon and Schuster, 1994.

Williams, John A., and Dennis A. Williams. *If I Stop I'll Die: The Comedy and Tragedy of Richard Pryor.* New York: Thunder's Mouth Press, 1991.

Wonham, Henry B. *Mark Twain and the Art of the Tall Tale.* New York: Oxford University Press, 1993.

———, ed. *Criticism on the Color Line: Race and Revisionism in American Literary Studies.* New Brunswick: Rutgers University Press, 1995.

The Comic Texan in Film:
A Regional Stereotype
in the National Imagination

Don Graham

The comic Texan is one of a few regional stereotypes that have leaped from the provinces to lodge permanently in the national pantheon of memorable icons, becoming something instantly recognizable, instantly usable. Like the old chicken-and-egg story, one might legitimately ask which came first, the Texan or the comic Texan? Probably the Texan, but we must not forget that one of the first Texans was Davy Crockett, a considerable humorist in his own right and a figure whose real identity always seemed to be mixed up with imaginary ones, as occurs in the Crockett *Almanacs*.[1]

The earliest comic generic Texan was composed of about equal parts of Southwestern humor and dime novel. Nineteenth-century humorist Alexander Sweet sums up this view of the Texan in his essay "That Typical Texan," published in 1882:

> The typical Texan is a large-sized Jabberwock, a hairy kind of gorilla, who is supposed to reside on a horse. He is half alligator, half human, who eats raw buffalo and sleeps out on a prairie. He is expected to carry four or five revolvers at his belt, as if he were a sort of perambulating gun-rack. He also carries a large assortment of cutlery in his boot. It is believed that a failure to invite him to drink is more dangerous than to kick a can of dynamite. The only time the typical Texan is supposed to be peaceable is after he has killed all his friends, and can find no fresh material to practice on.[2]

Sweet's "mythical personage," as he terms it, which "figures so largely in the Yankee mind and dime novels," was just that: a myth with little basis in reality. The closest embodiment of the figure in actual history would have been somebody like Big Foot Wallace, whose Crockett-like adventures, as recorded by John C. Duval, certainly contain strong admixtures of heroic exploits salted with a humor of exaggeration and belligerence. The rhetorical similarity between Big Foot Wallace and famous yarn spinners of Southwestern humor such as Sut Lovingood and Simon Suggs is apparent in a typical remark. The occasion is the appearance among him and his men of a pretentious "Author" who wants to write about the Wild West and who brandishes a very small pistol. Wallace observes, "I wish I may be kicked to death by grasshoppers if he didn't fish up out of his breeches pockets a little pepper-box of a thing about the size and length of my big toe."[3]

Except for the first influential manifestation of the comic Texan, the place to look is not in the annals of Sweet but in the work of Charles Hale Hoyt (1859–1900), a popular farceur of the 1890s, now largely forgotten, whose plays earned him both fame and wealth. Asked why he didn't take the theater seriously, Hoyt remarked, "I do. There is nothing funny about a game that is earning me $100,000 a year. That's serious money."[4] One of Hoyt's biggest successes was *A Texas Steer* (1890), which was immensely popular in its day. At one time there were five touring companies performing the play throughout the country. It enjoyed a long shelf life, too. As late as 1939, a shortened version of the play was published to provide a text for production, under the title *A Texas Steer: A Modern Acting Version of Charles H. Hoyt's Famous Comedy,* by Randolph Carter. There were also two silent film versions, one in 1915 and another in 1928.

Compared to Sweet's typical Texan and Duval's outsized frontier hero, the comic Texan as defined by Hoyt's *A Texas Steer* is pretty mild milk, a character played more for laughs than puissance. Hoyt's hero is a west Texas cattle king named Maverick Brander. Brander's pushy, ambitious wife coerces him into running for Congress as a means of breaking into Washington society. Brander hates the thought of leaving "the wilds of west Texas" and wonders out loud, "I'm an honest man. What would I do in Congress?"[5] Once ensconced in the capital, he continues to wear his rancher's garb and is repeatedly mistaken for a member of a Wild West troupe. Homesick for Texas, he has a metal horse installed in his office. He likes to mount this contraption and pretend he's riding the range. In one scene, perched on horseback, wearing his Stetson, boots, and a string tie, he ropes a corrupt African American ("darkie," in the lexicon of the day) named Fishback, an instance of two stereotypes in startling juxtaposition. Brander's slightly vulgar wife and his buxom, high-spirited daughter, Bossy, who calls herself "a gawky Texas girl in a frightful dress," round out this Texas family. Although the Branders strike Washington as not "tame," after a couple of years they win acceptance, thanks in large part, as Bossy shrewdly observes, to their wealth.

While Brander learns to dress less flamboyantly, the rougher side of his Texas background remains in high relief through the presence of three outlandish Texas cronies: Yell, Bragg, and Blow. Yell is a "great-boned Texan," and Bragg and Blow "look as much like Yell as possible." Their names tell everything about these three archetypal good old boys. They are loud, they like to brag (about Texas of course), and they never adjust their Wild West hyperbole to the usages of polite society. During a fancy dinner party late in the play, Yell, Bragg, and Blow break out their pistols and start a riot. Earlier we see a similarly crude side to their characters when Yell explains how he handled voting procedures in Brander's election: "Hell! I put through three Chinamen and a Mexican who was half nigger! We ain't particular in Texas." Indeed the play is so racist that it is hard to imagine its ever being produced again.

The crowning relevance of *A Texas Steer* to future representations of Texas in newspapers, magazines, movies, TV, advertising, and fashion occurs in a prophetic passage. Brassy Gall, a conniving Washington lobbyist who tries to enlist Brander's aid in a pork-barrel project, expatiates on the promise of Texas:

> The time was when we regarded Texas as the refuge of the criminal and the home of the coyote and cactus but since Mr. Brander has been here, our eyes have been opened. We have learned to appreciate the greatness and future glory of Texas! He has taught us that Texas is the coming Empire State! Gentlemen, thanks to the efforts of Mr. Brander, Texas is becoming the center of commerce and the home of science, literature, and the arts! (38)

Yell, drunk, interrupts with a cry: "Three cheers for literature." Then Gall continues: "And mark my words, gentlemen, in five years, and maybe less, New York will go to Texas for its fashions."

Three cheers for literature indeed. The list of twentieth-century Texas authors who have laced their work with Texas humor is a long one. C. L. Sonnichsen's anthology, *The Laughing West, Humorous Western Fiction Past and Present* (1988), includes, however, only two Texas authors, Larry L. King and Dan Jenkins, but Sonnichsen admits in his introduction that Larry McMurtry deserves a place as well. Humor is a prominent strain in much of McMurtry's work and is featured in such novels as *The Last Picture Show* (1966), *All My Friends Are Going To Be Strangers* (1972), *Cadillac Jack*

(1982), *Lonesome Dove* (1985), and *Texasville* (1987). Perhaps we should simply note that a sense of comedy informs all of McMurtry's fiction.[6]

The origins of the comic Texan in film, not surprisingly, lie in popular literature, beginning in the nineteenth century. The rich body of Texas humor in popular journalism and fiction offered a ready-made fund of material for filmmakers. Silent film versions of *A Texas Steer* disseminated in a powerful visual way the iconography of the comic Texan. Easily the best is the 1928 film starring living legend Will Rogers as the ideal embodiment of Maverick Brander—an instance of seemingly perfect casting. The Oklahoma cowboy humorist breathed an air of naturalness into the Texas rancher and won plaudits from the *New York Times*. Rogers also wrote most of the titles and did a fine job of capturing the vernacular humor of the play. Rogers's Brander says, for example, that his home town of Red Dog, Texas, is a place where "men are men and the plumbing is improving." (The stage play also has a very funny exchange about Red Dog. Gall says of the town, "All it needs is some good society and a little more rain," to which Brander rejoins, "Some good society and a little more rain—that's all Hell needs.")

The stage and film versions of *A Texas Steer* are among the most important early vehicles for transmitting the image of the Texan to a large audience. Andy Adams, who had been a real cowboy, was so annoyed by its stereotypical portrayal of Texas cattlemen that he wrote the trail-drive classic *Log of a Cowboy* (1903) to tell the story correctly. The Texas steer image was popular enough to be echoed in a 1939 John Wayne Republic Studio Western titled *Three Texas Steers*. Incidentally, one has to wonder if Hoyt or Hollywood ever knew the meaning of the word "steer" (a castrated male bovine). The term seems at best an odd choice to represent Texas machismo.

There were, of course, other and earlier cinematic portraits of the comic Texan, but it is impossible to identify the first comic portrayal of the Texan in film because of the paucity of information concerning lost silent movies. The first film to feature Texas materials has a title that sounds comic today: *Texas Tex*. From what we know about it, *Texas Tex* appears to have been a routine, primitive Western. Filmed in Denmark in 1908, it dealt with the daring-do of a Texas cowboy hero who has to rescue his girlfriend from a band of Sioux Indians. In the next decade several of silent-movie star Tom Mix's Westerns contained comic elements, and Mix's Texas persona is often that of a scamp, as in films like *The Heart of Texas Ryan* (1917). In more famous Mix films like *Riders of the Purple Sage* (1925) there are far too many serious issues, such as the penchant of Mormons for polygamy, to leave time for comic development. In other early Westerns, there were early prefigurations of the comic sidekick—as in the big cattle-drive epic *North of 36* (1924)—the sort of role that Walter Brennan would bring to perfection in

Red River. But the comic sidekick, a generic staple of B Westerns, does not appear to be imbued with unique Texas characteristics.

The comic Texan became a stock figure in Westerns throughout the 1940s and 1950s. Often he is presented as a braggart, a windy teller of tall tales, a vulgarian who is overly chauvinistic about his state, a supporting figure good for some guffaws but not center stage, not the protagonist. *Giant* (1956) has several of them in the background, including Chill Wills, who virtually made a career out of the part. These Texans are both crude bumpkins and millionaires. They talk like hicks but own their own airplanes.

The modern-day incarnation of the full-blown comic Texan appears most completely and successfully in *The Wheeler Dealers.* The film premiered in Dallas at a most inopportune time: 20 November 1963. All that month the Dallas *Morning News* had carried a series of advertisements for this new movie starring James Garner and Lee Remick. The advertisements featured photos not of the stars but of native Texan Chill Wills, a mainstay of cinematic images of the Texan for over thirty years. A series of Texas brag jokes accompanied the photos—for instance, "Didja Hear the One about the Texan That Bought a Kid for His Dog?" Another ad appealed to nativistic sentiments: "If you're a born Texan (or even a transplanted one), you've gotta see us make fools of those Yankee New Yorkers."[7]

Like most popular incarnations and most art—Harold Bloom would say like 100 percent of all art—*The Wheeler Dealers* was hardly sui generis; it didn't spring from the brow of some simple bard of the plains. Before and behind *The Wheeler Dealers* lay, as we have seen, a long tradition of the comic Texan. A Yale graduate with a degree in Romance languages, Garner's character is a pretend-Texan, replete with boots, Stetson, string tie, and an accent dripping with sounds from the provincial plains. He assumes the Texas persona, another character explains, because "the best way to rub up against money was to be a Texan." A masterpiece of the comic Texan subgenre, *The Wheeler Dealers* presents the Texan as a good-humored archetype of charm and savvy, a figure of irresistible appeal, a modern Maverick Brander.

The plot takes Garner from barren, dusty west Texas oil fields to the financial world of New York City where he wheels and deals. Garner buys the taxi that he hails to drive him into the city from the airport, saying it's cheaper that way; when he leaves, he'll just sell it and take a tax write-off. He goes to an elegant French restaurant, orders his steak burned with a side order of greens, and then buys the restaurant because the young woman he is with likes it. The formerly haughty maître d' is now very nice to him indeed. Garner's Texan swaggers and cajoles and grins his way through a series of financial ups and downs.

The funniest wheeling and dealing in the movie comes when Garner and a pretentious New York artist form a partnership and ransack Europe, collecting abstract expressionist paintings. Showing off his hotel suite full of Kandinskys and de Koonings, Garner brags, "Me and my boy Stan, we been wildcattin' all over the place." Their ventures in capitalist art speculation prove so attractive that Garner's pals from Texas want in on the action. There are three of them, all direct descendants of Hoyt's Texas steers. Yell, Bragg, and Blow are reincarnated here as R. J., Ray Jay, and J. R. Played by Phil Harris, Charles Watts, and, de rigueur, Chill Wills, the three men form a hilarious trio. They fly to New York on their private jet with its own steam room festooned with longhorn replicas. They wear Stetsons, boots, string ties, and are never without a bourbon and branch water in their hand. They view the art stacked around Garner's hotel room in terms familiar from their wheeler-dealer oil backgrounds and talk knowingly, lovingly, of acreage, depletions, and overrides.

In the wake of the Kennedy assassination, however, it stopped being easy for outsiders, or even locals, to see Texans as lovable millionaire good old boys, at least not for a good many years; a sinister dimension had been added. What happened to the comic Texan after November 22 is starkly simple: he suddenly turned dark and treacherous, becoming a monster of paranoia and xenophobia—in short, a hysterical, power-mad, ultra right–wing conspirator capable of anything in the name of Americanism. General Midwinter in *The Billion Dollar Brain* (1967), based on a Len Deighton novel, is a stark example. Although he dresses like a comic Texan—he wears department-store-bought Western-style pants, a Western shirt with pearl buttons, and a black string tie—there is nothing funny about him. He never smiles or laughs; instead, his face is always grim, filled with paranoid hatred. He has a war room that "makes the Pentagon look like a room in the Alamo." "I love the sound of gunfire," he says. He equates Europe and Washington as centers of polluted air, in contrast to Texas, which has the cleanest air in the world. He hasn't been out of Texas in twenty-five years, and it shows. This humorless, egomaniacal, anti-Communist puritan is the comic Texan transformed into the ugly Texan.

It is altogether fitting that the way the world ends in Stanley Kubrick's apocalyptic Cold War comedy, *Dr. Strangelove, or How I Learned to Stop Worrying and Love the Bomb* (1964), is with a Texan astride an A-Bomb, emitting a loud cowboy whoop as he rides the bucking bomb downward to its fail-safe target in the heart of Russia. The Texan, played by Slim Pickens, is named King Kong and represents a younger version of Chill Wills. We know he is a Texan because he wears boots and a Stetson and has an accent as thick as red-eye gravy. In the novel on which the film is loosely based, *Red Alert* (1958), by Peter Bryant, the B-52 commander hails from "Dothan, Alabama, but he had spent most of his life before joining the Air Force in Cincinnati, which accounted for his lack of Southern accent." The transformation of this character into a Texan can be credited to scriptwriter Terry Southern, a native Texan. In a discarded passage in the script, Major Kong's Texas credentials are even more explicit. At one point he inventories the contents of his flight crew's survival kits: "nine packs of chewing gum; one issue of prophylactics; three lipsticks, three pair of nylon stockings. Gee, a fella could have a pretty good weekend in Dallas with all that stuff." The film was released early in 1964, and the filmmakers changed the reference from Dallas to Las Vegas because of the wholly negative aura of Dallas in the post-assassination months. The translation of the traditional image into a darker, modern one, consistent with the times, is notable.

It wasn't until *Urban Cowboy* (1980) that the Texan was rehabilitated from over a decade of vilification and once again restored to his status as unspoiled son of the plains. As in *A Texas Steer,* the Texas cowboy hero, removed from his rural paradise, finds himself most at home in the city when he is astride a mount. In the case of *Urban Cowboy,* of course, the mount is a moving machine, a barroom bucking bronco, an automated version of the steed Will Rogers straddles in *A Texas Steer.* John Travolta, that temporary Texan from New Jersey, dresses the part, wearing boots, Stetson, pearl-buttoned shirt. He is not of course a comic Texan, but he is eminently recognizable on any stage. His uncle is played by Barry Corbin, the heir apparent to Slim Pickens and Chill Wills in the grits 'n gravy department. *Urban Cowboy,* a sort of dance Western, marks one more moment in the long tradition of the Texan in film.

In his 1961 book *The Super-Americans, New Yorker* author John Bainbridge sought to explain the interest Texas holds for the rest of the nation. "Texas," he wrote, "is a mirror in which Americans see themselves reflected, not life-sized but, as in a distorting mirror, bigger than life. They are not pleased by the image. Being unable to deny the likeness, they attempt to diminish it by making fun of it."[8] The comic Texan, as I have tried to suggest, is a particularly rich addition to the panoply of national stereotypes, and by no means dead. At the installation of Ronald Reagan into the National Cowboy Hall of Fame in 1989, Reagan told a hoary Texas joke that delighted his Oklahoma audience. Talking about his own ranch, he recalled, "You know, it reminds me of a story about a woman from New York who met a rancher from Texas and asked how big his property was. He said thirty-five acres. 'You call that a ranch?' 'No 'm, downtown Dallas.'"

By using the comic Texan, Reagan placed himself in good company. T. S. Eliot, after all, included in *The Waste Land* a Texan: Stetson, the Westerner at the end of Part 1, "The Burial of the Dead," a soldier-warrior who fought in an ancient war. Maybe the Eliot reference is stretching things a bit, but that, too, is in the best tradition of the comic Texan, from the nineteenth century to now.

Notes

1. For a vigorous discussion of the twin faces of Crockett, popular icon and the actual historical figure, see Jeff Long, *Duel of Eagles: The Mexican and U.S. Fight for the Alamo* (New York: William Morrow, 1990), 104–7.

2. Alexander Sweet, *Alex Sweet's Texas: The Lighter Side of Lone Star History,* ed. Virginia Eisenhour (Austin: University of Texas Press, 1986), 85. This piece appeared originally in *Sketches from Texas Siftings* (1882).

3. John C. Duval, *The Adventures of Big Foot Wallace,* ed. Mabel Major and Rebecca W. Smith (1936; Lincoln: University of Nebraska Press, 1966), 117. Interestingly, Bigfoot Wallace appears as a character in one of Larry McMurtry's recent novels, *Dead Man's Walk* (1995), but lacks the humor of the original and is killed off by McMurtry in a direct violation of the known facts about Wallace's life.

4. Douglas L. Hunt, "The Life and Work of Charles Hoyt," *Bulletin of Birmingham-Southern College* 39:1 (January 1946), 30.

5. All quotations from the play are from *A Texas Steer or "Money Makes the Mare Go,"* in Montrose J. Moses, ed., *Representative American Dramas National and Local* (Boston: Little Brown, 1926).

6. For a good discussion of McMurtry's "comic genius," see D. G. Kehl, "Thalia's 'Sock' and the Cowhide Boot: Humor of the New Southwest in the Fiction of Larry McMurtry," *Southwestern American Literature* 14:2 (spring 1989), 20–33; and C. L. Sonnichsen, ed. *Texas Humoresque: Lone Star Humorists from Then till Now* (Fort Worth: Texas Christian University Press, 1990).

7. Don Graham, *Cowboys and Cadillacs: How Hollywood Looks at Texas* (Austin: Texas Monthly Press, 1983), 73. Graham's commentary and extensive filmography point to many other manifestations of the comic in Texas films.

8. John Bainbridge, *The Super-Americans* (Garden City, New York: Doubleday, 1961), 6.

Popular Humor in Print

The "Funny Republican": P. J. O'Rourke and the Graying of Boomer Humor

Thomas Grant

During the 1920s, when many, mainly young people flocked to cities and the nation became predominantly urban, voters elected three avuncular conservative presidents in a row from small-town America: Harding, Coolidge, and Hoover. The generational conflict pitting youthful, liberalizing attitudes against traditional, conservative values created a cultural environment divided over fundamental issues. Conditions were ripe for young, irreverent journalists eager to attack and expose vice and folly—"bunk," to use a term coined in the 1920s.[1] Few journalists relished the challenge more than H. L. Mencken, who hit his satiric stride in the 1920s terrorizing sanctimonious and hypocritical moralists and politicians as well as the "booboisie" too easily gulled by them. Although he adopted the morally superior stance and denunciatory tone of the Juvenalian railer, Mencken never seriously intended to eliminate fraud and abuse. He needed his victims, and the times obliged him handsomely. For him, America was a "carnival of buncombe," a glorious, gaudy show where he was content being the dazzled spectator with a front-row center seat. "No other country houses so many gorgeous frauds and imbeciles as the US," he marveled in 1928. "I love this country as a small boy loves the circus."[2]

As befit a devotee of spectacle, Mencken cultivated the public persona of the cosmopolitan carouser, Falstaffian in his appetite for fatty foods, German beer, and big cigars. Like Shakespeare's rotund bombastic boaster, Mencken enjoyed most of all being onstage himself, whether in print or at the (men only) Baltimore bar, entertaining his select audience—a "forlorn intelligentsia," he called it—who shared his disdain for a commercial society paralyzed by corruption, demagoguery, and ballyhoo. What he called his "articulate noise"[3] could also be heard coast-to-coast, making him the nation's most influential arbiter on cultural matters. "So many young men," observed Jake Barnes in *The Sun Also Rises,* "get their likes and dislikes from Mencken."

61

When the Jazz age crashed in 1929, and the nation had to sober up and face a world dangerously balkanized, Mencken found himself bereft of his favorite adversaries. Increasingly out of touch, he turned bitter and resentful but continued to make himself heard until silenced by a stroke in 1948, eight years before his death. Recently, several ambitious young journalists have attempted to put on Mencken's mantle—or at least, to *sound* like him. These neo-Menckenites are baby boomers who emerged from the universities in the early 1970s—during another Republican ascendancy—in a decade that, like the 1920s, was driven by generational conflict between rapidly liberalizing attitudes and swiftly retrenching conservative values.

Two such writers came to the attention of the conservative wing of what Kevin Phillips called in 1970 "the emerging Republican majority"—reminiscent, perhaps, of Mencken's "forlorn intelligentsia." They achieved fame and fortune when Ronald Reagan, another avuncular conservative Republican from rural America, was elected president in 1980. The first is R. Emmett Tyrrell, Jr., editor-in-chief of *The American Spectator,* now the nation's highest-circulation conservative magazine; syndicated columnist; and author of two books of Menckenian "prejudices," *Public Nuisances* and *The Liberal Crackup,* both of which have sold briskly. The other is P. J. O'Rourke, humor columnist for *Rolling Stone* and author of many books of humor, including several in the debunking style of Mencken. Both journalists affect the Mencken pose of the cosmopolitan carouser devoted to manly appetites, including a taste for cigars—that is, if the claims of magazine puff pieces, TV talk show interviews, and book jacket hype can be taken at face value. Like Mencken they regard politics and culture in America as a "circus," and they're happy hurling insults at the performers from choice ringside seats. But whereas Mencken was cheerfully democratic in his choice of victims, many of whom hardly deserved his withering scorn, his imitators are unabashed Republican Party loyalists. Both Tyrrell and O'Rourke are ex-liberals who direct their contempt at Democratic Party luminaries, media celebrities deemed "liberal," feminists, and homosexuals. These are the avowed enemies of the neo-conservative establishment whose political advancement Tyrrell and O'Rourke serve—as well as, of course, their own. Insofar as what they write is funny, it can be called white man's humor. It delights in alleviating male boomer anxieties, but it also panders to their resentments and even at times strokes their prejudices—mainly against those groups who have threatened their hegemony, particularly women and blacks. It's out to settle scores. It's also highly processed, slickly packaged—fast-food humor. Tyrrell can take credit for opening this franchise of "humor McMencken," but his own product is so shamelessly a bland imitation of the original spicy recipe—even down to his plagiarizing of the master's now archaic vocabulary—that it's beneath comment, except to indicate how lucrative bashing liberals for laughs has become since the Carter interregnum.[4]

O'Rourke, on the other hand, is a wide-ranging and incisive wit who has successfully modernized the Mencken persona, style, and delivery. He has also absorbed the styles of humorists who inspired Mencken, particularly Twain, Bierce, and Wilde, as well as those of Mencken's contemporary wits, particularly Evelyn Waugh and Robert Benchley. On the climb up to fame and fortune, O'Rourke was ingratiatingly charming and even hip. Then in the 1980s he "came out" as the self-professed "funny Republican," just when the Republican Party seemed destined to binge lavishly into the 1990s. Since 1990, however, O'Rourke has turned rancorous, gloating and shrill—as did many of his male boomer admirers. Humorists in America, most notably the ones he admires and quotes in epigrams, didn't grow old very gracefully, and neither has he, yet the graying process certainly calls for close examination.

Like several of our best humorists, notably Ring Lardner and James Thurber, P. J. O'Rourke came out of the upper Midwest (Toledo, Ohio) and migrated to the big city, seeking a niche in the burgeoning magazine scene in the 1970s. He came from wealth and privilege as the crown prince of a large and influential family—or so he suggests in a miniature mock-medieval epic, "The King of Sandusky Ohio," published in the *National Lampoon* (May 1975). O'Rourke attended Miami University of Ohio in the late 1960s and went on to graduate school in the writing program at Johns Hopkins. While living in Baltimore, Mencken's hometown, he helped found a leftist alternative magazine—although by his own admission later it was, like the weight-watcher's beer, radical lite: "*Harry* was filled with the usual hippie blather, yea drugs and revolution, boo war and corporate profits. But it was an easy-going publication and not without a sense of humor. The want-ads section was headlined 'free *Harry* Classified Help Hep Cats and Kittens Fight Dippy Capitalist Exploitation.'"[5]

In the early 1970s, O'Rourke surfaced in New York City, working on an alternative newspaper called the *New York Ace,* which was attempting to upstage the *East Village Other* with two-color printing and wisecracks in the style of the *National Lampoon.* His work apparently brought him to the attention of writers on the *National Lampoon,* which he joined in 1974. The magazine by then had separated from its parent, the *Harvard Lampoon.* In 1970, Media Publications of New York had bought limited rights and moved operations to Madison Avenue. During the early 1970s, the magazine held to high Harvard standards for literary parody and learned burlesque, attacking political authority, subverting pop-cultural trends, and smashing gender stereotypes. Contributors delighted in trespassing boundaries of taste that continued to hold at the *Harvard Lampoon* but were receding everywhere else in post-Woodstock, post-Watergate America. The slippery times inspired 'pooners to be outrageous, offensive, even shocking. The goal was always, according to former 'pooner Tony Hendra, in his memoir, to "go too far."[6] But the new corporate owners wanted to reach a wider, less discriminating audience of baby boomers, still mostly male. Thus, sophisticated topical satire was gradually supplanted by leering, misogynist, bawdry, visual slapsticks, and sick jokes. Harvard 'pooners who had originally nurtured the new venture to respectable success feared they were being sold out to the growing "youth market" and did sell out, to the immense personal profit of a few. New recruits from outside the Ivy league, like O'Rourke, obliged the new corporate, Madison Avenue strategy by feeding male fantasy with frat humor geared to ex-frats highlighted by smutty sophomoric tales about adolescent male sexual conquests—in effect, *Animal House* humor.[7] One marketing scheme began with catchy titles, and O'Rourke's were among the most provocative: a typical example was "How to Drive Fast on Drugs While Getting Your Wing-Wang Squeezed and Not Spill Your Drink" (March 1979).[8] The article spun out a sort of urban tall tale, with O'Rourke the ring-tailed roarer of the new frontier, the suburb:

> When it comes to taking chances, some people like to play poker or shoot dice; other people prefer to parachute-jump, go rhino hunting, or climb ice floes, while still others engage in crime or marriage. But I like to get drunk and drive like a fool. Name me, if you can, a better feeling than the one you get when you're half a bottle of Chivas in the bag with a gram of coke up your nose and a teenage lovely pulling off her tube top in the next seat over while you're going a hundred miles an hour down a suburban side street. You'd have to watch the entire Mexican air force crash-land in a liquid petroleum gas storage facility to match this kind of thrill.

While some veteran contributors called such 'poon porn "loathsome" (Hendra, 378), contrary to the original and deliberately pointed dissent that had driven the magazine, the shift in emphasis worked. Circulation boomed as the humor went too far in one direction, becoming coarser, more misogynist, and even racist, stroking ever more blatantly the prejudices of the targeted audience, mostly white male boomers. According to Hendra, the person most responsible for diverting the *National Lampoon* away from wide-ranging satire to prurient backlash white male humor in the mid-1970s was the corporate-appointed editor-in-chief, P. J. O'Rourke (Hendra, 390).

O'Rourke became sufficiently well-known and well-practiced to be able to freelance in slicker, more mainstream magazines such as *Playboy, Esquire, Vanity Fair,* and even *House and Garden,* which increasingly welcomed topical humor. In 1974 he became resident humorist—using the parody title "International Affairs Desk" Correspondent—at *Rolling Stone,* a trendy youth magazine at the time pitched to the same male boomer audience. Sixties boomers had left the Animal House rioting at the frat house and were graduating into the real world of getting and spending. A humor niche opened up for a kindred spirit who understood boomer anxieties and could lighten them with laughter. Again, O'Rourke obliged his generation, and in 1987 he came out with *The Bachelor Home Companion: A Practical Guide to Keeping House Like a Pig,* an accomplished burlesque of how-to books in the droll, understated style of Robert Benchley. He exploits for comic effect the disparity between his Walter Mittyish fantasy as a 1980s plutocratic libertine and the unstable realities of the single life in a period of declining opportunities:

> I always wanted to be a bachelor when I grew up. My friends may have had fantasies about raking the yard, seeing their loved ones in pin curlers and cleaning the garage on Sundays, but not me. I saw myself at thirty-eight lounging around a penthouse in a brocade smoking jacket. Vivaldi would be playing on the stereo. I'd sip brandy from a snifter the size of a fish tank and leaf through an address book full of R-rated phone numbers. (7)

Instead, men are marooned in a world they never made. O'Rourke offers a few survival tips—about cooking, for example:

> All real bachelor food is fried, preferably in butter or bacon fat or lard and never in chrysanthemum oil or mung-sprout shortening or any other kind of fake grease that tries to pass itself off as good for you. Grease is the key ingredient in bachelor cooking. Grease makes food taste greasy, which is better than having it taste like a bachelor cooked it. And if you roll the grease food around in flour before you cook it, you've got three of the four Unmarried-Male Food Groups: fat, grease, starch, and sugar. (You can get the sugar, too, if you have a Mai Tai with dinner.) (53)

This is "regular guy" humor, addressed, he says, to "assistant district sales

managers, Dekes and Phi Delts in off-campus housing, divorced guys, young
men who've been told to get the hell out of the house by their parents, and
any fellow whose girlfriend won't marry him because her first husband was
such a bummer. That is, to every male in a house without pot holders" (4).
But it's also gender-neutral. Even feminist former sorority sisters on the
same career paths could presumably savor it.

Feminists and their male allies would not likely be as pleased by
Modern Manners: An Etiquette Book for Rude People (1989), a burlesque
sequel to *Bachelor Home Companion* pitched to boomers who have reluc-
tantly departed bachelorhood and faced up to marriage, career, and other
obstacles to old-fashioned male fun. It's a rule book for a world without
rules, complete with acerbic epigrams from famously disgruntled male wits,
such as Byron and O'Rourke's fellow Ohioan, Ambrose Bierce. In choosing
his muse, O'Rourke has abandoned the amiable Benchley for the more
acidic Oscar Wilde. "The world is going to hell," he proclaims. "All we can
do is look good on the trip" (xvii). O'Rourke, who had discarded the beery
frat house toga for the klutzy bachelor's kitchen apron, now dons the
country club blazer and bow tie and strikes the Wildean pose of the suave,
world-weary libertine. The sly, disarming pose allows him to sneer at 1960s
radicals for their bad behavior, appealing to boomers who have, like him,
wised up and repudiated their misspent youth. For example, in giving advice
about "Acting Cute," O'Rourke oozes glib charm while he quips,

> Once you know what you're doing is wrong, it's easy to
> learn how to get away with it. The first technique of misbe-
> havior is to be cute. When the generation born after World
> War II began to act up, they wore feathers in their hair, put
> paint on their noses, and went around sticking chrysanthe-
> mums down rifle barrels. *Life* magazine adored it—it was so
> cute. But later they began doing things which were much
> less cute, like threatening to vote, and it became necessary
> to kill them at Kent State. Of course, "hippies" were also
> violating a basic principle of cuteness; they were getting
> old. To be cute you must be young. If you had a great big
> adult dog and it whined all night, tore up your shoes, and
> messed on the rug, you'd have it gassed. But when a puppy
> does these things, it's cute. (51)

Clearly, O'Rourke knows how to push boomer buttons—how to provoke,
offend, go too far. However, when truly taboo subjects challenge him to
really go too far and reach the summit of bad taste—subjects like rape,

incest, and abortion, for example—O'Rourke can only grope and fumble, as if squeamish about controversies that were then still taboos. Thus, he hovers cleverly on the edge of giving offense, as in the opening line under "Incest": "It is very bad form to screw your children except in your will" (109). When he crosses boundaries of taste or decorum, he goes after victims he knows are, to his audience, the most vulnerable. For example, "Wife swapping is never done in the best circles of society. Wives can rarely, if ever, be traded for anything useful like a set of golf clubs" (109).

On his travels beyond the country club, both around America and abroad, as *Rolling Stone*'s roving correspondent, O'Rourke shows he can tell funny stories that are also astutely observant of human foibles, particularly sham and pretense. In *Holidays in Hell* (1988), a collection of pieces from *Rolling Stone,* he recounts his misadventures as a modern-day Mark Twain, a new innocent abroad. He strives to be impressed by local culture only to give way to chauvinist mockery while at the same time searching desperately for the nearest Hilton Hotel bar. His satiric vignettes are witty and incisive, at times what and how Twain would write today—for example:

> In place of celebrated palaces, our era has celebrated parking spots, most of them in Rome. Romans will back a Fiat into the middle of your linguine al pesto if you're sitting too close to the restaurant window.
> The "sermons in stone" these days are all sung with cement. Cement is the granite, the marble, the porphyry of our time. Someday, no doubt, there will be "Elgin Cements" in the British Museum. Meanwhile, we tour the Warsaw Pact countries—cement everywhere, including, at the official level, quite a bit of cement in their heads. (8–9)

The farther O'Rourke ventures from the comforts of the Hilton Hotel bar and into the outback, the more he's challenged to find the comically incongruous in the authentically bizarre and even shocking. The results are predictably uneven. He's at his best when he can familiarize a scene by focusing through the lens of American pop culture. During a rather chilling week wandering around South Africa in the late 1980s, for example, a pause before the Voortrekker Monument in Pretoria inspires a bit of mock amazement:

> It was, God help me, "Wagon Train" carved in stone. There was no mistaking the pokey oxen and prairie wagoneers parked in a circle for a combat-ready campout. The gals all

had those dopey coal-scuttle bonnets on and brats galore doing curtain calls in their skirts. The fellers all wore Quaker Oats hats and carried muskets long as flagpoles. Horses pranced. Horizons beckoned. Every man jack from Ben Cartwright on down stared off into the sunset with chin uplifted and eyes full of stupid resolve. Every single give-me-a-home-where-the-buffalo-roam bromide was there, except the buffalo were zebras, and at that inevitable point in the story where one billion natives attack completely unprovoked, it was Zulus with spears and shields instead of Apaches with bows and arrows. The Zulus were, of course, everything Apaches were always depicted as doing before we discovered Apaches were noble ecologists—skewering babies, clobbering women and getting shot in massive numbers. (161)

During the late 1970s and early 1980s, when these representative humor pieces were originally published in magazines, O'Rourke remained by and large neutral politically, though it's apparent from scattered digs at liberals that he shifted from left to right, following his audience. In 1987 he published *Republican Party Reptiles*—another collection of previously published humor pieces—where, in the introduction, he "comes out" as "the funny Republican"—just when the Reagan Revolution was entering its second stage with the predictable election of Reagan's vice president, George Bush. It's a mock "Apologia Pro Vita Sua," meant in apparent jest:

We are the Republican Party Reptiles. We look like Republicans, and think like conservatives, but we drive a lot faster and keep vibrators and baby oil and a video camera behind the stack of sweaters on the bedroom closet shelf. I think our agenda is clear. We are opposed to: government spending, Kennedy kids, seat-belt laws, being a pussy about nuclear power, busing our children anywhere other than Yale, trailer courts near our vacation homes, . . . all tiny Third World countries that don't have banking secrecy laws . . . and jewelry on men. We are in favor of: guns, drugs, fast cars, free love (if our wives don't find out), . . . cleaner environment (poor people should cut it out with the graffiti), a strong military with spiffy uniforms . . . and a

> firm stand on the Middle East (raze buildings, burn crops,
> plow the earth with salt, and sell the population into
> bondage). (xv–xvi)

Republican Party spokesmen stereotypically look like nerdish, three-piece suit types such as George Will, with tightly vested opinions and buttoned-down attitudes. They are sometimes capable of sly wit of the sort uttered sparingly by conservative elder, William Buckley. O'Rourke casts himself as the opposite— an unapologetic libertine, openly hostile to the alleged enemies of male pleasures, rude and contentious, even lethal—that is, "reptilian." The book includes, from his apprenticeship on the *National Lampoon,* several of O'Rourke's raunchier tales of male conquest, nurturing happy memories in aging boomers of frat fun at the old Animal House. The book is dedicated "to the memory of Warren G. Harding," a clean strike perhaps at Harding's conservative disciple, Ronald Reagan. But the book is also an announcement: the 1920s—when men were men (and mostly Republican), women knew their place, as did blacks, and organizations like country clubs kept undesirables (like liberals) out—are back and roaring again. The dedication also conjures up Harding's great nemesis, H. L. Mencken, perhaps intentionally, for O'Rourke seems to be shedding other influences to become Mencken redux, complete with flashing cigar(ello). The Mencken debunking stance and tone took over in 1991 when O'Rourke came out with his own Menckenian diatribe (written by *Rolling Stone's* "White House Correspondent"—doubtless another mock honorific title) against the national political establishment. In O'Rourke's view, this establishment—a "carnival of buncombe"—has degenerated into, as the title of his book announces, *A Parliament of Whores.* O'Rourke has earned his press credentials by acquiring an impressive command of the system—party nominations, election campaigns, Supreme Court hearings, and the lobbying process—and why it's gummed up. This is knowledge that Mencken, holed up in Baltimore, never bothered with. However, O'Rourke is full of sweeping and unsupportable indictments of the system yet is conspicuously short on particular cases or culprits. Such blanket attacks focus maximum attention on the humorist himself, who exercises his talent for facile hyperbole delivered in cheerfully derisive tone—debunking in the style of Mencken. Predictably, the familiar liberal luminaries O'Rourke knows his boomer audience has come to detest best oblige his special gift for witty caricature; for example:

> You would have to go miles down under the ocean in a
> bathysphere to find anything as ugly as the plaintiffs in the

> 1990 Supreme Court flag desecration case, though their
> wacky old left-wing lawyer, William Kunstler, was also quite
> a sight. But Kunstler—with eyebrows the size of squirrels
> and mouth, mind and long, gray tresses going every which
> direction and who was wearing a hobo literature-professor
> type suit no doubt carefully pre-rumpled at the special
> Pinko Dry Cleaner and Valet that they have in New York
> ("Be a Liberal or Just Look Like One"), where you can also
> get your hair uncut and your shoes scuffed. (75)

O'Rourke is not so loyal a Republican that he can't mock a party stalwart
whose buffoonery merits it—most vividly, George Bush,

> the tall schmo with the voice up his nose, the one who was
> running for president but nobody could figure out why be-
> cause he kept getting his tongue in a clove hitch and calling
> every whatchamajigger a "thing," . . . a skinny, inconsequen-
> tial doofus, an intellectual smurf and moral no-show who'd
> wound up in the White House by default. (38)

As in *Holidays in Hell,* O'Rourke can be a stylish yet insightful reporter on
"hell" in America—that is, when he resists showing off and attends to a compelling story. For example, from a police cruiser he evocatively lays bare the
nightmarish farce that is drug enforcement in Washington, or anywhere in
America:

> [At two in the morning] it's like ordinary life with the clock
> on backward, except nighttime people don't move the same
> way daytime people do. The whores parade in wide ellipses
> and figure eights. Or nighttime people don't go anywhere
> at all. The little kid lookouts sit stock still. There's a
> distinct walk to nowhere the dealers have—the self-enforced
> confidence of the pimp roll combined with the leery, kinky,
> darting turns of the head that set a couple of pounds of
> gold "dope rope" swaying until you wonder if the fellow's
> neck vertebrae will hold. Then there's the dumb strut of the
> buyers—the asshole college kids, the stoner white trash from
> the trailer suburbs and the local jerks with the Third World
> briefcases blaring stuff they'd get arrested for saying if they
> said it without a beat. (114)

The self-professed former recreational druggie of *National Lampoon* has put his experience to good journalistic use. When real system scroungers pop up, O'Rourke swings into attack, singling out other boomer enemies, such as the AARP:

> How can we keep gilding the gramps [with "old-goat en-titlements"] and still have anything left over from the gross national product to invest in machinery for making crude plastic cowboy hats to sell to Japanese tourists (which is what our benefit-beggared economy will be reduced to by 2030)? Well, we could ask our wizened deadbeats to go Dutch, make at least some of the richer ones pay the freight on what society sends their way. (223)

At other times in *Parliament of Whores,* O'Rourke blunts the force of his debunking by bullying society's victims and the liberals he thinks foolishly dote on them. For example, at a pre-"March for Housing Now" rally held beside the Washington Monument in 1989, O'Rourke reports,

> I did hear one woman say she was homeless. She was a big, resentful woman—the kind who's always behind the counter at the Department of Motor Vehicles when you go to re-new your car registration. She was co-chairhuman of some-thing or other, and she was declaiming from the podium: "I've got five kids! We live in one room! We're homeless!" No, ma'am, you're not. Your housing may be as bad as your family planning, but you're not homeless. (186)

Other lobbyists for what O'Rourke calls the "Perennially Indigent" include

> Angry black poverty pests making a life and a liv-ing off the misfortunes of others.
> Even angrier feminists doing their best to feminize poverty before the blacks use it all up.
> College bohos dressed in black to show how gloomy the world is when you're a nineteen-year-old rich kid. (187)

People of whatever color and background who exploit a failing system for personal gain or advantage certainly deserve exposure to mockery. But O'Rourke is sparing only with stick figures, making glancing strikes that are hardly worth a serpent's effort at coiling. He's in search of the easiest scapegoats, and he finds them, but only on the political Left. Apparently there are no mockable "special interests" on the Right—just as there are no suburban Republicans who cruise the District of Columbia for drugs. But perhaps a critic protests too much, for isn't O'Rourke just kidding? Looking back, many of the inside-the-beltway stories in *Parliament of Whores*, like the example above, seem entirely made up, invented far from the scene, perhaps out in some cushy, air-conditioned suburban study.

In *Give War a Chance* (1992), a later collection made up of humor pieces from *Rolling Stone* and the *American Spectator*, O'Rourke tries to remain the suave, Wildean libertine with a quiver full of wicked barbs to fling—ever leftward. Today, he's past 50, and his cool, unflappable facade is cracking with age. The "funny Republican" act is surely wearing thin. In the introduction he recites the same familiar litany of charges against liberals, describing them as "daffy," whiny, sanctimonious, loving only society's victims, and hating wealth and success. The mockery sounds overwrought, the style is congealed, and the images are moldy; for example:

> Liberal self-obsession is manifested in large doses of quack psychoanalysis, crank spiritualism, insalubrious health fads and helpless self-help seminars. The liberal makes grim attempts to hold on to his youth—fussing with his hair, his wardrobe, his speech and even his ideology in an attempt to retain the perfect solipsism of adolescence. . . . At the core of liberalism is the spoiled child—miserable, as all spoiled children are, unsatisfied, demanding, ill-disciplined, despotic and useless. Liberalism is a philosophy of sniveling brats. (xxii)

In passages such as these, O'Rourke forsakes the real world of fools and knaves for a twilight zone where liberal-phobic conservatives listen for reverberations of old Mencken volleys that will mirror their resentments. Over the years, O'Rourke at his best has shown himself to be a worthy successor to Mencken, however partisan politically. Now, however, he's reduced to aping the master in his dotage, becoming tediously repetitive, peevish, and shrill. At other times in this collection he departs present reality for the 1950s, that later period of Republican hegemony (and a time when Mencken's writings were reprinted and widely read), and advocates another anti-Communist purge—this one more thorough than the last. "God knows the problem is not a lack of Commies," he begins in "Notes Toward a Blacklist for the 1990s." "There are more fuzzy-minded one worlders, pasty-faced peace creeps and bleeding-heart bedwetters in American now than there ever were in 1954" (123). What follows is a two-page list of every known liberal individual, publication, and organization (although surely the *L* word has been by now utterly exhausted of comic usefulness). He may be, as always, just kidding, but many of his admirers stand ready to put his mock plan into action. Fortunately, comic absurdity prevails, for his imagined "Commies" will get what O'Rourke cutely calls "the Burt Reynolds/Loni Anderson treatment":

> the worst punishment for dupes, pink-wieners and dia-lectical immaterialists might be a kind of reverse black list. We don't prevent them from writing, speaking, performing and otherwise being their usual nuisance selves. Instead, we hang on their every word, beg them to work, drag them onto all available TV and radio chat shows and write hun-dreds of fawning newspaper and magazine articles about their wonderful swellness. (126)

What O'Rourke imagines done to the enemies of the Right has been done to him, not as a punishment but as a reward. He's gotten what can be called the "Rush Limbaugh/Howard Stern Treatment"—fame, notoriety, wealth.

As if in recognition of O'Rourke's prolific and unremitting bashing of liberals, the Cato Institute, a libertarian think tank, named him recently its "H. L. Mencken Research Fellow." If bestowed in earnest, it's a title, however well deserved, any wit of true libertarian independence should re-fuse. Removed from a ringside seat at the American "circus" and elevated to a corporate box high above, a humorist inevitably becomes complaisant and self-indulgent, too distracted by the blandishments of corporate sponsorship to see the passing show. That O'Rourke has succumbed to being a conser-vative establishment shill is all too apparent in his most recent collection from *Rolling Stone*, entitled *All the Troubles in the World: The Lighter Side of Overpopulation, Famine, Ecological Disaster, Ethnic Hatred, Plague, and Pov-erty* (1994). The once curious and irreverent innocent abroad of *Holidays in Hell* has aged into the ugly American. Backed by an expense account and accompanied by a staff photographer, O'Rourke travels about such impov-erished places as Bangladesh, Haiti, and North Vietnam in his leased Mer-cedes. He searches out the grosser incongruities to mine for snide quips, which he then tosses about like coins to beggars. Searching for the evil ones who have caused "all our troubles," O'Rourke rounds up the usual liberal suspects, whom he terms "professional worriers," "Masters of Sanctimony," or "New Agers" who "will believe in anything but facts, environmental softies who think the white rats should be running the cancer labs, or bong-smoke theorists who would have the world as stupid as they are" (12). While tooling around Somalia in press-credentialed comfort, O'Rourke compares himself, the tough-minded realist, to soft, back home sentiments:

> Compared to Mogadishu, starving children would be cute. In fact, somewhere in the psychic basement of the sob-sister sorority house, in the darkest recesses of the bleeding heart, starving children *are* cute. Note the big Muppet Baby eyes, the etiolated features as unthreatening as Michael Jackson's were before the molestation charges, the elfin incorporeity of the bodies. Steven Spielberg's E. T. owes a lot to the Biafran-Bangladeshi-Ethiopian model of adorable suffering. (67)

Boomer humorists such as P. J. O'Rourke may be regarded as satirists by their admirers because these humorists ridicule the admirers' enemies. But they have no point of view nor principle other than exercising their right to sound irksome and outrageous in order to entertain a market audience for fun and profit. They often trade on facile stereotypes that further polarize groups; it's a style of humor that thrives in the frenetic 1990s media environment that elevates style over substance, attitude over conviction, the quotable insult over telling wit. What a shame O'Rourke has squandered the opportunity to unmask actual knavery and folly with the ferocious impartiality of a true libertarian. Instead, he has become the Republican Party hit man. The viper has metamorphosed into a chicken: chicken McMencken.

Notes

1. On debunking in the 1920s, see Edward A. Martin, *H. L. Mencken and the Debunkers* (Athens: University of Georgia Press, 1984), especially chapter 2.

2. Quoted in J. James McElveen, "H. L. Mencken," in Perry J. Ashley, ed., *American Newspaper Journalists, 1925–1950* (Detroit: Gale Research, 1984), 193.

3. "American Culture," in *A Mencken Chrestomathy*, ed. H. L. Mencken (New York: Vintage Books, 1982), 181. On the "carnivalization" of American speech in satiric humor before Mencken, see David S. Reynolds, *Beneath the American Renaissance: The Subversive Imagination in the Age of Emerson and Melville* (Cambridge: Harvard University Press, 1989), 444.

4. See Hendrick Hertzberg's highly critical review of *The Liberal Crackup*, in *New Republic* (8 April 1985), 30–33; and James Wolcott, "Young Whippersnappers," *Esquire* (September 1980), 14, 17.

5. "Second Thoughts About the 60s," in *Give War a Chance* (New York: Atlantic Monthly Press, 1992), 91. For biographical facts I have relied on Franz Lidz, "Winning Through Denigration," in *Johns Hopkins Magazine* (June 1980), 14–20; and Tony Hendra, *Going Too Far* (New York: Doubleday, 1987).

6. Hendra, *Going Too Far*, "Introduction." The story of the *National Lampoon* splintering off from the *Harvard Lampoon* is told by Thomas Grant in "Laughter Light and Libelous: The *Lampoon* from Harvard Yard to Madison Avenue," *Markham Review* 13 (spring–summer 1984), 33–40. For a critical dismissal of lampoon humor, see Arthur Lubow, "Screw You Humor," *New Republic* 179 (21 October 1979).

7. In his witty but acerbic memoir about working on the *National Lampoon*, Tony Hendra has only contempt for O'Rourke, who Hendra considers merely clever and too sycophantic with higher management. He appears already to be preparing himself to shed radical chic and embrace his true conservative calling: "O'Rourke was a narc, a very good narc who hit all the right notes, but whose police-issue shoes showed beneath his bell-bottoms" (339).

8. This article was reprinted in *Republican Party Reptiles* (NY: Atlantic Monthly Press, 1987), 128.

Works Cited

Ashley, Perry J., ed. *American Newspaper Journalists, 1925–1950*. Detroit: Gale Research, 1984.

Hendra, Tony. *Going Too Far*. New York: Doubleday, 1987.

Martin, Edward A. *H. L. Mencken and the Debunkers*. Athens: University of Georgia Press, 1984.

Mencken, H. L. *A Mencken Chrestomathy*. New York: Vintage Books, 1982.

O'Rourke, P. J. *All the Troubles in the World: The Lighter Side of Disaster, Ethnic Hatred, Plague and Poverty*. New York: Atlantic Monthly Press, 1994.

———. *The Bachelor Home Companion: A Practical Guide to Keeping House Like a Pig*. New York: Atlantic Monthly Press, 1987.

———. *Give War a Chance*. New York: Atlantic Monthly Press, 1992.

———. *Holidays in Hell*. New York: Random House, 1989.

———. *Modern Manners: An Etiquette Book for Rude People*. New York: Atlantic Monthly Press, 1989.

———. *A Parliament of Whores: A Lone Humorist Attempts to Explain the Entire U. S. Government.* New York: Atlantic Monthly Press, 1991.
———. *Republican Party Reptiles.* New York: Atlantic Monthly Press, 1987.

The Mark Twain of Baseball?: A Proposal for Humor Research of Turn-of-the-Century American Sportswriting

David G. Lott

Over the years, American sports journalism, whether print or broadcast, has relied on humor (or certainly intended humor) as one of its staple features. Newspaper and magazine commentary on the baseball strike of 1994–95, for example, provided an abundant source of satire. In a *Sports Illustrated* essay entitled "The Big Strikeout," Steve Rushin posited that union chief Donald M. Fehr once underwent a "sense-of-humorectomy," that owners' representative Richard J. Ravitch "had his personality removed by a pioneering team of microsurgeons" ("both men courageously await charisma donors"), and that fans would have been better off singing, to both sides of the dispute, "Buy me some peanuts and Cracker Jack? I don't care if you never come back" (86). Elsewhere, in "Casey at the Bank," an updated version of "Casey at the Bat" (1888), published in the *Chicago Tribune*, Jeff MacNelly characterizes baseball's decaying appeal to its youthful audience: "Willy's now a killer whale, and Mickey's just a mouse; DiMaggio, some guy named Joe, who sold coffee house to house" (A23). And not long ago a lawyer for the players' union observed in confidence, "There was a lot of satirical stuff printed, especially early on. I remember that somewhere Don Fehr was described as appearing to be 'trapped in a perpetual Maalox moment'" (personal telephone interview).

Despite being fertile ground for humorous expression, sports journalism (or "sporting journalism," as it was once known) has been largely ignored by scholars of humor studies. Researchers seem to have branded it with the proverbial "double whammy" of scholarly disinterest: being journalistic, it has generally been considered nonliterary; being about sports, it has often been regarded as frivolous. My purpose here is to help compensate for this absence of attention in three ways: first, by acknowledging one of the innovators of humorous sports reporting in the daily press, Charles Dryden; second, by expanding on a prior evaluation of his humoristic repertoire; and third, by offering a rationale for further inquiry into efforts by Dryden and other sporting journalists of his period.

An article by Dryden written during the baseball season of 1903 and published in the Philadelphia paper *The North American* is revealing as a forerunner of the strike-related excerpts just cited. In this article Dryden parodies not a baseball song but a typical speech by a team owners' spokesman who is reacting to a player strike:

> The Creator in His infinite wisdom has seen fit to place the ball fields and bat bags of this country in the keeping of a few intelligent Christian gentlemen. We own the plants, by divine right. If the players decide to go ahead and blast out base hits for 28 cents a ton and furnish their own powder we will have no more trouble. Otherwise the operators will close the fields for all time or import new men, if we have to send to Upper Sandusky for them. (June 15, 1:6)

In fact, Dryden has fabricated this strike scenario under the pretense that he is predicting what will happen a couple of years down the line if the two major leagues attempt to merge. Still, he attributes the speech to then National League president Pulliam and is clearly lampooning the team owners of his day as sanctimonious and stingy. In Dryden's portrayal these owners see themselves as divinely ordained keepers of the baseball kingdom, yet they maintain the language of the industrial magnate, depicting the players as replaceable factory grunts who are left to "blast out" hits at the meager rate of "28 cents a ton" and even "furnish their own powder."

The owners are not the only targets of satire in this 1903 installment. The players' representative in Dryden's scenario, a veteran second baseman named Tom Daly, is treated with high burlesque:

> The great strike leader was loudly applauded as he left the hall. Spurning the carriage, which the strikers had placed at his disposal, Mr. Daly walked away. . . .
>
> Though high in the councils of organized labor, Mr. Daly is a plain man of unassuming habits, and it is his delight to hear his friends address him as Tom. (June 15, 6:6)

The thought of a sixteen-year veteran player like Tom Daly, during this notoriously rugged era in baseball, "spurning the carriage" or being delighted at hearing his own friends call him by his actual first name is ridiculous enough. But Dryden throws in for good measure another type of high burlesque, a mock-tragic account of Daly's fellow strikers:

> They barely eke out a living toiling full time. . . .
>
> The operators [the owners] always exact in advance the rental of the miserable shanties the strikers inhabit on the hills of Harlem, so that any shortage on pay day is taken from the mouths of women and children. Sometimes the small sons of players earn a few peanuts carrying water and bats in the base-ball yard, but the opportunities for these little food winners are too rare to help the family much. (June 15, 6:6)

Of course, the tight-fistedness of the owners is also caricatured in this high tragedy.

While these satiric treatments might not seem to be anything out of the ordinary to contemporary readers, it appears that Dryden was, in his day, one of a handful of journalistic innovators to infuse humor into their sports coverage. So thought Stanley Walker, city editor of the *New York Herald Tribune*. Writing in 1934, three years after Dryden's death, Walker asserted,

> Until Dryden began writing in San Francisco in 1890, reports of most sports events had been written with much of the unearthly beautiful, pungent style of a decision by the Supreme Court of the United States. Dryden picked on striking features of a game or player. He would comment on the size of a player's feet, or his whiskers, and would spin it through his story as a sort of theme song. Soon Dryden's stuff was read as much for his comical treatment as for the news it contained. . . .
>
> Dryden stimulated, if he did not actually originate, the idea that sports were worth writing about, and that they could be written differently from a market report. . . . He created a young and lively language for sports. (117–18)

Dryden's obituaries had rendered similar assessments in 1931. The *Chicago Tribune* referred to him as "one of the most popular baseball writers of his day," who "became famous for the unique manner in which he reported ball games" (27:5). The (Chicago) *Daily News* called him "one of the first and greatest of all baseball humorists" (17:8). The *New York Herald Tribune,* moreover, ventured that "the facile wit of Charles Dryden . . . not only made him one of the leading baseball writers of the country but founded a style of reportorial writing. The style is now generally followed in sports pages from New York to California" (19:7).

A few observers went beyond recognizing Dryden as one of the pioneers in humorous sports coverage and claimed he was simply an extraordinarily gifted humorist. In 1928, for example, while Dryden was still alive but no longer reporting, sportswriter Hugh Fullerton wrote,

> The greatest of all the reporters [of baseball,] and the man to whom the game owes more, perhaps, than to any other individual, was Charles Dryden, the Mark Twain of baseball. In any other line of writing he probably would have been accepted as one of our greatest humorists. His books of reminiscences are classics and his Percy the Trained Flying Fish one of the choicest bits of American humor. (188)

Echoing Fullerton's high praise was the *Chicago Herald and Examiner* obituary of 1931, which described Dryden as "perhaps the most famous of all baseball writers and considered by many as the greatest humorist of his day" (19:2). The *Herald and Examiner* went on to judge that Dryden and Ring Lardner (who began his journalistic career in 1905) "made satirical baseball writing an art" (19:2).

These various observers were all journalists, who likely had a vested interest in inflating the reputation of one of their own (the epithet "greatest humorist of his day," for instance, seems a little excessive). Or these writers could have been former colleagues and even friends wishing to laud Dryden, especially just before and after his death (Dryden was severely paralyzed by a stroke more than three years before he died in 1931) (Fullerton, 188). Nonetheless, preliminary investigations into the primary source material, the Dryden columns themselves, suggest that at least some of his contemporaries' assessments are well-founded.

In an article for *Aethlon: The Journal of Sport Literature,* I argued that in a month's worth of reporting from 1903, Dryden demonstrates an impressive command of a number of stylistic devices known to critics of literary satire: the high and low burlesque, as well as their offshoots mockepic, parody, and travesty (Lott). Having now explored a full season of Dryden reports, I wish to add the technique of the tall tale. In the following passage, from *The North American,* for instance, Dryden describes an incident involving Philadelphia Athletics' pitcher Rube Waddell:

FOUL BALL AND BEAN TRAGEDY

Once again has Mr. Waddell figured as chief actor in a baseball tragedy. He cannot be checked, it seems. In the seventh inning, "Rube" hoisted over the right field bleachers a long foul fly that landed on the roof of the biggest bean cannery in the city [Boston].

In descending, the ball fell on the roof of the engine room and jammed itself between the steam whistle and the stem of the valve that operates the same. The pressure set the whistle blowing. It lacked a few minutes to 5 o'clock, yet the workmen started to leave the building. They thought quitting time had come.

The incessant screeching of the bean factory whistle led engineers in neighboring factories to think fire had broken out, and they turned on steam. With a dozen whistles in full blast, a policeman sent in an alarm of fire. . . .

Just as the engines arrived, a steam cauldron in the first factory, containing a ton of beans, blew up. The explosion dislodged Waddell's foul fly and the whistle stopped blowing, but that was not the end of the trouble. A shower of scalding beans descended on the bleachers and caused a small panic. One man went insane. When he saw the beans dropping out of a cloud of steam, the unfortunate rooter yelled: "The world is coming to an end, and we will all be destroyed with a shower of hot hailstones."

An ambulance summoned to the supposed fire conveyed the demented man to his home. The ton of beans proved a total loss. (August 12, 5:4)[1]

Another fantastic occurrence purportedly befell Athletics' players Jack Taylor and Mike Kahoe. As in the prior excerpt, Dryden's extensive digression comically belittles the ball game at hand:

One day last fall, so the story goes, [Taylor and Kahoe] surrounded a duck pond in the woods. The hunters crept up from either side, peeped through the bushes, and beheld the pond literally packed with ducks. At a signal Taylor and

Kahoe blazed away with both barrels right into the middle
of the flock.

To the surprise and chagrin of the hunters, the
birds arose in a body and started to fly away, without
leaving so much as a feather in the pond. Taylor looked at
Kahoe, and Mike looked at him. Both were about to toss
their $100 guns into the water, when a strange thing
happened.

"It was the queerest sight I ever witnessed," said
Mr. Kahoe while relating the adventure last night. "When
the flock got up a couple of hundred feet, dead ducks com-
menced to drop one after another. Then they came down
in bunches, while a great cloud of feathers blew off to the
leeward. For about a minute, the sky rained ducks. You
see, the flock was so tightly packed in the pond that the
survivors, after our shots, carried the dead ones up with
them. Then, when the flock loosened up a bit, to escape in
different directions, the dead birds naturally dropped out of
the bunch. Jack and I collected eighty-four fine, fat ducks
and concluded not to hunt anymore that day." (September
17, 5:4)

In addition, like much of the literary humor of his era, Dryden's
elaborate tales do not always live up to today's standards for politically correct storytelling. This one features Albert "Chief" Bender, a pitcher for the
Athletics who was one-quarter Chippewa:

An event unique in the history of baseball occurred here
today. Between four and five hundred cigar stores closed up
in the afternoon in order that the proprietors and clerks
might see a real Indian before they died.

Of all the people in the game Mr. Bender least
expected such an honor. He was quite overcome. For years
the proprietors and clerks had gazed upon the wretched
wooden effigies in front of their doors until they regarded
them as true representatives of a noble race. As an object
lesson Mr. Bender was a complete success. The cigar store
clerks endured the first shock when Mr. Bender was not
pushed out to the slab on rollers. No meat axe gleamed in
his right hand, and he did not hold a bundle of leaf tobacco
in the other. In fact he does not handle the filthy weed in

any form, and so far as he is concerned the cigar people have cruelly slandered the Redman. (May 22, 5:1)

Dryden was not afraid to treat readers of high political standing irreverently. Here, Dryden finds a subtle way to insult the governor of Pennsylvania, who had just passed a libel law in response to journalistic practices he considered offensive:

> DRYDEN HEARS RUMORS THAT ATHLETICS LOST. . . .
> FILLED WITH FEAR OF LIBEL LAW HE MERELY INTIMATES
> THAT WADDELL WAS HIT HARD
>
> Owing to the rumor that an alleged Governor is declared to have signed what is thought to be a bill, it is currently believed that we find ourselves to be up against it. Should the feelings of any person be bruised he can slam the hooks into our alleged bank account and collect for libel. . . . Competent eye witnesses, many of whom are thought to have been sober, aver that the sun appeared to be shining at the time. Danger lurks in every line of this statement. Though he spells it differently, old Sol [the sun] may be the same kind of man as the alleged Governor, and they might get together, it is said, and pull off a libel suit.
> (May 15, 1:3)

Through a rather convoluted pun, Dryden manages to imply that the governor is not honorable, thus challenging both the libel law and its esteemed proponent.

Dryden's technical ingenuity during this season warrants the acclaim afforded him later by several of his contemporaries. Such ingenuity, if it could be shown to extend throughout a long career, should surely merit the attention of scholars of humor studies, especially those concentrating on the turn-of-the-century period. And while unearthing the work of an innovative comic stylist might prove rewarding, situating this stylist within the broader context of the journalistic humor of his day could yield even more significant findings.

Critic Norris W. Yates once surmised that "between 1900 and 1920 the humorous column of the urban daily, conducted in each case as the personal organ of one writer, grew to become the most important single medium of American humor" (32–33). Consider how well details about Dryden fit the trappings of Yates's thesis. First, according to the (Chicago) *Daily News,* Dryden began his career in 1889 and retired in 1921 (17:8).

Second, according to all sources, he wrote for city newspapers. In his Philadelphia *North American* columns of 1903, he always had a byline, his reports
regularly appeared on the front page (granted, the Athletics were a popular
news item as defending league champions), and a small photograph of his
face would sometimes sit above his story. In contrast, the same attention-
getting format was not given to the column of the Philadelphia Phillies' reporter of the same year.

Beyond these surface similarities, Yates has made other assertions
that may be relevant to Dryden's case. The critic has described turn-of-the-
century Chicago as "particularly rich in columnists," citing as examples humorists Eugene Field, George Ade, Finley Peter Dunne, and Ring Lardner
(34). Meanwhile, sportswriter Hugh Fullerton claimed that Dryden had been
hired by Dunne himself at a Chicago paper (188). Further, Dunne, like
Lardner, had covered baseball before moving on to greater fame as a columnist (Betts, 54; Yates, 34). Dunne, in fact, has also been credited with a
key role in originating—several years prior to the time Dryden began writing
his columns—the practice of humorous baseball reporting (Betts, 54).
Dryden, then, may have been influenced by some of the more notable humor
columnists of the period.

True, Dryden did not write the same sort of broad-ranging newspaper column as these humorists. He reported on baseball games, while digressing constantly to suit his fancy. Nonetheless, his accounts contained the
same mixture of small-town informality and urbane perspective that Yates
has noted as a crucial trademark of column writing of the time (33). Dryden
would place "Rube" Waddell in the center of a high tragedy that featured,
in addition, the earthiness of baked beans and the workings of the city
factory. Note the similar juxtaposition of the dignified "Mr. Waddell" with
the countrified "Rube," as well as more obvious rural/elite strands, in this
excerpt:

> One thing we are proud to say of him, and that is he
> [Waddell] admires the superior intellect wherever it is
> found. For several hours yesterday Rube carried the blanket
> for an educated dog, and helped the trainer put the flea-
> bitten prodigy through its paces. The educated dog, whose
> name is Ted, has been to Europe, and Ted's knowledge of
> the foreign theatrical circuit also appealed strongly to Mr.
> Waddell. (June 24, 5:6)

Seen in the light of Yates's evaluation, Dryden might be judged not only as
an early craftsman of humorous sporting coverage but also, as a few of his

contemporaries believed, as one of the important humorists of the new century.

Of course, this is all speculation. Since the current project has been unable to turn up a single close examination of Dryden's work to date, who knows where further investigation would actually lead? In light of current evidence, it appears that turn-of-the-century sporting journalism holds promise for humor scholars. And not just because of Dryden. Along with the Chicago school of humorous baseball reporters (founded in part by Dunne in the 1880s), historian John Rickards Betts once listed thirteen baseball writers who, like Dryden, may have played a crucial role in sustaining fan interest during the corrupt 1890s. As Betts observed, "It may well have been the baseball writers who really carried the game through those dark years" (54–56). Since so many writers kept us entertained through the course of the game's most recent dark moment, doesn't it seem plausible that the impulse to be humorous was a shared one in Dryden's time as well?

Notes

1. This and further citations are to the appropriate date, page number, and column of *The North American*.

Works Cited

Betts, John Rickards. "Sporting Journalism in Nineteenth Century America." *American Quarterly* 5 (1953), 39–56.

Chicago Herald and Examiner, 12 February 1931.

Chicago Tribune, 12 February 1931.

Daily News [Chicago], 12 February 1931.

Dryden, Charles. *Philadelphia North American,* 15 May, 22 May, 15 June, 24 June, 12 August, 17 September 1903.

Fullerton, Hugh. "The Fellows Who Made the Game." *Saturday Evening Post,* 21 April 1928, 18–19, 184–88.

Lott, David G. "Notes on an American Dryden: New Directions for Literary Investigation of the Sports Pages." *Aethlon: The Journal of Sport Literature* 11:2 (spring 1994).

MacNelly, Jeff. *The Washington Post,* 2 February 1995.

New York Herald Tribune, 13 February 1931.

Rushin, Steve. "The Big Strikeout." *Sports Illustrated* (12 September 1994), 86.

Telephone interview (5 December 1994).

Walker, Stanley. *City Editor*. New York: Frederick A. Stokes, 1934.
Yates, Norris W. *The American Humorist: Conscience of the Twentieth Century*. New York: Citadel Press, 1965.

Humor High and Low: An Introduction

Steven H. Gale

I live on a river in central Kentucky. One afternoon some years ago I was out with one of my dogs, walking along the riverbank under some large oak trees. I saw a squirrel running along one of the branches about twenty feet off the ground. Suddenly, it slipped and fell to earth with a thud! After a moment of stunned silence, the squirrel muttered something to itself, got up, and scampered back up into the tree. I thought that the event was funny, probably because I did not expect a squirrel to fall out of a tree. The squirrel was not hurt, but the accident did not seem to be funny to it, and my dog did not run off to tell her companions that she had seen something amazing, a squirrel falling out of the sky, so I suppose that it was not funny to her either. When a squirrel falls out of a tree, that is not funny to the squirrel any more than it would be funny to a human being suffering the same mishap; at the same time, while another animal observing the event might be shocked because squirrels are sure-footed and therefore are not supposed to fall out of trees, probably only a human would find the event amusing.

Maurice Charney's *Comedy High & Low* complains that there is no common ground for the discussion of comedy, no equivalent of Aristotle's *Poetics,* no shared vocabulary, conventions, or assumptions. Indeed, the problem of how to approach humor critically has become even more complicated as certain trends that Charney noted have become more pronounced. Researchers in the areas of audience response, communication theory, philosophy, medicine, semiotics, gender studies, biology, physiology, anthropology, sociology, and other disciplines have added new dimensions, and perhaps confusing new elements, to the field of humor studies over the past several decades.

Definitions are always important keys in research. Not long ago I edited a volume more than thirteen hundred pages long, entitled *Encyclopedia of British Humorists*. The project included essays on 204 humorists by 119 scholars from seven countries (the United States, Canada, England, Ireland,

Scotland, France, and Australia) and a variety of disciplines (literature, theater, history, library science, sociology, political science, business). During
the editing process I not only was not surprised by but eagerly anticipated
finding points of debate scattered throughout the two volumes. What did
surprise me, however, was debate over a situation that I had taken for
granted: the inclusion of satire as a subgenre of humor. Several of the con-
tributing scholars wrote to me asking whether their subject author's satiric
works should be discussed along with the humorous writing. I had always
assumed that satire was considered a type of humor. In hindsight, I also
found it interesting that this question had not been raised in connection with
my companion text, the *Encyclopedia of American Humorists,* published eight
years earlier. I wondered whether the time differential or the diversity in
nationality of the humorists or the scholars were significant, or if it were
purely a matter of coincidence, or perhaps something else entirely. I am
inclined toward the coincidence theory, though I still wonder if satire is
perceived differently by British critics than by American critics, especially in
the study of British literature. I certainly would not want to go so far as to
say that the British put on a more serious face than do the Americans when
examining either literature or humor. The question remains unresolved.

In any case, the essential, primal questions remain as well: Should
literary critics create a unified theory that will provide a reasonable approach to dissimilar queries, such as, What is humor? Why is something
funny? How do individual authors create comedy? What purpose does
laughter serve biologically or sociologically? Furthermore, if we were to create a unified theory, how would we go about doing so? Interestingly, and as
a prime example of the confusion over terminology and the aesthetics of
humor studies, while Charney begins with the assumption that comedy is
"discontinuous, accidental, autonomous, self-conscious, histrionic, and ironic"
(p. x), he also opts to use examples from stage comedy and not from comic
fiction because, "It seemed . . . that the examples from fiction would conflict
with those from the theatre. Since the two arts of comedy are not really
comparable, it would only confuse matters to speak of them together" (ix).

Charney seems to me to have taken a wrong turn here. In any analysis of *humor,* there must be some essential components across all genres.
Charney may be right in that there are seemingly incompatible elements that
do not permit a one-for-one exchange in an analysis of the humor in drama
and prose (live action versus the act of reading, for instance), but that is a
function of how the genres operate—the nature of the modes of expression
rather than the nature of what is being expressed. Further work is needed
toward an understanding of the distinction between those two poles; the
definition of "high" as opposed to "low"; and the ways serious humor, exemp-

lified in the work of Mark Twain, differs from popular humor, exemplified in the writing of Dave Barry. We need to consider the elements of style, subject matter, audience, and author's intent. We scholars need to give shape to the overall generic study, to provide a recognizable direction by moving toward a set of shared definitions, but not necessarily to provide a final definition of humor. We need only hope that our dialogue can begin with an identified shared base.

Humor is probably the most nationalistically defined of the literary genres. In some ways it may seem that the notions of high and low humor do not apply as rigorously in American literature as they do in British literature. The distinctions between Geoffrey Chaucer's *The Canterbury Tales* and John Cleese's scripts for *Monty Python's Flying Circus* are easily identified. But, can't we make the same distinctions between the writings of Twain and Barry? Certainly, slapstick humor exists side-by-side with word-play in the works of both authors. Perhaps belonging to America's nominally classless society has led scholars and the public alike to ignore such a question. Also, the development of humorous writing in America has reflected the history of the nation, and a lot of that history has neither been nor been perceived as high class.

It is quite likely that Benjamin Franklin would have categorized some of his satiric essays as high comedy; they were, after all, witty and patterned along the lines of the English high comedy of Jonathan Swift, Joseph Addison, and their ilk. At the same time, there can be no doubt that the majority of humor produced during colonial days in what was to become the United States did not approach the intellect and subtlety of Franklin's works, even if the out-and-out copies of British exemplars are included. For example, two of Franklin's more literarily famous near contemporaries also wrote humorous accounts—though it may be that for a modern audience, the appellation humorous is accurate more by comparison with what else was being published at the time than for the outright laughter they produced. George Alsop authored the witty and satiric *A Character of the Province of Maryland* (1666), and William Byrd, who numbered among his friends the great British dramatic comedy writers William Congreve and William Wycherley, penned *The History of the Dividing Line* (written, 1738; published, 1841). Unlike Franklin, however, Alsop and Byrd wrote about the quotidian events that they engaged in and graphically described the dirty streets, drunken servants, and country bumpkins whom they met in terms that make them akin to the later Local Colorists, who are definitely considered writers of low comedy.

The standard critical paradigm for American literary critics has depended on the frontier tradition as defined by a constellation of major critics—Constance Rourke in *American Humor: A Study of the National Character* (1931), Bernard DeVoto in *Mark Twain's America* (1932), Walter Blair in *Native American Humor* (1937), and Mody C. Boatright in *Folk Laughter on the American Frontier* (1942)—in the nationalist era preceding World War II. Their work was buttressed by the assumptions of crucial early-twentieth-century historians: Frederick Jackson Turner, most seminally, in *The Frontier in American History* (1920), and Vernon L. Parrington in *Main Currents in American Thought* (1927–30). While there has been considerable subsequent discussion of this aspect of American history, these volumes have been extremely influential in the development of certain points of view in American literary criticism. Only at the end of the twentieth century have their assumptions come under serious reconsideration, although the economic theories of historians Charles Beard and Mary Beard established a potent alternative from early on.

Among the common elements described in these various studies is how rough the frontier was, and how American humor reflected that roughness to the point that even today, the stereotype is of physical, even brutal humor (especially in the writings of those from the Old Southwest—Augustus Baldwin Longstreet, William Tappan Thompson, George Washington Harris, Thomas Bangs Thorpe, and a host of others), which includes boasting and exaggeration (as found in the work of Mike Fink and Davy Crockett). Examples that contribute to this stereotype are plentiful: *Georgia Scenes* (1835) and "The Big Bear of Arkansas" (1854) have nothing to do with high humor or wit; neither do Simon Suggs nor Sut Lovingood. At the same time that Franklin was producing erudite, polished essays, it is clear that the precursors of these Old Southwest humorists were actively creating an oral heritage in just this brand of humor. Another way of looking at the main species of humorous traits typically used to define American humor, then, is to compare the colonial tradition, as epitomized by Thomas Chandler Haliburton's Sam Slick, with that of the Old Southwest, which is an obvious outgrowth of the backwoods genus.

As Rourke points out, the figures of the Yankee and the backwoodsman emerged early and almost full-bodied as the prototype of the American character. These are two quite distinctive, contradictory types, but were they respectively high and low? Rourke comments, "Yankee humor was gradual in its approaches, pervasive rather than explicit in its quality, subtle in its range. Backwoods drawing was broad, with a distinct bias toward the grotesque, or the macabre. Backwoods profusion was set against Yankee spareness. . . . the Yankee as a figure stood alone. . . . The backwoodsman was likely to appear in pairs."[1] Elsewhere she states that the two characters, along with the Negro, "sprang from humble life . . . were looked down upon or scorned by someone, often by whole sections of society. They formed the hard and bony understructure of the nation." It is out of this conglomeration that American humor emerged, and Franklin notwithstanding, this brand of three-strained humor was alive and well during the colonial period, even if it was not widely recorded or published.

How accurate is the stereotyped equation of American humor with low humor? In Hartford, Connecticut, a group of writers known as the Hartford Wits (John Trumbull, Timothy Dwight, and Joel Barlow) became famous in part for their light verse. Written about forty years after *The History of the Dividing Line*, Trumbull's *M'Fingal* (1775–82), a political satire, was cast as a mock epic, a form in favor among English writers such as Alexander Pope a generation earlier. After the turn of the nineteenth century, Washington Irving continued the high humor tradition, which he used in his parodies of conventional histories, with *A History of New York*, in which his style approximates that of Oliver Goldsmith. Generally speaking, the high humor of this period incorporated American themes, characters, and locales, but it was English in accent. Yet, among the first American writers to incorporate the language and manners of the frontier into their humor were Irving's partner in *The Salmagundi Papers*, James Kirke Paulding (*Letters from the South* [1813]), and the artful fabricator of American historical idealizations, Mason Locke Weems. In his "Awful History of Young Dred Drake" (1812), Weems describes the commotion when a group of men get together and try to out-boast one another: "'*Here I come, gentlemen!*' roars a third, '*Here I come! a screamer! yes, d—n me, if I an't a proper screamer; JUST FROM BENGAL! HALF HORSE HALF ALLIGATOR, AND WITH A LITTLE TOUCH OF THE SNAPPING TURTLE.*'"[2] This type of flyting became a standard element of the stereotypical definition of American humor for many years, yet the differences between this low humor and Irving's high humor are obvious.

Perhaps any consideration of high and low in American humor has to recognize their fusion. The satiric works of James Russell Lowell, who was once regarded as the American counterpart to the German poet Johann Wolfgang von Goethe, supply examples of dialect humor that, as French critic Daniel G. Royot has noted in an essay in the *Encyclopedia of American Humor*, "served as a significant link between Yankee lore and the comic fiction of the late nineteenth century" (300). Birdofredum Sawin, a character in Lowell's *Biglow Papers* (first series, 1848; second series, 1867), is representative:

> *Ez to my princerples, I glory*
> *In heving' nothin' o' the sort;*

I ain't a Wig, I ain't a tory
I'm just a canderdate, in short'
Thet's fair an' square an' parpendicular
But, ef the Public care a fig
To hev me an'thin' in particler
Wy, I'm a kind o' peri-Wig.[3]

Lowell was also an editor of the *Atlantic Monthly* magazine, a bastion of Boston Bluestocking sensibility that also gave great impetus to the local color movement that was an especially dominant strain in American humor in the 1870s and 1880s. The whole history of American humor magazines, in fact, shows this tension, stretching from *The Philadelphia Bee* in 1765 through *Puck, Judge,* and *Life* in the nineteenth century to *Captain Billy's Whiz Bang* and *Ballyhoo* in the 1920s and 1930s to *Mad* and *Spy* and components of *Esquire* and *Playboy* in the 1990s.[4]

Related to magazine humor is the strain of comic newspaper writing that has continued from the *American Magazine and Monthly Chronicle* in 1757 to William T. Porter's *The Spirit of the Times* to the present. In these journalistic venues the differentiation between high and low humor has been seen as the difference between urban humor and the humor of the people. The writing of Literary Comedians—like Artemus Ward in *Artemus Ward, His Book* (1862), David Ross Locke as Petroleum V. Nasby in *The Nasby Papers* (1864), Josh Billings in *Josh Billings, His Sayings* (1865), and Finley Peter Dunne in *Mr. Dooley's Opinions* (1901)—are filled with the components that define the humor of the people: primarily, humor that is expressed in the vernacular, with popular idioms and spelling, often appearing in newspaper pieces. This is the tradition of the oral tall tale. It is also a showcase of democratic ethics and American political awareness, very different from the more literary and belletristic humor of Charles Dickens and William Makepeace Thackeray, who were writing in England at the same time. George Ade, Damon Runyon, and Will Rogers, in the first half of the twentieth century, were more tempered than Longstreet, Thompson, and Harris, but there is a definite connection between these two groups of writers. Similarly, there is a connection between Ade, Runyon, and Rogers and contemporary writers such as the *Chicago Daily News'* Mike Royko, Andy Rooney, Art Buchwald, Erma Bombeck, and Dave Barry. Throughout, newspaper humorists have tended to write in the vernacular about everyday events and people and to fill their writing with references to popular culture in ways that clearly distinguish them from the Algonquin wits, though a sense of dry wit seems more prevalent in the twentieth-century practitioners than in their forebears.

This background helped produce Twain, who is recognized as the premier American humorist. Although he included all of these elements in his novels, Twain is deemed to be a writer of high comedy. Again, the question arises, how is it that Twain is categorized as such while Ward, Locke, Billings, Dunne, and the satiric Ambrose Bierce in *The Cynic's Word Book* (1906; later retitled *The Devil's Dictionary*) are not? Possibly it was not until the appearance of Twain that this question, in retrospect of course, could even be asked. His writing is so clearly superior to the work of those who preceded him that it became possible to make such a distinction, not that he or his contemporaries would have thought to ask the question themselves. In part, the answer is the same as would be posited to explain why Twain would be considered a major author: his style and themes, particularly in *Adventures of Huckleberry Finn* (1884), are in a sense derivative, but they also transcend that background and make his work both universal in nature and uniquely his own—a situation undoubtedly true for all major authors. Nineteenth-century American humorist Frederick Swartwout Cozzens observed that any rules defining wit and humor can be overthrown when a "comet" of a wit or a humorist comes along and breaks through the established rules by his unlicensed originality.[5] It is through the ways in which he brings these elements together in an exploration of significant themes that Twain, more than any other American writer up to his time, establishes the reputation of American literature. Moreover, it is this amalgam, with special emphasis on the significant themes, that establishes Twain as a writer of high humor.

In the nineteenth century, the Romantic movement that had flourished in Europe moved across the Atlantic Ocean to the United States, where it emerged as local color and dialect writing, which may differ significantly from frontier humor. In this milieu Marietta Holley ("Josiah Allen's wife") wrote poetry, drama, and fiction from the female point of view. In works such as her best-selling *Samantha at Saratoga* (1887), she drew on the regional detail tradition of the local colorists, the sentimental conventions of the 1850s, and the vernacular humor of the literary comedians.[6] By the end of the century the pendulum swing away from Romanticism had already begun. Because the excesses of Romanticism naturally lend themselves to humorous observations, it might have been expected that the reaction against Romanticism would be expressed in humorous ways. Instead, the mainstream reaction was tempered by a new perception of the world—a perception brought on by World War I. Nevertheless, humor was alive and well in a number of venues. The Roaring Twenties/Jazz Age allowed for new possibilities of expression. Langston Hughes had moved from Missouri to Harlem, in New York City, where he created the character of Jesse B. Simple and others. In stark contrast to that setting, college campuses were one of the most fertile breeding grounds for future humorists—and had been for some time.

As was true in the past, much of the humor that appeared in college humor magazines was a combination of high (because of the inexorable influence of the setting) and low (because of the irreverent exuberance of youth). The Columbia University *Cap and Gown* (1868; later the *Acta Columbiana* under the editorship of John Kendrick Bangs), the *Yale Record* (1872), the *Harvard Lampoon* (1876), Princeton's *The Tiger* (1882), the *Brown Jug* (1920), the Dartmouth *Jack-O-Lantern* (1909), and the like were so popular that *College Humor* was created in 1921 to reprint the best of the campus offerings outside the ivied halls, and cheaper imitations with "lower" content soon followed. Numbered among those who worked on college humor magazines before moving on to productive and prosperous careers as humorists are Robert Benchley, Art Buchwald, Bennett Cerf, Elliott Nugent, S. J. Perelman, Budd Schulberg, Max Shulman, and James Thurber.

February 21, 1925, is an important day in the history of humor, for under the editorship of Harold W. Ross, in the premiere issue of the *New Yorker,* the concept of high humor in the United States was reintroduced. Under Ross's leadership, many of the most important American humorists of the twentieth century contributed to the journal and defined what is known as the *New Yorker* style: the epitome of high humor as practiced by a group of literati, including Alexander Woollcott, Franklin P. Adams, George S. Kaufman, Max Benchley, and Dorothy Parker—all members of the celebrated Thanatopsis Literary and Inside Straight Club that met at the Hotel Algonquin in New York City. Indeed, the list of contributors to the *New Yorker* is a who's who of humor: in addition to members of the Algonquin Round Table, the list includes S. M. Behrman, Sally Benson, Marc Connelly, Clarence Day, Ralph Ingersoll, Nunnally Johnson, Ring Lardner, Lois Long, H. L. Mencken, Leonard Q. Ross (Leo C. Rosten), Thorne Smith, Jean Stafford, Frank Sullivan, and E. B. White. Benchley, Perelman, Thurber, and White were most responsible for establishing the *New Yorker*'s tone and polished style and perfecting the character of the "Little Man."

The "casuals," Ross's term for the short prose pieces he published, exemplify high humor. No matter which of the writers above was the author, each piece contained certain attributes. The casuals are characterized by human, cultivated, sensitive qualities. The style is one of lyrical softness combined with an unhurried, gentle, relaxed, urbane pose. On occasion a manic humor breaks through the superficial "pretense of controlled humor," and while the writers sometimes appear a bit dilettantish, they are seldom foppish, silly, or stupid. Quiet as opposed to ranting, they are amused, yet wistful; romantic and wise, they are at times innocently foolish. If their personae are pretentious at the beginning of a story, they are not pretentious at the end.

Much the same can be said about the cartoonists whose works are packed into the pages of the *New Yorker*. The tone and style of the single-line format favored by Ross has become identified with the magazine through the works of the century's major cartoonists, contributors such as Charles Adams, Peter Arno (Curtis Arnoux Peters), George Booth, Sam Cobean, Whitney Darrow, Jr., Chon Day, Robert Day, Eldon Dedini, Dana Fradan, Al Frueh, John Held, Jr., Syd Hoff, Helen Hokinson, Edward Koren, Arnie Levin, Robert Mankoff, Joseph Mirachi, George Price, Gardner Rea, Mischa Richter, Ronald Searle, Danny Shanahan, William Steig, Saul Steinberg, Richard Taylor, Thurber, Robert Weber, Gahan Wilson, and Jack Ziegler.

The world that both the prose and the cartoon characters inhabit is typically seen from the perspective of bohemian New York, whatever the actual setting of the story, with allusions to books, art, films, the theater, restaurants, ritzy shops, and hotels playing an important part in the background. The themes tend not to be about isolated incidents but instead about events that are extendable to a category of episodes in significant areas of human life.

The Great Depression, which began in 1929, might have dampened American humor, but no evidence of this exists. The screwball comedies of the 1930s and 1940s demonstrated that humor can be used as a weapon against reality. While the comic one-reelers that preceded this genre tended to be low humor (the Keystone Cops, for instance), the personae of many comedians—such as Charlie Chaplin, Harold Lloyd, and Buster Keaton—had a high-class quality that added to the piquancy of their work. With the screwball comedies, the high-class tone became paramount (if one is going to fantasize, after all, one is not likely to fantasize about the dreary world of the Depression but instead will look for relief in tales about people who do not have to worry about money and in whose good fortune we can share, even if only vicariously). The luxurious settings and suave and witty repartee of William Powell and Myrna Loy in *The Thin Man* (1934; adapted from Dashiell Hammett) and the literate banter of Spencer Tracy and Katharine Hepburn in *Adam's Rib* (1949; scripted by Ruth Gordon and Garson Kanin) exemplify the emergence of high humor on a popular level.

Since the turn of the century, American humor has remained a mix of the high and the low. William Faulkner's mainstream novels contain considerable humor that is related to that of the Old Southwest (*The Reivers* [1962], for instance). John Hersey's *A Bell for Adano* (1944) and *Mr. Roberts* (1946) are more along the midline of comedy, but they pave the way for the literary black and ironic humor of Vladimir Nabokov (*Lolita* [1955], a fine example of high humor), J. D. Salinger (*The Catcher in the Rye* [1951]), Joseph Heller (*Catch-22* [1961]), and Kurt Vonnegut, Jr., as well as the Jewish novelists Saul Bellow, Bernard Malamud, and Philip Roth (*Good-bye, Columbus* [1959]; *Portnoy's Complaint* [1969]). John Barth's parodies and burlesques, Thomas Berger's blending of fact and fiction, J. P. Donleavy's picaresque novels filled with misanthropic themes, Bruce Jay Friedman's surrealistic fantasies, Key Kesey's grotesque comedic explorations, and the novels of Thomas Pynchon and Terry Southern have also made their authors famous in this genre.

Not surprisingly, stage and screen show much the same tendencies as book publishing and periodicals. Native humor has been present on the American stage since Royall Tyler's *The Contrast,* which premiered in 1781. A light comedy, the play is reminiscent of the dramas of Englishmen Oliver Goldsmith and Richard Sheridan; like most of the literary prose and poetry of the period, the tone of Tyler's play is essentially that of high humor. By and large, the stage comedy since that time has been at a higher level than that represented by the burlesque theater, but it has seldom risen above the level of musical comedy or the work of Neil Simon. In the case of motion pictures, even leaving aside the Three Stooges, this trend has persisted as well. Recently, the emphasis has been on low humor, and discouragingly so, as evidenced by the immense popularity of the anti-intellectual *Home Alone* (1990) and the trend-setting dumb-and-dumber crop of the mid-1990s. The Marx Brothers, although they dipped into low humor frequently, are among those who strode the middle ground, and the humor of Woody Allen is without a doubt an extension of the high humor style and subject matter found in the works of Benchley, Parker, Perelman, and Thurber.

Television, the most popular of the entertainment media, retains its reputation as a wasteland, with few exceptions. Geared for the average eight-year-old, there are more situation comedies of the *Laverne and Shirley* or *Gilligan's Island* tenor than there are of the more sophisticated blends of high and low found in shows such as *M*A*S*H* or *Mad About You.* To some extent the current slide toward the juvenile in television humor may be a result of the incorporation of stand-up comics in starring rolls; very few of today's stand-up comics fit the high humor mold. Some of those popular in the early part of the century (George Burns and Gracie Allen, Jack Benny, Fred Allen, Bob Hope, Henny Youngman), along with a few mavericks (Garrison Keillor) were closer to high humor than those who attracted large followings in the 1960–90 period (Lenny Bruce, Rodney Dangerfield, Bill Cosby, Eddie Murphy, Richard Pryor, Tim Allen), but even those in the former group were closer to the Yankee/backwoods tradition than that of the Algonquin wits. The American equivalents to the low humor brand of silly comedy of the Two Ronnies, Dame Edith, Bennie Hill, the Goonies, and the Pythons are Milton Berle, Sid Ceasar and Imogene Coca, Ernie Kovacs, Soupy Sales, Buddy Hackett, Jonathan Winters, Robin Williams, and some of *Saturday Night Live,* none of whom would pretend to rank themselves among the practitioners of high humor. Ethnic situation comedies show even less reflective characteristics.

Rourke reconciles the shrewd Yankee/wild backwoodsman strains of American humor by asserting that they both depend on fantasy: "Neither invited the literal view or the prosaic touch" (68–69). While this may be true, it does not address the high/low dichotomy inherent in American humor to a greater extent perhaps than in any other national humor. Touching on the source of the dichotomy, Rourke explains that America is the great melting pot literarily, as well as racially and culturally. In a series of essays in Stanley Trachtenberg's *American Humorists, 1800–1950,* the editor and several other scholars consider American humor from a regional perspective.[7] Trachtenberg examines Eastern humor, which he finds "is associated with the urban centers, which remain its imaginative source if no longer its demographic focus. It is knowing, sophisticated, understated, self-deprecatory, ironic. It acknowledges the complexity not only of the content of experience but of its process." This sounds a great deal like the definition of high humor. Sandy Cohen comments on the cruelty and physical violence that are mainstays in Southern and Southwestern humor, both of which grew out of the oral folk story and tall tale (and still exist in the routines of Tennessee Ernie Ford, Brother Dave Gardner, Moms Mabley, and Jerry Clower). Nancy Pogel demonstrates that Midwestern humor is down to earth, filled with rural horse sense expressed in proverbs. This type of humor predominated in the 1930s, 1940s, and even into the 1950s, propelled by national exposure through the medium of radio. The Midwestern outlook on life, with its glorification of the simple and its distrust of sophistication, is seen in Herb Shriner, Charlie Weaver, Jack Paar, Max Shulman, and Johnny Carson. In his survey of Western humor in Tractenberg's volume, David B. Kesterson concludes that its raw, untamed, exaggeration grows less identifiable and prevalent as the twenty-first century arrives.

Perhaps what can be seen in the commentaries of these humor scholars is that while momentary differences in American humor are evident throughout the country's history and in various locales, there is also a pattern that extends across time and geography—that of the concurrent and ubiquitous mix of high and low humor. Whether the Yankee or the backwoods or the *New Yorker* paradigm is used, an interesting blend results that is more accurate than the traditional stereotype, and this blend may require a redefining of the terms high and low humor. For instance, is the definition dependent on style, theme, or both? Taking another tack, does high humor come with a nation's maturing? Is the appellation high humor, therefore, merely a synonym for civilized? The distinctions enumerated by many critics would seem to indicate that this is so.

The absolute distinction between high and low humor is artificial when applied to American humor, but it is useful from a scholarly point of view, provided that it does not become a red herring. With the realization that additional signifiers may be applied, the study of American humor is opened another notch in terms of the function and operation of the humor itself and the examination of that humor as a reflection of our national character. The existence of another context in which American humor can be studied provides for ancillary facets that may be explored as well, allowing for further extension and amplification of our understanding of the subject at hand.

Notes

1. *American Humor: A Study of the National Character* (New York: Doubleday Anchor, 1953), 68.

2. *The Drunkard's Looking Glass,* 6th ed. (1818), quoted in Hennig Cohen and William B. Dillingham, *The Humor of the Old Southwest* (Boston: Houghton Mifflin Riverside Editions, 1964), 6.

3. *The Biglow Papers, First Series, A Critical Edition,* ed. Thomas Wortham (DeKalb: Northern Illinois University Press, 1970), 114.

4. See Frank L. Mott, *A History of American Magazines,* 5 vols. (Cambridge: Harvard University Press, 1938–65); and David E. E. Sloane, *American Humor Magazines and Comic Periodicals* (Westport, CT: Greenwood, 1987), an analytic bibliography covering the genre from 1765 to 1985.

5. Cozzens, in a lecture before the Mercantile Library Association in New York City on 27 January 1857, as reported in "Mr. Fred S. Cozzens' Lecture on Wit and Humor," *New-York Daily Times,* 28 January 1857, p. 1.

6. See Jane Curry, *Marietta Holley* (New York: Twayne, 1996), TUSAS, no. 658, for a concise and compelling presentation of Holley's work.

7. Stanley Trachtenberg, ed., *American Humorists, 1800–1950,* parts 1–2 (2 vols.), of *Dictionary of Literary Biography,* vol. 11 (Detroit: Gale Research, 1982), 585–622.

Works Cited

Charney, Maurice. *Comedy High & Low.* New York: Oxford Press, 1978.

Cohen, Hennig, and William B. Dillingham, eds. *Humor of the Old Southwest.* Boston: Houghton Mifflin Riverside Editions, 1964.

Curry, Jane. *Marietta Holley.* New York: Twayne, 1996. Twayne United States Authors Series, no. 658.

Gale, Steven H., ed. *Encyclopedia of American Humorists.* New York: Garland, 1988.

——. *Encyclopedia of British Humorists.* 2 vols. New York: Garland, 1996.

Lowell, James Russell. *The Biglow Papers, First Series, A Critical Edition.* Ed. Thomas Wortham. DeKalb, IL: Northern Illinois University Press, 1970.

Mott, Frank L. *A History of American Magazines.* 5 vols. Cambridge: Harvard University Press, 1938–1965.

Rourke, Constance. *American Humor: A Study of the National Character.* New York: Doubleday Anchor, 1953.

Royot, Daniel G. "James Russell Lowell." In *Encyclopedia of American Humorists,* ed. Steven H. Gale. New York: Garland, 1988.

Sloane, David E. E. *American Humor Magazines and Comic Periodicals.* Westport, CT: Greenwood, 1987.

Trachtenberg, Stanley. *American Humorists, 1800–1950,* parts 1–2 (2 vols.). *Dictionary of Literary Biography,* vol. 11. Detroit: Gale Research, 1982.

Weems, Mason Locke (Parson). *The Drunkard's Looking Glass.* 6th ed. 1818.

Gender Issues

Talking Back to the Culture: Contemporary Women's Comic Art

Nancy A. Walker

In his introduction to *The Comics as Culture*, M. Thomas Inge notes that "along with jazz, the comic strip as we know it perhaps represents America's major indigenous contribution to world culture" (xi). One reason for the importance of the comic strip in American life may be the American habit of self-mockery, which we can trace to the late-eighteenth-century work of Joel Barlow and Royall Tyler, early practitioners of a flourishing tradition of American humor. Barlow's mock-epic about cornmeal mush, *The Hasty Pudding,* and Tyler's satiric drama *The Contrast,* which pokes fun at newly minted Americans who ape European manners, can almost be imagined taking place in a series of frames that reflect back to us our own habits and foibles from the pages of the morning newspaper. While many comic strips over the years have had a strong element of fantasy, featuring superheroes and talking animals, the central thrust of the American comic strip has been to represent facets of American life and values, from Mary Worth selling apples on the street during the Depression to Dagwood's penchant for sandwiches and naps.

Yet in a twentieth-century culture of comics in which it takes Rex Morgan, M.D., forty-seven years to recognize and reciprocate his nurse's love for him, questions emerge about the roles women have played as characters in—and more important, as creators of—comic strips. While some of the best-known comic-strip characters are female—such as Blondie, Nancy, and *Peanuts'* Lucy—they inhabit strips by men, no doubt because most syndicated comic strips are created by men. Like stand-up comedy, the comic strip has been one of the most difficult areas of humor for women to enter, perhaps because it is so public and its audience so judgmental, and perhaps, as Betty Swords, creator of the 1974 *Male Chauvinist Pig Calendar,* has said, "Women don't make the jokes because they are the joke" (69). With some notable exceptions, such as Dale Messick, creator of *Brenda Starr,* women who succeeded as creators of comic strips before the 1970s did so by perpetuating familiar stereotypes of women—or by creating cartoons about children, which was how Swords entered the profession in the 1950s.

One question to consider is whether women as creators of comic strips can really change the way this particular humorous medium reflects the values of the culture. Are readers of daily newspapers so conservative that papers would lose advertising revenue if most women characters were not dumb blondes or bitches? In his 1977 book *Women in the Comics,* Maurice Horn expressed the view that women would have little interest in making such changes. Having acknowledged that female cartoonists had faced discrimination in the past, Horn continued:

> While women should certainly be given the same chance in this field as well as any other, as a matter of fairness and right, the mere presence of more women cartoonists would not, in my view, lead to any appreciable improvement in the image of women in the comics. (It is naive to believe that female cartoonists would be motivated by nobler goals than male cartoonists, just as it was childish to assume that female politicians would be prompted by loftier ideals than male politicians, as recent history has clearly shown.) (11–12)

It is tempting to deconstruct Horn's statement because it includes assumptions significant for a consideration of women's involvement in any field, not just the production of comic strips. We can note, for example, that Horn neatly shifts responsibility for what women are able to accomplish in the medium from the men to the women. Male editors have been unfairly discriminatory, he acknowledges, but with that barrier down, the issue becomes women's "nobility" and "idealism," in which he professes to have little faith. Further, this profession is based on the false analogy with women in politics, about whom Horn betrays more than a little bitterness, arising from his disillusionment with a nineteenth-century belief in women's greater moral purity. Finally, it is not at all clear what Horn would consider an "improvement" in women's comic images—even were we to assume that such improvement was the goal of the female cartoonist.

In fact, the motivations of women who draw comic strips are as various as the women themselves, and a desire simply to improve the image of women in comics is pretty far down the list. Nicole Hollander, the creator of *Sylvia,* has said she wants to "express a sense of outrage at all the things that bombard me from television, from newspapers and magazines, from other people's opinions about how everything should be" (Coburn, 147). A common Hollander motif shows Sylvia talking back to her television set. When, for example, a young girl in a television commercial asks, "Mom, can a douche make you feel more confident?" Sylvia retorts, "Not like a good stock portfolio." In addition to expressing outrage at media messages, Hollander states that her Sylvia character can "[cut] a problem down to size. That's important," she continues, for "otherwise, more women would be jumping off the tops of buildings" (Coburn, 147). Cathy Guisewite, whose comic strip *Cathy* has been controversial among feminists, also creates her strip out of a personal response to the culture. She says, "The strip is how I work out my anxieties" ("Life Imitates Art," 30), and she has identified women's "four basic guilt groups" as "food, love, mother, and career" (*Reflections,* viii). "I never," Guisewite continues, "set out to make the strip a voice for anything in particular, but have always just written about the things that were either happening to me or the people around me" (*Reflections,* viii). Lynn Johnston, who bases her strip *For Better or For Worse* in large part on her own family, reports quite simply, "I am every character (even the dog)" (*It's the Thought,* 6).

I employ the work of these three women as examples of the contemporary comic strip used as a personal, individual response to cultural realities in part because all three of these women began to be published around the same time Horn published *Women in the Comics,* and thus they are a part of the future he was trying to imagine. Whether these three strips have effected an "appreciable improvement" in the image of women in the comics is a matter for debate. Are a cigarette-smoking, beer-drinking, no-nonsense writer, a thirty-something career woman riddled with anxieties, and a beleaguered wife and mother improvements over the bimbo and the bitch? That, I think, is not the issue. It is not the business of the comic strip—or of humor in general—to present ideal images, except, perhaps, by inversion. By pointing to absurdity, folly, stupidity, and foible, humor suggests the possibility of a saner, more rational and humane world. Hollander, Guisewite, and Johnston are but three of a growing number of women using the medium of the comic strip to present their perceptions of and commentary on contemporary culture. And because it is the nature of contemporary American political life to be concerned with areas that in other periods might have been considered personal—areas such as sexual preference, child-rearing, and even eating habits—women's comic art must be considered political, whether overtly or subversively. Whether it is Sylvia making fun of Dan Quayle or Cathy bemoaning the tyranny of bathing-suit designers, women's comic strips provide distinctive voices in current political debate.

In one sense, this is nothing new. As Alice Sheppard has demonstrated in her book *Cartooning for Suffrage,* a number of turn-of-the-century female political cartoonists endeavored to show the absurdity of keeping women away from the ballot box. But as Trina Robbins points out in *A Century of Women Cartoonists,* during much of the first half of the twentieth century, syndicated comic strips by women were devoted to the adventures of infants, small children, and adolescent girls—often beautifully executed. The most famous of these cute kids were the Kewpies, drawn by the enormously talented Rose O'Neill. The competent adult woman, with a mind and life of her own, made her entrance with Messick's *Brenda Starr, Reporter* in the early 1940s. *Brenda Starr* was an action strip featuring an assertive, red-haired newspaper reporter who does almost anything to get a story and who is surrounded by a cast of bizarre characters. The Brenda Starr strip was quite literally rescued from the wastebasket by the female assistant to the head of the Chicago Tribune–New York News Syndicate, who grudgingly accepted it for syndication, but refused to run it in his own newspaper, the *New York Daily News,* and his resistance to Messick's strip was shared by other men in the media business. Trina Robbins speculates on the reasons for this reaction:

> There had been plenty of women drawing comics for the past forty years, and there is no record of men strongly criticizing their work. However, all the previous comics by women had been comparatively light—cute animals and kids, pretty girls without a care in the world, rotund grandmas spouting homespun philosophy. These comics might be considered "girl stuff"—a genre the men didn't care to work in or took [sic] seriously. But with *Brenda Starr,* Dale Messick was trespassing on male territory. (66–67)

That was the 1940s. But it is interesting to see how Horn described Messick's comic strip in 1977, just as a new generation of syndicated strips by women was going into circulation. Speaking of the decade of the 1940s, when several new strips began that featured what Horn rather condescendingly terms the "working girls," he singled out *Brenda Starr* as the most successful of these, characterizing the strip's central character as "A tempestuous and flamboyant creature . . . , the red-headed Brenda exhibited more than her share of neuroses. . . . Perpetually torn between the demands of her career and her romantic proclivities, her life proved a long litany of frustrations" (129). Rather, that is, than focusing on Brenda Starr's adventurous spirit or her strength, Horn views her as an unhappy, neurotic woman. That he is uneasy precisely because she refuses to live a traditional domestic life seems clear when he later describes her as "fierce-tempered" and "fickle-hearted": "Romance (usually doomed) dogged her footsteps, as she turned down suitor after eligible suitor in her pursuit of the secretive Basil St. John. In 1976 Dale Messick relented, however, and allowed her heroine to join Basil in wedded bliss" (156). Even, then, while acknowledging and seeming to deplore negative stereotypical images of women in the comics, Horn reveals about alternative images a decided ambivalence that has been widely shared in the mainstream media.

Such attitudes may help to explain why *Cathy* and *For Better or For Worse* appear in far more daily newspapers than does *Sylvia*. *Cathy* and *For Better or For Worse* operate on principles that are in many ways precisely opposite those that animate a strip such as *Sylvia*. The first two rely mainly on realism, whereas *Sylvia*, for all the rich specificity of its artwork and the actual issues with which it deals, uses fantasy as a central component. The "four basic guilt groups" *do* have an impact on the contemporary woman, as they do on Cathy, and sometimes the dog does find and eat all the Easter eggs, as in one of Lynn Johnston's strips. In contrast, Hollander's strip sometimes features alien creatures with antennae and cats who wear funny hats; strips may be set in the Middle Ages, the future, or even in heaven; and some are clearly labeled "fantasy." In addition, whereas Cathy and Elly largely react to cultural realities with dismay or consternation that is shown clearly on their faces, Sylvia talks back to her world without moving a muscle. Finally, while *Cathy* and *For Better or For Worse* frequently provide commentary on social issues—most notably, in Johnston's strip, the sequence in which Elly's teenage son deals with his friend Lawrence's homosexuality—*Sylvia*'s content often approaches the direct political satire of a strip such as *Doonesbury*.

The work of some newer, lesser-known comic artists further illustrates that contemporary women's comic strips represent a diverse set of personal perspectives and comic techniques. Barbara Brandon's *Where I'm Coming From*, the first syndicated comic strip by a black woman, features nine characters, all African-American women in their twenties and thirties, who talk to each other about relationships, jobs, politics, and racism. The typical Brandon strip shows one of her characters talking to another one—usually on the telephone—about a particular irony or absurdity of contemporary life as experienced by African-American women but relevant for the rest of us as well (fig. 1). In a 1992 strip, for example, Brandon's character Lekesia reports that her boss has announced the office will not close on the Martin Luther King, Jr., holiday but that any black employee who wants to may take the day off. In the final frame, Lekesia muses, "Now am I wrong or is *he* missing the point?" Men are never pictured in the strip, though the women frequently talk about them, and as if to underscore the "girl-talk" nature of the strip, only the women's heads are pictured, not their bodies. This is quite deliberate on Brandon's part, and the technique has a political intent, as she explains: "For too long in our society, women have been summed up by their body parts and not by their brains. I want to change that" (Thomas, B5).

Figure 1: *Where I'm Coming From* © Barbara Brandon. Distributed by Universal Press Syndicate. Reprinted with permission. All rights reserved.

   While Brandon's *Where I'm Coming From* is nationally syndicated in mainstream newspapers (as was her father's strip, *Luther*), lesbian comic artist Alison Bechdel is published in what is usually referred to as the "alternative" press, through self-syndication. A collection of Bechdel's strips, *Dykes to Watch Out For,* published in 1986, deals primarily with the perils and pitfalls of lesbian relationships. Whereas Johnston's *For Better or For Worse* can feature a sequence about homosexuality within an otherwise traditional, family-oriented strip, Bechdel's strip appears primarily in the gay and lesbian press. Yet, depictions of the culture's diversity are becoming more acceptable in the mainstream press. Bechdel's *Dykes to Watch Out For* is also published in the monthly *Funny Times,* where it shares space with the humorous prose of Dave Barry, Molly Ivins, and Bailey White, and the comic art of dozens of men and women, including Nicole Hollander. And although nineteen newspapers canceled *For Better or For Worse* within the first week of the Lawrence story, 70 percent of the responses Lynn Johnston and her syndicate received about the series were positive. Notwithstanding the risk that Johnston knew she was taking, she remains convinced that "it was the right thing to do" (*It's the Thought,* 108).

Despite the welcome diversity of contemporary women's comic strips, they have in common a direct response to the culture that surrounds them. As Jaye Berman Montresor has pointed out, "while male cartoonists have traditionally drawn from fantasy, female cartoonists have made it explicit in their strips that they are drawing from life—their own and those around them" (337). Indeed, it is interesting to note that whereas women have traditionally been associated with drawing children, on today's comic pages a number of the most widely circulated strips by men use children as the central characters—for example, *Peanuts, Calvin and Hobbes, Nancy,* and *Curtis.* In a sense, we could say that women's comic art has come of age as its creators explore what it is like to be adult women.

In this respect, women's comic strips follow in the tradition of American women's written humor, which "talks back" to the culture, essentially by telling comically heightened versions of women's real stories. Instead of employing the tall tale of Mark Twain or Thomas Bangs Thorpe, creating linguistic absurdity as have S. J. Perelman and Woody Allen, or indulging in whimsy, female comic artists locate their humor firmly within a reality they in turn critique. One way of analyzing this critique is to use the concept of containment. To what extent are the women characters contained, both artistically—within the frame of the strip—and culturally? Put another way, do they talk back from the inside or the outside?

In one sense, Barbara Brandon's and Alison Bechdel's characters are outsiders and their situations are uncommon. As African-American and lesbian women, they belong to groups accorded minority status in American culture. To some extent the way the strips are drawn reinforces this fact. Each strip departs from comic-strip traditions: Brandon's has no frames around the individual parts of the sequence, and the women are represented only by their heads and sometimes their hands. In Bechdel's *Dykes to Watch Out For* the women have bodies, but they are often unclothed. Also, instead of following a narrative line, Bechdel's strips are sometimes "do's and don'ts," guides to lesbian social and sexual behavior (fig. 2). In part precisely because she is not on the comic pages of daily newspapers, Bechdel is free to create both single-panel and multiple-panel comics, as does Nicole Hollander. A position outside mainstream syndication provides a flexibility not available to those who write for the "family" newspaper. Tom Inge has pointed out that the comic strips in daily papers reinforce mainstream cultural values—the family as the "basic social unit," ethical behavior in professional life, and so forth—whereas comic artists whose work appears in the alternative press have "the incredible luxury of unrestricted artistic freedom." Inge continues by suggesting that the work of the latter group "holds the promise of a politically untrammeled comic art of the future"

(Introduction, 632). While Barbara Brandon's strip does appear in the mainstream press, its large size means that it is not on the comics page but instead the editorial or lifestyle page. This is fine with Brandon, who has said, "I don't want to be on the funny pages. I want to be separate" (Hickey, E1).

Figure 2: "The Unrequited Crush" by Alison Bechdel from *Dykes to Watch Out For,* published by Firebrand Books, Ithaca, NY. Copyright © 1986 by Alison Bechdel.

We would expect, then, that strips such as *Cathy* and *For Better or For Worse* would be more conservative—that they would "talk back" in different ways and about different issues. Indeed, this is largely the case. But I believe these five comic strips are best seen as occupying places on a continuum, with Brandon and Bechdel on one end, arguing that the lives and problems of black and lesbian women be taken seriously and on their own terms; Johnston and Guisewite on the other end, presenting dilemmas with which large numbers of women can identify; and Hollander somewhere in the middle, occupying the insider and the outsider positions simultaneously.

Despite the sexual explicitness of *Dykes to Watch Out For,* Bechdel often presents situations that will seem familiar to heterosexual readers. In "The Unrequited Crush," part of her "Lesbian Etiquette Series," Bechdel presents do's and don'ts that most of us would find sensible in any instance of unrequited love. Readers are advised that while it is acceptable to collect "small mementoes" (in this case, used facial tissues and toothpicks) and seek the support of one's friends, the don'ts include calling to hear her voice and then hanging up, and having her name tattooed on one's body. The "luppies" (lesbian urban professionals) she presents in another strip have the same values and aspirations as any group of yuppies. Some strips, of course, are more firmly located in the gay experience, such as one in which a masculine-looking woman is challenged at the entrance to the women's restroom. But even here Bechdel is working with the general theme of the human tendency to equate appearance with identity, and she commonly deals with issues that affect us as human beings—love, relationships, competition, jealousy, identity—and in the process suggests that our similarities are more important than differences in sexual orientation.

Brandon's *Where I'm Coming From,* while featuring only black women characters, conveys the implicit message that young black women do not all have the same values and aspirations. Brandon works against media stereotyping by creating a gallery of characters to represent various realities of contemporary black culture. Lekesia is the most politically active of the group, staunch in her support of the rights of black women, and Monica speaks out against all forms of racism. Nicole and Sonya, on the other hand, are more concerned about relationships with men; Nicole constantly searches for the right man, while Sonya thinks only about her boyfriend, Kenny. Some of Brandon's characters are professional women; some are primarily concerned with their appearance. Their educational levels differ. Perhaps because the various characters address problems, stresses, and constraints they confront as women, Brandon's strip has sometimes been compared to Guisewite's *Cathy*—a comparison that does not please Brandon, who has said, "I feel I have a larger responsibility." And indeed there are fundamental differences between the two strips. As one commentator puts it, "Instead of obsessing about whether their boyfriends play too much golf, they worry about whether the man will be around when the child is born" (Hickey, E1). In addition, because Brandon's characters form a community of women who confide in each other, they often provide reality checks for each other, as Judy does for Nicole in one strip. Nicole is happily telling Judy about a new boyfriend who has been married, divorced, and engaged three different times. To Nicole, this means "he's a man who is not afraid of commitment," but at the end of the sequence Judy comments wisely, "it shows he doesn't know the meaning of the word." What *Cathy* and *Where I'm Coming From* actually have most in common is not the extent to which the characters are at the mercy of life's pressures but rather the technique the two artists use of having the characters address readers face-to-face, as if carrying on a dialogue with the world outside the strip.

At the other end of the spectrum of "talking back" are *For Better or For Worse* and *Cathy*. With the exception of the final frame of a *Cathy* strip, in which Cathy presents the "moral" of that particular strip, both Johnston and Guisewite allow readers to look in on a series of episodes in a continuing story that may last for several weeks. *For Better or For Worse* centers on Elly and her responsibilities as wife and mother, and its issues are the same as those featured in the mid-century "domestic" humor of Jean Kerr and Shirley Jackson: the pressures of housework, and children's foibles and pranks. Part of what updates Johnston's strip to the 1990s is Elly's struggles with technologies that her children take for granted. One strip, for example, shows Elly tapping away on her typewriter when her teenage son decides to introduce her to the miracle of the computer. After several panels in which he discusses menus, files, and commands, the final panel shows Elly happily back at her typewriter. While Elly's husband is generally supportive and involved in the life of the family, some strips echo the perceptions of earlier women humorists that husbands fail to understand the complexity of domestic responsibilities. Elly, however, makes sure that John understands (fig. 3).

Figure 3: *For Better or Worse* ● Lynn Johnston Prod., Inc. Reprinted with permission of Universal Press Syndicate. All rights reserved.

In general, *For Better or For Worse* celebrates family life (88). Elly worries sometimes about aging and appearance—in one strip in which she is pleased at being able to swim well after the age of forty, she concludes, "That definitely proves one thing . . . cellulite floats" (*It's the Thought,* 72).

Guisewite's Cathy, on the other hand, is obsessed with her appearance—as she is with her mother, her relationships with men, and the stresses of her job. In fact, the *Cathy* strip has been almost uniformly attacked by feminist readers for showing a thirty-something career woman who is so much at the mercy of her culture. *Cathy* would seem to bear out Horn's bleak prediction, made in 1977, that future female comic artists would not necessarily present more positive images of women. While it is not my aim to rescue Cathy from her detractors, I would like to point out two things. First, without conflict of some sort, there is no humor; the real and the ideal must be at odds with one another. For this reason, *Cathy* is a more *comic* comic strip than is *For Better or For Worse.* Second, it is through the very recognizable reality of the *Cathy* strip that Guisewite and her character talk back to the culture. Food, mothers, men, and jobs are actual issues for women, and if Cathy doesn't deal with them very well, neither do many of us. Guisewite's strip suggests this may not be entirely our fault.

In many *Cathy* strips, both women and men are unable to communicate their real feelings. When Cathy's boyfriend Irving takes her to a nice restaurant, for example, the following dialogue ensues:

> CATHY: This is a beautiful restaurant, Irving. What's the occasion?
>
> IRVING: Why? Does there have to be an occasion?
>
> CATHY: No. I just thought you might want to talk about something.
>
> IRVING: Why? Do *you* want to talk about something?
>
> CATHY: No! I don't want to talk about anything. Are you sure you don't want to talk about anything?
>
> IRVING: No. I don't want to talk about anything. Are you sure you don't want to talk about anything?

When the waitress asks, "Ready to order?" Cathy responds, "No, thanks. We're still searching for each other's hidden agenda."

As much as Cathy would like to find the perfect bathing suit, she often shows her disgust with the fashion industry by running from the store (fig. 4). It would be difficult *not* to feel pressured by a mother who has devoted her life to trying to run yours. And about food and dieting, Guisewite has this to say: "The very fact that I can look through fifteen years of dieting strips and remember what I was eating when I wrote almost every single one of them should give some clue as to why food has the importance in Cathy's life that it does" (*Reflections*, 215). As is the case with Lynn Johnston's strip, *Cathy* is comic strip as autobiography; "talking back" is a matter of presenting one's own reality to the public.

Figure 4: *Cathy* © Cathy Guisewite. Reprinted with permission of Universal Press Syndicate. All rights reserved.

Nicole Hollander's *Sylvia* talks back to the culture from the position of both insider and outsider. Like Johnston's Elly, she is a mother; unlike her, she is a single mother. Like Cathy, she recognizes that food can be a problem. In many strips messages appear on Sylvia's refrigerator door: "the temple of doom," "do not open—guard dog inside," "there's nothing in this refrigerator that a normal, well-adjusted person needs," and more simply, "don't." When a voice from her television set intones, "you are what you eat," Sylvia responds, "I am a Fritos corn chip." She and her daughter are often at odds, as are Elly and her children, and Cathy and her mother, but in Sylvia's case the roles are usually reversed: it is Sylvia's daughter who tries to get Sylvia out of the bathroom and often thinks her mother is outrageous. In fact, Sylvia's appeal is that she makes no attempt to conform to the wishes or expectations of others, in either her behavior or her opinions. She is a fifty-something woman who frequently appears dressed in a bathrobe and a hat, smoking a cigarette, and drinking a beer. Hollander made a deliberate decision about her character's age:

> I think I created someone who is a little bit older than I am now so I could see how I might act when I get to be that age. I am really furious about age and the way that old people are treated. Specifically, I'm thinking of how women become invisible after a certain age. No one listens to them; no one sees them. There is this image of what middle-aged women look like, and I can see that some women have made a decision to look like that—dowdy, matronly, an "I

will wear my polyester pantsuit and I will blend into the background and I will have a permanent" look. So Sylvia is a support—a personal one if nothing else—for not doing that. (quoted in Coburn, 146)

One of Hollander's strips comments on this very circumstance, with Sylvia in her role as advice columnist. At her typewriter to write about "getting old in America," Sylvia at first cannot think of anything to write, and by the final frame she has written only "Best to do it somewhere else." Thus, Hollander has overturned a stereotype by giving voice to a silenced segment of the culture. Sylvia talks back to that which she finds outrageous in politics, the media, and human relationships. Sometimes she sounds as though she is advising Guisewite's Cathy and acknowledging that we often replace one bad habit with another: "Does money slip through your fingers? Is your motto 'why pay less?' Meet with a group of like-minded people to pore over Neiman-Marcus catalogs, select expensive items, fill out the order form and then burn it, while chanting in unison: 'I don't need to shop. I can eat instead.'" In fact, it is often the outrageous nature of Sylvia's advice that reveals the absurdity of the situation she comments about.

Hollander's *Sylvia* is more overtly political than almost any comic strip besides *Doonesbury*. Like Molly Ivins, she enjoyed taking pokes at Ronald Reagan's absent-minded presidency. In a strip featuring only Sylvia's television set and her cat, a television announcer's voice conveys the following information: "The Washington press corps was stunned today when President Reagan suggested mud wrestling as a substitute for affirmative action. A staff aide said later that the President had misunderstood the question, but refused to say what question the President thought he was answering." But *sexual* politics more often captures Hollander's attention, especially when some "authority" pronounces women's proper role (fig. 5). Sometimes the two kinds of politics come together, as they did in debates about the Equal Rights Amendment. When a voice from Sylvia's television set says, "There's no place for special treatment in the business world. If women want time off to bear children, they can't expect to be treated as equals," Sylvia responds, "Okay, give men time off to bear children."

While Sylvia's no-nonsense responses to the culture constitute the most obvious example in women's comic art of talking back to those forces that seek to manipulate women's lives, all five of these strips force readers to see beyond the humor to realities of sexism, racism, homophobia, and other forms of discrimination. In this regard, all are to some degree political in intent. Equally important is their use of autobiographical elements—as reflections of what their creators have experienced—which they use to make the comic strip a conversation in which we may mutually explore contemporary women's lives. Precisely this point has been made by Lynn Johnston, who admires Guisewite's *Cathy:* "It's like talking to a good friend, letting it out to a good friend. . . . There are times when you want to say, 'That's too true to even put down on paper'" (Kruh, F5).

In these contemporary women's comic strips whose creators "talk back" to the culture, it is significant that the language of the strip is at least as important as the visual element. As especially Brandon's *Where I'm Coming From* illustrates, these are strips about conversations—not the visual pratfalls of *Beetle Bailey* or the elaborate travel fantasies of *Calvin and Hobbes.* Sylvia and Elly are at least part-time writers, providing symbolic evidence of the strips' creators' desire to communicate. Overwhelmingly, these are representations of real women in the real world, telling it like they wish it were not.

Figure 5: Cartoon from *The Whole Enchilada,* by Nicole Hollander. Copyright © 1986 by Nicole Hollander. Reprinted by permission of St. Martin's Press Incorporated.

Works Cited

Bechdel, Alison. *Dykes to Watch Out For.* Ithaca, NY: Firebrand Books, 1986.

Brandon, Barbara. *Where I'm Still Coming From.* Kansas City, MO: Andrews & McMeel, 1994.

Coburn, Marcia Froelke. "On the Draw." *Chicago* (August 1984), 145–47, 180.

Guisewite, Cathy. *Reflections.* Kansas City, MO: Andrews & McMeel, 1991

Hickey, Elisabeth. "Black Woman Cartoonist Is First to Hit Syndication." *Washington Times,* 17 September 1991, E1.

Hollander, Nicole. *The Whole Enchilada.* New York: St. Martin's Press, 1986.

Horn, Maurice. *Women in the Comics.* New York: Chelsea House, 1977.

Inge, M. Thomas. *Comics as Culture*. Jackson: University Press of Mississippi, 1990.

———. Introduction. *Journal of Popular Culture*. Special issue on "The Comics as Culture" 12 (spring 1979), 631–39.

Johnston, Lynn. *It's the Thought That Counts*. Kansas City, MO: Andrews & McMeel, 1994.

Krier, Beth Ann. "Life Imitates Art for Cathy the Cartoonist." *Los Angeles Times,* 7 May 1987, B2–B3.

Kruh, Nancy. "Cathy Defuses Issues With Humor." *Dallas Morning News,* 17 November 1991, F1, F4–F5.

Montresor, Jaye Berman. "Comic Strip-Tease: A Revealing Look at Women Cartoon Artists." *Look Who's Laughing: Gender and Comedy,* ed. Gail Finney. Langhorne, PA: Gordon and Breach, 1994.

Robbins, Trina. *A Century of Women Cartoonists*. Northampton, MA: Kitchen Sink Press, 1993.

Sheppard, Alice. *Cartooning for Suffrage*. Albuquerque: University of New Mexico Press, 1994.

Swords, Betty. "Why Women Cartoonists Are Rare, and Why That's Important." In *New Perspectives on Women and Comedy,* ed. Regina Barreca. Philadelphia: Gordon and Breach, 1992, 65–84.

Thomas, Keith L. "Homegirls in 'Toon Town." *Atlanta Journal,* 13 January 1992, B1, B5.

"Old Maids" and Wily "Widders": The Humor of Ruth McEnery Stuart

Judy Sneller

In the last half of the nineteenth century, Northern women like Ann Stephens, Phoebe Cary, Sara Willis Parton, and Marietta Holley were making their mark as literary humorists. The work of these women has recently received some well-deserved critical attention thanks to the efforts of Jane Curry, Linda Morris, Nancy Walker, and Zita Dresner, to name a few.[1] Unfortunately, little sustained critical attention has been given to Southern women writers as humorists, even though they were also creating a powerful body of regional humor at the turn of the century. Perhaps the idea of proper "Southern Ladies" daring to write humor in their war-decimated homeland is a stretch of belief, even for contemporary humor critics.

Nevertheless, from 1888 until the time of her death in 1917, New Orleans native Ruth McEnery Stuart was so popular for her humor that she was believed by some to "out rank all Southern humorists" ("Sharps and Flats"). She won national acclaim not only for her humorous stories and poems but also for dialect readings she gave throughout the nation. At one point Stuart was so popular for her "local color" stories about life in Louisiana and Arkansas that an article in the *Bookman* proclaimed, "now there is no woman whose work is more widely known and loved, and whose personality has a further reaching influence" (Tutwiler, 633). The critical neglect of Stuart, once lauded as a "sort of very Southern goddess" for her humor, is an oversight because her humor can provide unique insight into the intersection of gender, race, and region at the turn of the century (Field). In fact, it is Stuart's strong regional identity that ultimately inhibited her ability to see gender and racial subordination as linked and equally worthy issues to be challenged with her humor.

Stuart's humor consistently reflects her interest in both The Woman Question and The Negro Question. Like most other Americans in the last decades of the nineteenth century, she tried to (re)assess what rights and roles women and newly freed slaves would have in the United States. In the postwar South the reigning cultural ideal for white middle- to upper-class women like Stuart was still the "Southern Lady," a model that in some ways was simply a more fragile and leisured counterpart of the Northern pious, pure, domestic, and submissive "True Woman."[2] In spite of this, Stuart was a self-proclaimed feminist who once boldly declared, "'I never questioned . . . the inherent right or righteousness of the women's cause. It seemed instinct with me'" ("The South Old and New"). Overlooking the fact that her beloved Louisiana was ranked by some as "perhaps the last among the supporters of the woman suffrage idea," Stuart used much of her humor to challenge indirectly the traditional, restrictive models of white Southern womanhood (Spiers 18–19).

Stuart also maintained an unflagging loyalty to the defeated South, for she knew first-hand the poverty and humiliation that followed its defeat. Her wealthy, aristocratic New Orleans family was impoverished by the war, and years later the war's painful legacy is still felt in Stuart's comment, "The recollections of my childhood . . . are very strange and troubled; it is as if the atmosphere upon my mental canvas were dimmed with the fire and smoke of war" (Steadman). Unfortunately, part of Stuart's lifelong loyalty to the Confederacy was her support of the region's postwar attempt to redefine an "Old South" ideology based in part on the tradition of maintaining white supremacy. For example, the Jim Crow laws of the 1890s enabled Louisiana whites to impose a legally sanctioned system of segregation, and by 1898 blacks in that state had been completely disfranchised through educational and property qualifications (Dethloff and Jones). Ironically, of course, by supporting such a reactive ideology, Stuart was also approving a system that was not only racist but also unabashedly sexist, a patriarchy in which white men dominated not only supposedly ever-grinning "Sambos" but also mythically passive and dependent "Southern Ladies." As a few examples will illustrate, Stuart's attempt to create a truly feminist humor fails because her portraits of strong and independent Southern white women cannot be reconciled with the negative stereotypes of black women that dominate her work.[3]

A good example of Stuart's portrayal of postwar Southern white women is "The Woman's Exchange of Simpkinsville," in which she positively transforms a number of traditional images of Southern women into more dynamic and independent models of womanhood.[4] In this story, set in the small town of Simpkinsville, Arkansas, Stuart indirectly expresses her wish to redefine gender roles to match the very changed social and economic circumstances of the postwar South. The Misses Sarey Mirandy and Sophia Falena Simpkins are twin sisters—no longer young—who find their family fortune depleted after the war. When they for the first time must work for a living, they realize that all their background has prepared them to do as

"Southern Ladies" is to sew, cook, and calculate figures, so they decide to operate a woman's exchange, where women of the community bring in goods of various kinds to be sold by the sisters in return for a 10 percent commission on the sales. The sisters eke out a modest income from the exchange, and although it initially seems somehow "wrong" to the sisters (and their community), they also begin boarding an occasional traveler. Stuart emphasizes the change in social relations wrought by the economic disaster of the war by noting, "It seemed odd that its leading family . . . should have been first to put a price on the bread broken with a stranger" (331–32).

In both appearance and actions the spinsters adjust to their new roles—and with gusto. Stuart contrasts the old days, when the sisters' delicate wrists and arms were decorated with a "succession of bracelets," with the present, when burns from oven doors adorn them. Stuart does not note these changes with a sense of nostalgia or dismay but emphasizes the positive repercussions of the sisters' new, more active engagement with the day-to-day business of their community. For example, she reflects that "it was . . . a new, youth-restoring life to be always professedly and really busy with work that left no time for repinings" (327). The sisters even embark on what is for them a drastic change in their appearances. When Sophia proposes that their habitual, totally black dresses could have "'a little white ruchin' in the neck an' sleeves . . . not meanin' no disrespec's to the dead, but in compliment to the living,'" Sarey replies, "'Well. . . . Seem like our first duty *is* to the livin'" (333). Furthermore, both agree that a little white piping might even keep their overnight lodgers from feeling compelled to "'talk religion to us like they do'" (334).

The Simpkins sisters' new strength and independence are contrasted with the character of their revered dead brother, Sonny, who was a genteel but ultimately weak man. Sonny is mocked by his boyish name and his depiction as an absent-minded professor who had "never grasped the changed situation after the war" and who meets an unheroic death when he falls out of a tree while hunting birds for his collection (312). When a traveler from the Smithsonian discovers Sonny's rare bird collection and offers to buy it, the sisters gratefully accept and are thereby restored to their former upper-class status in the community. Significantly, however, Stuart does not portray the sisters as closing their business and returning to lives of genteel inactivity. On the contrary, they see the funds as supplying their exchange with "just the lubrication it needed for smooth and happy working" (355).

In "The Woman's Exchange," therefore, Stuart not only mocks the stereotypes of the supposedly leisured, genteel "Southern Lady" and the ever-dependent, reclusive "Old Maid," but she also suggests that the ideal of the dashing and heroic "Southern Gentlemen" needs revision. The humor in this story never laughs at the many gentle Southern women whose lives were so drastically refashioned by the war but instead mocks the social codes that refuse to afford women equal opportunities in education, politics, and economics—thereby perpetuating a narrow, subordinate view of women's rights and roles. As Helen Taylor insightfully notes about this story, "Stuart is giving cautious welcome to the New South" and is using it to point to the strength derived from women's ability to adapt to new economic and social circumstances (124).

"The Second Mrs. Slimm" is another story in which Stuart portrays postwar white women who may have once been called "Old Maids" but who now work at occupations outside the home and who, as in the Simpkins family, are stronger than the men around them.[5] Here, Ezra Slimm, a genteel widower "quite diminutive in size," is trying to figure out how to get a new wife in his small Arkansas town when all the local women know who "wore the pants" in the Slimm marriage (37–38). Ezra recalls the dark day he had nerve enough to "talk back" to his wife, Jinny, and how she "'took it upon herself to lay me acrost her lap an' punish me'" (38–39). Jinny was an ultra pious woman who believed her tiny husband but "a pore lost sinner" (39). Ezra remembers the little devils she used to print on the butter pads to warn him of evil and recalls that "the nearest I ever did come to answerin' her back . . . was the way I used regular to heat my knife-blade good an' hot 'twix' two batter-cakes an' flatten that devil out *de*lib'rate. But he'd be back nex' day, pitchfork an' all" (40–41). Ezra wearily concludes that he misses the little devils "about ez much ez I miss her" (40).

Ezra believes his dilemma solved when he reads about a distant school mistress, Miss Myrtle Musgrove, who had "abolished the use of the rod" in favor of "the law of kindness" (41). Ezra feels Myrtle must be a gift from Providence, so he writes her a love letter and begins daydreaming of her hanging on his every word and favoring him with dazzling smiles. However, when Ezra finally dares to visit her, his dreams of demure and dainty Southern belles are dashed when a "stout, matronly woman" introduces herself as Myrtle. To Ezra's relief, Myrtle announces that her profession is "the only husband I shall ever take," but she is willing to introduce him to three likely young women (47). Ezra meets one likely freckle-faced lass but longs to meet a "radiant . . . red-haired creature" he spotted earlier (45). Myrtle agrees to find the red-haired vision, but not before telling Ezra that although whipping had been abolished at school, "that girl thought one of her boys needed it, and she followed him home, and gave it to him there, and his father interfered, and—well, *she whipped him too*" (48–49). Needless to say, Ezra changes his mind about meeting her. The story ends with the second Mrs. Slimm (a freckle-faced lass) delivering their first child, whom Ezra gratefully names Myrtle.

In this story Stuart again challenges the stereotype of the "Old Maid," updated here as the single career woman. Although such a stereotype has traditionally been used to demean women, Stuart surrounds it with outrageous exaggeration to suggest that it is indeed too laughable a stereotype to take seriously. As Nancy Walker has pointed out, the frequent use of female stereotypes by women humorists "suggests that rather than endorsing or even accepting these extremes of women's behavior, the authors are rejecting the cultural forces that have created them" (*Serious Thing,* 65). Furthermore, Myrtle may seem at first glance to be the stereotypical "Plain Jane" spinster, but she is *not* ultimately a comic figure. She is, in fact, the most compassionate, practical, and logical character in the story, a woman who is happy and motivated by the life she has built for herself. Stuart uses Myrtle, and a number of other white female protagonists throughout her fiction, to redefine restrictive gender roles for white women.[6] Indeed, Stuart's humor consistently mocks the stereotype of the unfulfilled "Old Maid," thereby suggesting that late-nineteenth-century Southern women *do* have other options besides the fragile domesticity and genteel submission upheld by traditional models of white Southern womanhood.

Unfortunately, Stuart's stories about Southern black women offer an immediate and striking contrast to these progressive portraits of empowered white women. By consistently depicting black women as "Black Widders" and "Misfits," Stuart reveals the restricted sexual and social roles she anticipated for black women in the supposedly new South. Stuart's demeaning stereotypes of black women not only mark them as comic inferiors at whom white readers can laugh but also suggest they threaten the foundations of white patriarchal order. Such negative images suggest that black women are outside acceptable (that is, white) society and models of womanhood. Indirectly, these images seek to recreate an Old South relationship between the races that keeps blacks unthreatening and subservient to white power and knowledge. Much of this facet of Stuart's humor attests to John Burma's contention that although humor is often considered a benign literary tool intended only to amuse, "a not inconsequential amount of humor . . . has as its primary purpose the continuation of race conflict" (714).

First of all, Stuart's many "Black Widder" stories employ outlandish, exaggerated humor that does more than provoke innocent laughter from white readers. Like the "Mammy" and "Mulatto Temptress" stereotypes used by other popular writers during this period, Stuart's "Black Widders" and their intricate plots to remarry relate to white fears about black women's sexuality (Burma, 711). Such fears were not new, especially for white antebellum plantation women who lived with the knowledge that their husbands often regularly visited the cabins of black slave women and fathered children who played with their own. However—perhaps as a way to explain or justify both the master's actions and the wife's seeming acceptance of such an intolerable situation—the sexual abuse of black women often resulted in the labeling of them as wanton whores, not victims. As Catherine Clinton has observed, the perpetuation of the myth of the promiscuous "'slave wench' . . . demeaned black women by equating them with animal sexuality— and project[ed] onto them the sensuality denied to the plantation mistress" (222). Then, too, in New Orleans the liaisons between genteel white men and free black women also implanted in white minds the idea that black women were sexually promiscuous and immoral.

Lize Ann Johnson in "The Widder Johnsing" is representative of Stuart's many immodest and immoral "Black Widders."[7] For the first ten pages of the story, Lize Ann is present only in her hysterical wailings over the death of her third husband, Jake (95). Portraying her grief in a theatrical manner not only robs it of dignity but sets up a contrast between white genteel "order" and the supposedly innate tendency of blacks to be emotional and irrational, for Stuart quickly interjects, "No negro ever resists any noisy demonstration of grief" (104). The gossiping women at the funeral call Lize Ann a notorious man chaser who had buried two other husbands and who they predict will soon be looking for another.

The black widow is soon spinning her web, for she arranges for Brer Langford, a "handsome bachelor . . . the best catch in the parish," to help ease her pain (108). Stuart describes his many visits to Lize Ann in language that accentuates this black woman's sexuality, sensuality, and craftiness. For example, on his first visit the pastor is amazed to find Lize Ann transformed from an old widow to a "round, trig . . . youngish woman" with a "shapely bosom" (112). When he happens to walk through her bedroom, "the white bed, dazzling in its snowy fluted frills, reminded him of its owner" (115). An array of mouth-watering food always happens to be on hand, and when Lize Ann asks him to fetch some milk, the reverend finds a bottle of beer instead, which she insists she keeps only for "faintiness." The pastor agrees to drink it, declaring that a *Christian* man is the only one who should trust himself with the wine cup "'case a sinner don' know when ter *stop*" (115).

However, this black widow does not rely only on the five senses to snare her victim. Stuart again places this black woman outside the rational by aligning her with deviltry and superstition. When alone, Lize Ann throws herself to the floor laughing. With "eyes fairly dancing," she stokes her fire and proudly thinks to herself, "'I does wonder huccome I come ter be sech a devil, anyhow? I 'lowed I was safe ter risk de beer. Better get a dozen bottles, I reck'n; give 'im plenty rope, po' boy'" (118). Three months and many feasts later, Lize Ann's schemes pay off and she becomes Mrs. Langford—and just in time, too, for there was only *one* bottle of beer left.

From beginning to end, this and other Stuart "Black Widder" stories use humor to portray black women as irrational, immoral, and sexually promiscuous—and therefore threats to the established social structure who should be banished to the margins of proper white society.[8] Although Stuart's motivation for the stories may have been to launch a comic assault on black women's equality in the New South, she actually weakens the case for *all* women's increased autonomy through her demeaning depictions of scheming women happy only when safely confined within the patriarchal institution of marriage.

While Stuart's "Black Widders" focus primarily on black women's morality and sexuality, she also depicts them as grotesquely comic misfits who are unable to cope with freedom without white assistance. According to George Lampugh, popular magazine fiction from 1875–1900 frequently depicted the flight of rural blacks to the city as a disastrous mistake that could be corrected only by returning to the supposedly happy (and poorly paid) life of the plantation worker (187). In "Queen O' Sheba's Triumph," Stuart portrays a black woman from Arkansas as a grotesque urban migrant whose only "triumph" is achieved in death.[9] From the outset, Queen of Sheba Jackson is described as one whose physical ugliness, outlandishly ironic name, and bizarre actions mark her as a comic grotesque. When she arrives in New York City she is set apart from the white urban norm by her odd dress, country habits, and black drawl. However, Sheba is not just a grotesque because she is a country bumpkin who dresses wrong and looks funny, for her role as an uneducated black woman substantially contributes to her status as an ugly undesirable—namely, a misfit. Although famous for her cooking in Broom County, she finds in New York that her biscuits "counted for naught, and that her frying-pan was unavailable" (56). The uneducated Queen of Sheba soon finds herself a "plebe on the down grade," who finally ends up a scullion in a Harlem boarding house where she was aware that she "was the very lowest in the social order" (57, 61). To save face, however, she manages to send a good photo of herself to her Arkansas friends to convince them she has "made it big" in the city.

When Sheba's friends announce they are coming to visit, she engages on a darkly comic, even gruesome, plot to hide her dire straits. Since her only possession is a life insurance policy for a first-class burial, she arranges to have a stately (mock) funeral conducted *now* in exchange for a pauper's grave later. The plot becomes even more macabre when she secretly attends the funeral, collapses and dies from exhaustion, and really *is* buried by her friends. Having failed to construct a new life for herself in the urban North, this black woman's "triumph" was possible only in suffering and death. The quest of the black Queen of Sheba, unlike Stuart and a score of other *white* Southern women who moved to the North to pursue writing careers near the turn of the century, ends not in empowerment or upward social mobility but in poverty, loneliness, and death.

Regrettably, the many grotesques found throughout Stuart's fiction exhibit none of the positive attributes accorded to the grotesque by either Mikhail Bakhtin in his study of carnival or Mary Russo in her consideration of the potential power of the female grotesque as a political tool for women.[10] For Bakhtin the grotesque body of carnival imagery is deeply positive, regenerative, and even cosmic in its significance (18–30, 303–67), whereas Russo tentatively suggests that the female grotesque might be used to destabilize the *potential* idealizations of female beauty (213–229). Thus, although "Queen O' Sheba's Triumph" could potentially have made a positive feminist statement, it fails because of Stuart's inability to provide portraits of black women as admirable and independent members of society.

Admittedly, Stuart had no well organized, comprehensive solution for either The Negro Question or the The Woman Question, but as the foregoing examples suggest, she did enter into these ideological debates through her humorous writing. She used her humor to indicate an awareness of the patriarchal nature of society and to suggest innovative transformations of white middle-class women's rights and roles in American society. However, Stuart's regional identity as a member of the aristocratic plantation South affected her ability to frame racial issues in anything but reactive terms, regardless of the gender implications. As recent scholarship has shown, such a strong regional identity was not uncommon for Southern women of this period. Elizabeth Fox-Genovese concludes, "Gender, race, and class relations constituted . . . the elements from which they fashioned their views of themselves" (43), and Anne Goodwyn Jones notes that Southern women often identified not only with a specific area of the South but with the *idea* of the South, with "the South as a region of mind" (47). Unfortunately, for Stuart, part of that regional "idea" was maintaining white supremacy, and she was never able to resolve the logical inconsistency between her portraits of empowered white women and demeaned black women. Her work consistently uses humor to portray empowered images of single, white Southern women who negate the dependent "Old Maid" image, and at the same time employs demeaning portraits of single black women who uphold the image of the promiscuous, scheming "Black Widder" and the grotesque "Comic Queen." In the final analysis, Stuart was unable to create a truly feminist humor to reflect her optimism that a transformation of gender codes could occur for both white and black women.

Certainly we can wish Stuart's feminist voice was stronger and more courageous, and certainly we cannot condone the racism found in her stories. However, her humorous fiction deserves our attention because it may help us in late-twentieth-century America to understand more fully how complex and intertwined racial and gender issues are with regional identity and to recognize again what a powerful double-sided tool of social criticism humor can be. Stuart's friend Kate Chopin once praised her by noting, "I fancy there are no sharp edges to this woman's soul, no unsheathed prejudices dwelling therein wherewith to inflict a wound, or prick, or stab her fellow-man or woman" (11). My opinion is that Stuart, like most of us, had her prejudices about the important issues of her day, but in her fiction she attempted to keep them at least somewhat sheathed within the various guises of humor.

Notes

1. See, for example, Jane Curry, *Marietta Holley: Samantha Rastles the Woman Question;* Linda Morris, *Women Vernacular Humorists in Nineteenth-Century America;* and Nancy Walker and Zita Dresner, eds., *Redressing the Balance.*

2. See Barbara Welter and Anne Firor Scott for classic discussions of the "True Woman" and "Southern Lady," respectively.

3. Gloria Kaufman distinguishes between "feminist" humor and "female" humor by suggesting that feminist humor is nonaccepting and challenges the patriarchal status quo, whereas female humor ridicules women's inferior place in society but ultimately accepts it by offering no agenda for change (13).

4. *A Golden Wedding and Other Tales,* 307–55. All further references to this story will be made parenthetically.

5. *Moriah's Mourning, and Other Half-Hour Sketches,* 37–49. All further references to this story will be made parenthetically.

6. For example, see "Blink," in *A Golden Wedding and Other Tales,* 157–85; "The Afterglow," in *The Haunted Photograph,* 133–68; and "A Note in Scarlet," in *Holly and Pizen and Other Stories,* 93–158.

7. *A Golden Wedding and Other Tales,* 95–126. All further references to this story will be made parenthetically.

8. Another excellent example of one of Stuart's black widow stories is "Moriah's Mourning," in *Moriah's Mourning.*

9. *Holley and Pizen and Other Stories,* 48–91. All further references to this story will be made parenthetically.

10. Stuart also employs a number of demeaning images of black male grotesques in her fiction. See, for example, "Uncle Mingo's 'Speculatioms [*sic*],'" "Crazy Abe," and "Lamentations of Jeremiah Johnson," in *A Golden Wedding and Other Tales;* and "Solomon Crow's Christmas Pockets" and "Duke's Christmas" in *Solomon Crow's Christmas Pockets.*

Works Cited

Bakhtin, Mikhail. *Rabelais and His World.* Trans. Helene Iswolsky. Bloomington: Indiana University Press, 1984.

Burma, John H. "Humor as a Technique in Race Conflict." *American Sociological Review* 11:1 (February 1946), 710–15.

Chopin, Kate. "As You Like It." *St. Louis Criterion,* 27 February 1897.

Clinton, Catherine. *The Plantation Mistress.* New York: Pantheon Books, 1982.

Curry, Jane. *Marietta Holley: Samantha Rastles the Woman Question.* Urbana, IL: University of Illinois Press, 1983.

Dethloff, Henry C., and Robert R. Jones. "Race Relations in Louisiana, 1877–1898." *Louisiana History* 9 (fall 1968), 301–23.

Field, Flo. "Beloved Writer of Southern Tales Tells How the Stories are Born and Transcribed," [circa June 1915]. Ruth McEnery Stuart Collection, no. 139. Howard-Tilton Memorial Library, Tulane University, New Orleans.

Fox-Genovese, Elizabeth. *Within the Plantation Household: Black and White Women of the Old South.* Chapel Hill: University of North Carolina Press, 1988.

Jones, Anne Goodwyn. *Tomorrow Is Another Day: The Woman Writer in the South, 1859–1936.* Baton Rouge: Louisiana State University Press, 1981.

Kaufman, Gloria, and Mary Kay Blakely, eds. *Pulling Our Own Strings: Feminist Humor and Satire.* Bloomington: Indiana University Press, 1980.

Lampugh, George. "The Image of the Negro in Popular Magazine Fiction, 1875–1900." *Journal of Negro History* 57:2 (April 1972), 177–89.

Morris, Linda Ann. *Women Vernacular Humorists in Nineteenth-Century America: Ann Stephens, Frances Whitcher, and Marietta Holley.* New York: Garland, 1988.

Russo, Mary. "Female Grotesques: Carnival and Theory." *Feminist Studies/Critical Studies*. Ed. Teresa de Lauretis. Bloomington: Indiana University Press, 1986, 213–29.

Scott, Anne Firor. *The Southern Lady: From Pedestal to Politics, 1830–1930*. Chicago: University of Chicago Press, 1970.

"Sharps and Flats." *Chicago Record,* 19 March 1895. Ruth McEnery Stuart Collection, no. 139. Howard-Tilton Memorial Library, Tulane University, New Orleans.

"The South Old and New, as Pictured by Ruth McEnery Stuart." *New York Post,* 6 December 1913. Ruth McEnery Stuart Collection, no. 139. Howard-Tilton Memorial Library, Tulane University, New Orleans.

Spiers, Patricia. "The Woman Suffrage Movement in New Orleans." M.A. thesis, Southeastern Louisiana College, 1965.

Steadman, Arthur. "An Observor of Life and Not a Reader of Books" [circa 1895]. Ruth McEnery Stuart Collection, no. 139. Howard-Tilton Memorial Library, Tulane University, New Orleans.

Stuart, Ruth McEnery. *A Golden Wedding and Other Tales.* 1893. Reprint, New York: Garrett Press, 1969.

———. *The Haunted Photograph.* New York: Century, 1911.

———. *Holly and Pizen and Other Stories.* 1899. Reprint, Freeport, New York: Books for Libraries Press, 1969.

———. *Moriah's Mourning and Other Half-Hour Sketches.* New York: Harper & Brothers, 1898.

———. *Solomon Crow's Christmas Pockets.* New York: Harper & Brothers, 1898.

Taylor, Helen. *Gender, Race, and Region in the Writings of Grace King, Ruth McEnery Stuart, and Kate Chopin.* Baton Rouge: Louisiana State University Press, 1989.

Tutwiler, Julia R. "The Southern Woman in New York." *Bookman* 18 (February 1904), 624–34.

Walker, Nancy. *A Very Serious Thing: Women's Humor and American Culture.* Minneapolis: University of Minnesota Press, 1988.

Walker, Nancy, and Zita Dresner, eds. *Redressing the Balance: American Women's Literary Humor from Colonial Times to the 1980s.* Jackson: University Press of Mississippi, 1988.

Welter, Barbara. "The Cult of True Womanhood: 1820–1860." *American Quarterly* 18(2)(1) (summer 1966), 151–74.

"Quite unclassifiable": Crossing Genres, Crossing Genders in Twain and Greene

Karen L. Kilcup

Who *is* Sarah Pratt McLean Greene?

To begin with, she's a nineteenth-century writer with more than the customary trinity of names.

Writing to Greene concerning her first book, which she or her publisher had apparently sent him, Mark Twain commented,

> Dear Miss McLean—
> I am just as much obliged to you, all the same, but I have *already* read it—months ago—& vastly enjoyed & admired it, too; as did the rest of this family & the visitor within its gates. There was but one regret—that there wasn't more of it.[1]

Describing her experience as a teacher on Cape Cod, Greene's first novel, *Cape Cod Folks,* made her an internationally famous figure, in part because it provoked the first libel suit for fiction in the United States. A semi-auto-biographical story not originally intended for publication, the book's first edition retained many of the local people's names. As Greene herself explained the situation, the publisher "knew, of course, that the names were real ... but he said the names were good and the place remote, and he was sure no trouble would follow, and I believe that he was as magnificently innocent and undesigning in the matter as we."[2] Reviewers praised the book in the most generous manner: The *Buffalo Express* claimed, "it is a rarely powerful and realistic picture of simple life," while the *New York Star* observed, "every chapter is fresh and sparkling with life and humor, and we cannot help but eulogize the author for her masterly hand and genius of story-telling." The *Boston Herald* praised "the touch of a new hand, at once

129

original, intense, and dramatic, with a vein of humor and a power of sarcasm warranting the belief that in this work we have the beginning of a career and of a name."[3] Newspapers and magazines all over the United States and Canada lauded the novel, and Greene was favorably compared with such writers as Howells, James, Aldrich, and Hardy (Oakes, 56). Twain had six of her books in his Hartford library, and concerning *Flood-Tide,* the novel I will compare to *Adventures of Huckleberry Finn,* he commented in a letter to Howells about Miss McLean's "delightful unworldly people."[4]

Greene herself was far from unworldly, having been born into an affluent and influential Simsbury Connecticut family in 1856. She was well educated, first receiving careful intellectual nurturing from her mother and then attending Mount Holyoke Female Seminary in 1871–72 and 1873–74. After *Cape Cod Folks,* which went through eleven printings between its first publication in 1881 and the end of 1882, she settled into a long and prolific career, producing fourteen novels, a collection of sketches, and magazine stories and verse. Nineteenth-century anthologist of women's humor Kate Sanborn omitted Greene from her important collection *The Wit of Women,* asking, "why not save space for what is not in everybody's mouth and memory?"[5]

But is she (still) funny?

By way of introduction, I'll offer the following wedding oration, taken from *Flood-Tide* (1901):

> Aunt Rocksy Tate came forward, in mits.
>
> "It seems to me," she said practically, "you two have got about all the remarks you can chew on for this present time bein'. In the hard times and the poor sleddin' of my life, it's allas been a comfort to think 't 'So 'tis, and it can't be no tiser.' You, Bell, hain't got to be a great moon calf no longer, huntin' around for a beau. You've both played high line and ketched one another. Gettin' married has allas seemed to me in some ways like dyin' or other hariss-ments. When it's over, it's over, and hain't got to be gone through with no more. I wish ye sufficient jiy."[6]

On the surface this passage seems to represent another incarnation of the familiar figure, the wise innocent, but the entrance of humor in the senti-mental context of a wedding suggests the complicated dialogue between the two modes that underscores the engendering of American humor. Greene calls on conventions of the sentimental novel and on a tradition of American women's humor, such as that in Harriet Beecher Stowe's *Oldtown Folks,* to write novels that confuse and challenge categorization. One of Greene's early reviewers, echoing the perspective of many of her contemporaries, complained, "The novels of Mrs. Sarah Pratt McLean are quite unclassifiable. They violate the ordinary rules of fiction at every turn."[7]

As feminist literary scholars explore the sources and shapes of women's humor, the appeal of Greene's work becomes more evident and its difference from Twain's more comprehensible. In this connection Nancy Walker has argued that one impulse for nineteenth-century women's humor was the subversion of sentimentality; she observes of Kate Sanborn, for example, "she was both acknowledging and participating in a trend which ran counter to the prevailing sentimentality of women's literature in the 19th century." Walker goes on to assert that women like Fanny Fern, Caroline Kirkland, Frances Whitcher, Gail Hamilton, and Marietta Holley "consistently satirized the woman who wrote pious, sentimental prose and poetry," concluding, "If sentimentality in literature is the result of powerlessness, wit may be seen as its opposite: an expression of confidence and power."[8] While she qualifies this assertion with the observation that "sentimentality exerts a passive, often subversive power; wit, on the other hand, is a direct and open expression of perceptions, taking for granted a position of strength and insight" (6), Walker makes it clear that the two modes are at odds and that she privileges the latter. In a recent book on Frances Whitcher, Linda A. Morris reaffirms this view, which is based on Ann Douglas's cautionary account of the "feminization of American culture" in the nineteenth century.[9]

How does this discussion relate to Twain? Several critics, most notably Peter Stoneley, Gregg Camfield, and Laura Skandera-Trombley, have recently acknowledged his debt to sentimentalism. Stoneley argues for Twain's ambivalent use of the "feminine aesthetic" embodied by sentimentalism; while I acknowledge his ambivalence, I will argue that Twain employs sentimentalism far more affirmatively than Stoneley suggests.[10] Camfield points to the ways in which sentimentalism inflects Twain's portrait of Jim, and he draws the connection between sentimentalism and humor; I will expand on this insight as I explore Twain's gendered aesthetic.[11] Most relevant for this study is Skandera-Trombley, who points to Twain's connections between "the traditional masculine quest novel and the sentimentalized female novel" and observes, "While *Adventures of Huckleberry Finn* may lack traditional Southwestern masculine themes, what it is striking *for* is its similarity to the themes and plot structures that comprised female-authored fiction of the mid-nineteenth century."[12] I agree with Skandera-Trombley that Nina Baym is too hasty in claiming that men wrote against sentimental conventions, and I support her suggestion that Twain "was pragmatic enough to incorporate his audience's expectations as females and the themes of female-authored sentimental fiction into his writing" (34). I am less convinced that he used sentimentalism as a way of "challenging the doctrine of spheres and encouraging an epistemological shift" (31, 32) in relation to gender roles, although I think he challenges the "doctrine of spheres" in the sense that those spheres relate to segregations of genre. I will argue against the notion that the sentimental narrative "was an exclusively female format" (32), for when we look at Twain in connection with Greene, what we see in both is a mixing of genres—not an opposition, as Walker argues—that allows us more radically to interrogate notions of generic, and gender, purity.

In this chapter I ask what difference the author's gender makes in American humor, and I propose several answers: gender difference can influence the representation of character by including a woman's as well as a boy's and man's perspective; it may shape the writer's conception of audience and hence the text's relationship to that audience; and it often transforms the configurations of genre, especially interacting genres, in the development of its humor. The site for my exploration of these differences is the conjunctions between sentimentalism and humor, and the context is two sets of characters, the bad boy and the bad girl. Looking at Twain in connection with women writers—here, Greene—suggests both the different perspective of a woman humorist and the directionality and shape of Twain's own perspective.[13] Whereas Twain's bad boy forms the central mediating consciousness of *Adventures of Huckleberry Finn,* recalling Eileen Gillooly's point about the "reinforcement of ego" in much male humor (478), Greene's bad boy is one of many equally important perspectives in *Flood-Tide,* and his story is only one of several competing narratives. While Twain's humor is often more localized (and hence identifiable), Greene's lies in larger, often implied, textual collisions; furthermore, it is, as Gillooly proposes of some women's humor, "diffused throughout [the] text" (481). While the bad girl is ostensibly present and actually absent in *Adventures of Huckleberry Finn,* she emerges in complex and not always humorous form in Greene. The ultimate "bad girl" of humor, however, is Greene herself.

The bad boys in *Adventures of Huckleberry Finn* are plentiful and ambiguous in presentation, and Huck himself is, of course, the prototype of the bad boy described by John Crowley in his discussion of the "boy-book."[14] From the beginning, Huck is at the matrix (pun intended) between "sivilized" and "savage" that Crowley underscores, and the work of the Widow Douglas and Miss Watson is to bring him into the world of "self-knowledge, hard work, and moral responsibility" (Crowley, 7). About living at the widow's, Huck says, "the longer I went to school the easier it got to be. I was getting sort of used to the widow's ways, too, and they warn't so raspy on me. . . . I liked the old ways best, but I was getting so I liked the new ones, too, a little bit."[15] In tension with the "feminine" influences of the widow and Miss Watson is Pap's observation, "Now looky here; you stop that putting on frills. I won't have it. I'll lay for you, my smarty; and if I catch you about that school I'll tan you good. First you know you'll get religion, too. I never see such a son" (39). Both "frills" and "religion" are affiliated with a feminizing softness that Pap disdains and, because he (a grown, and hence more menacing, bad boy) disdains it, readers are left wondering from the start where Twain will eventually take a stand.

Like the narrative itself, Huck's attitude and his depictions of the collisions between "sivilized" and "savage" forces are expressed in ostensibly humorous terms, here and elsewhere—with his accounts of his encounters with Miss Watson among the liveliest. Nevertheless, the narrative holds this humor in tension with the sentimental mode at various levels. When Huck leaves the widow's and returns, at Tom Sawyer's urging, "the widow she cried over me, and called me a poor lost lamb, and she called me a lot of other names, too, but she never meant no harm by it" (2). Here Huck's inadvertent humor mitigates the sentimental reception given him and the sentimental role assigned to him by the widow, symbolized by her weeping and indicated by the preciousness of her language. Twain's humor suggests at one level that toward the bad boy such emotions are inappropriate. On the other hand, as Skandera-Trombley observes (32), Huck is an orphan, himself the stock of sentimental fiction; from this perspective, an important subtext of the story becomes whether or not Huck will find a home, especially given the detailed descriptions of his abusive father.

Not only is Huck the *object* of sentiment, however, this bad boy at times *acts* as sentimentally as the widow, as the encounter with the Grangerfords indicates. The funny thing about Emmeline is of course that she conventionalizes mourning that should be (and perhaps is) sincere, becoming a cultural self-parody. Much of the passage's infamous humor resides in the space between the approval of her image and her images by her family and by Huck, and the author's clear dislike. We have here an example of the individual, judging consciousness of the author, apparently detached from sentimentalism. But in spite of Twain's viciously funny portrait of Emmeline's obsession with death via her mourning pictures and poems, Huck—and Twain—sentimentalizes the living women of the family: "Miss Charlotte, she was twenty-five, and tall and proud and grand, but as good as she could be, when she warn't stirred up. . . . She was beautiful. So was her sister, Miss Sophia, but it was a different kind. She was gentle and sweet, like a dove, and she was only twenty" (137). Huck's language is wholly conventional, here and elsewhere, in its approbation of the sisters; furthermore, while he dislikes the violence between the two families and feels guilty for his inadvertent part in their mutual slaughter, he approves of the love affair and elopement of Harney and Miss Sophia, which provides the only "happy ending" to the feud. Humorous and sentimental modes interact here on the narrative level.

For the purposes of this discussion, the most significant feature of this narrative is its creation of a space opened by Huck being both the object of and participant in a sentimental fiction, both a sentimental object and a sentimentalizing subject. Whereas the humor resides in the ironic distance between Twain's perspective and Huck's on this loving and warring family, there seems to be much less detachment in relation to the wholly conventional Grangerford women. The (female) reader is invited to participate in the narrative via a perspective that reinforces conventions of sentimentalism and that may require her—if she does not conceptualize herself in this way—to identify against herself and to become the sentimental object embodied in the Grangerford sisters. Twain not only "incorporated his audience's expectations as females and the themes of female-authored sentimental fiction into his writing" (Skandera-Trombley, 34), he also endorsed and complicated these conventions via the tripartite relationship between himself, Huck, and the reader. As we shall see, with Greene, this multiple perspective is transformed into a "relinquishment of ego, a dispersion of self and meaning," with different consequences for the reader (Gillooly, 478).

For those who know nothing about Greene, it is important to observe that there are at least three interacting stories in *Flood-Tide,* representing the author's self-dispersion at the narrative level. This self-dispersion is also apparent in her assumption of a male narrator's voice, from which she frequently digresses. The story of our bad boy, Dinsmore (Dinny) Gleeson—whose name reflects the boisterousness, verve, and merriment of his personality—enacts the tension, and represents the continuity, between humor and sentimentality in *Flood-Tide.* This story also underscores the difference that the author's gender makes, because we see Dinny from a mother's perspective as well as from the narrator's and Dinny's own. Our introduction to this bad boy takes place when the narrator has relinquished his wife, Dinny's aunt, to the responsibilities of her profession as an herbalist, which frequently take her away from home. His view of her absence is decidedly different from Dinny's:

> "*I'm* glad Aunt Infra's gone!" said Dinsmore, from the lane, starting towards the bushes, however, and grinning, fiend-like, at my misery.
>
> "I know—so that you can live naked over in the cove, along with the crabs and devil-fish."

"Yep. Aunt Infra use' ter come over an' haul me
out when I'd only been in an hour. Ef the's anything I hate
'tis to be under pet'coat gov'ment."

"I'll look out for you with some trousers government, the best I can, Dinsmore."

"Pooh! You're nothin' but a fishin' captain. I'm a
sailin' captain." Rank with his freedom from moral re-
straint, Dinsmore turned a pair of heels to me and fled.
(43)

Like Huck, Dinny sees women as a civilizing force that will cut his hair "with
[the] old loose-geared shears," put him to work at the butter churn, or order
him to kill flies. Part of the humor in this passage resides at the level of
diction, with "crabs" and "devil-fish," Dinny's close associates, metonymically
representing his "fiendlike" character. This passage overflows its images to
resonate elsewhere, and "pet'coat gov'ment" becomes a refrain in the novel.
The passage also underscores Greene's dispersed humor, for while Dinny
breaks free of such female control here, he is ultimately under the control
and "sivilizing" force of the author herself. Dinny's story, this passage intimates, will be very different from his predecessor Huck's.

Only infrequently does authority assume a masculine visage in Dinny's life; his father is away at sea during much of the story, and his grandfather cannot hold his own against Dinny's appetite and imaginative force:

There sat the white-haired man, with smooth, pink cheeks,
his voyaging all turned to rest, and the old little boy, wise
and wrinkled with the consciousness of much weighty
sea-craft and with a mouth sullen from intercepted pie.

"Now, tell the story of Jonah, little son."

"Yah! I git licked for tellin' stories through the
week, an' now it's Sunday ye want me to reel off the biggest
yarn ever heered tell on!"

"Don't you think, Dinny, 't the Lord could rig up
a fish to suit himself?"

"Why don't he make somethin' like it now, then?"
said Dinsmore, his mouth watering at the imagination.
"The' ain't nothin' around now but cod and haddick."
(44–45)

Part of the problem of authority here lies in Dinny's hungry verbal inven-
tiveness, but part resides in the feminine ("smooth, pink cheeks") character

of his grandfather, whose restlessness has "all turned to rest." Apparently surrounded by "pet'coat gov'ment," Dinny frequently has recourse to the moral equivalent of "lighting out for the territories"—running off, sometimes with "little Everywheres," sometimes alone, but usually to engage in some form of mischief, whether "tinking ducks" with rocks or spying on the unwary. His mother takes a kind of perverse pride in Dinny's willfulness, but at times she cannot master him. Dinny himself affirms, "I'm a old bachelor, ma, and I'm allus goin' to be a old bachelor." When Dorna asks if he loves "his ma," Dinny replies, "with a note of some cynicism," "I love my ma . . . but I pity my pa" (226). Altogether, as Aunt Nag tells Dorna, "I ain't alone in thinkin' 't Dinsmore Gleeson is as eagle-wild as anything ever conceived of to the Bar." (293) In short, Dinny is as bad a boy as could be wished.

At some level, we are given to understand that Greene herself approves of Dinny and indeed shares his perspective—in particular, his desire to light out for the territories, perhaps reflecting her own desire to break out of gender roles. Just as Huck becomes at times an alter ego for Twain, so Dinny does here for Greene. Nevertheless, while Dinny and Huck possess many of the same characteristics, we view them differently because of the gender of the authors, for Greene's expanded and dispersed perspective includes not only Dinny's but also that of his mother, Dorna. Thus, while a large part of his appealing badness resides in his restlessness, Greene suggests it is this same restlessness that ultimately kills him. On an outing with Everywheres, Dinny falls to his death while trying to rescue his pet dove from a cliffside perch. This impending action is foreshadowed by a shift in the narrative voice at a moment when Dorna is putting him to bed and Dinny's inadvertent joke collides with a sentimental evocation of his innocence:

> "Afore you go off"—[Dorna] bent over him—"the' *is* love in your little obstrep'rous heart, ain't the', Dinny?"
>
> Dinsmore gripped her hand in a spasm of interrupted sleep. "I love *you,* ma."
>
> She put her lips to his heavy ear and said, yearningly, "Why don't you make more speed, little son, in tryin' to be a better boy?"
>
> "I don' know, ma, unless 'n it is—that seamen—is lazy." He was gone, blameless peace on his features, that asserted themselves innocent, almost white, in the pale light of the room. (296)

Described as a stereotypical sentimental innocent, Dinny remains an inveterate trickster who echoes in younger form the willfulness of Huck. Dinny's ostensible "escape" from "pet'coat gov'ment" occurs only through his death.

 While these events may seem to represent the transformation of the plot from humor to unacknowledged sentiment, however, they indicate more clearly the alliance of the two modes. Dinny's death and funeral in *Flood-Tide* are counterbalanced by the numerous accounts of his pranks and pratfalls; in spite of Greene's appeal to the sentimental image of mother and son—and even her gesture toward the adoption of the orphan Everywheres in the latter's place—the weight of the narrative falls as decisively on Dinny's dubious deeds. Furthermore, Dorna herself remains a comic figure even in sentimental grief. When she discusses with Everywheres why he should not sprinkle her cats with water, he asserts, "Sprinklin' don't make 'em suffer." She replies, "No, but it gives 'em a mean aspect, and they seem to take it more to heart 'n as if their necks was clean broke off an' taggin' along after 'em" (315). Greene's bad boys are *both* sentimental and humorous figures, and by establishing this continuity via Dorna, the mother, she seeks not only to evoke feeling in but also to provide solidarity among a community of female readers. Bringing into question Walker's assertion that "sentimentality in literature is the result of powerlessness," while "wit may be seen as its opposite," Greene situates the two modes together in complementary, assertive, and polyvocal fashion. Gender transforms not only the shape and valence of the character portrait here, it also alters the author's concept of her relationship with the audience. For contemporary readers, accustomed to the singular perspective of Twain, such a juxtaposition may seem confusing or even clumsy, but I believe Greene is attempting to invoke experiences, and especially the mother's experiences of the bad boy, from both the inside and the outside in order to enable the female reader's participation in this funny sad story. In contrast, Huck's "mothers"—his dead birth mother and Widow Douglas—are conspicuously silent.

 At one point Twain apparently does attempt to gain an inside-out view of female perspective: *Adventures of Huckleberry Finn* has no bad girls except Huck himself.[16] Since at one level the novel is an "adventure" story, this omission is not surprising, for respectable girls were not supposed to have adventures.[17] It is Huck the trickster who, as Sarah/Mary Williams, represents, in comic cross-dressed form, female adventuresomeness and restlessness. Again, female readers gain access to *Adventures of Huckleberry Finn* (and to Huck) through the conventions of sentimental narrative. A "bad girl," Sarah/Mary—like Huck—is (comically) an experienced (sentimental) storyteller; she tells Mrs. Judith Loftus, "My mother's down sick and out of money and everything, and I come to tell my uncle Abner Moore. He lives at the upper end of town, she says. I hain't ever been here before" (73). Just as Greene's approval of Dinny at one level indicates her desire to transcend gender roles, so does Twain's delight in the cross-dressed Huck suggest his pleasure in the sentimental.

Part of Huck's problem throughout the episode is that he is, quite literally, a bad *girl*. When he first puts on the girls' clothing, he rehearses his role: "I practiced around all day to get the hang of things, and by-and-by I could do pretty well in them, only Jim said I didn't walk like a girl; and he said I must quit pulling up my gown to get at my britches pocket. I took notice, and done better" (71). Playing a girl is simply another kind of adventure for Huck that requires more mindfulness of his own identity than usual. Before he knocks on the woman's door, he says, "[I] made up my mind I wouldn't forget I was a girl" (71). Ironically, Huck the con artist has been set up here, conned by the woman who tries to get him to tell her his "genuine story" after she pretends to have a wrenched arm. As she tells him later, "I spotted you for a boy when you was threading the needle; and I contrived other things just to make certain" (64). It is worth noting that the "differences" in behavior recorded by Mrs. Loftus are comically trivial, suggesting what Marjorie Garber observes of the transvestite more generally, that his/her presence calls into question not only categorical gender roles but also categorical thinking itself.[18] Twain refutes this disruptive function of Huck as transvestite, however, by framing the episode with Huck's remark, "I turned up my trowser-legs to my knees and got into it" (71). This scene does precisely what Greene's multiple representation of Dinny accomplishes: it calls into question gender and genre norms. Both Twain and Greene problematize categorical thinking not only in the content of their narratives— funny Dinny dies, Huck cross-dresses—but in the aesthetic that shapes their narratives.

If humor permeates the performances in this scene, it is achieved in part via sentimental narratives simultaneously embedded within it. Huck/Sarah/Mary's story of the sick mother inaugurates the genre, Judith Loftus's invention of Huck's "real" story as an apprentice resonates further, and Huck's final invention of himself as a runaway caps it off:

> So I said it wouldn't be no use to try to play it any longer, and I would just make a clean breast and tell her everything, but she mustn't go back on her promise. Then I told her my father and mother was dead, and the law had bound me out to a mean old farmer in the country thirty mile back from the river, and he treated me so bad I couldn't stand it no longer; he went away to be gone a couple of days, and so I took my chance and stole some of his daughter's clothes, and cleared out, and I had been three nights

coming the thirty miles, and hid daytimes and slept, and the
bag of bread and meat I carried from home lasted me all
the way and I had a-plenty. (78–79)

Again Huck's story has all the elements of a classic sentimental plot: the
orphan whose parents are dead, a villain, and a daring escape. Huck even
imagines a happy ending, saying, "I believed my uncle Abner Moore would
take care of me" (79). What we must recall again is that Huck's own "real"
"story" as an orphan, complete with an abusive (and by this time, dead) father, echoes the disingenuous one he formulates. Whether or not he intends
to do so, Twain gestures toward the shape of a possible "happy ending" for
Huck himself. While we might (or might not) argue that Twain's resistance
to sentimentalism ultimately triumphs, it simultaneously mirrors, enables,
and undercuts the humor in certain scenes by acting not as satire but as shadow narrative.

Interestingly, Greene's perspective on her bad girl is more detached
in many ways than Twain's is from Huck. Part of the reason for this detachment lies in her own gender, for while Twain has cultural approval for the
bad boy, Greene does not have the same authorization for her bad girl. She
must create a heroine who, without wholly confirming the confining cultural
norms of piety, purity, and selflessness associated with the sentimental heroine, manages to avoid the danger of the "painted lady."[19] Going beyond the
bad girl that she imagines in her second novel, *Towhead,* Greene's portrait
of Alpena in *Flood-Tide* essays a transgression of both personal and aesthetic
purity, for she compromises both conventional behavior and genre norms in
this portrait. One of our first pictures of Alpena reveals this adjacency to,
but departure from, the sentimental heroine: "Her white teeth were just
enough overlapped to provoke study; she looked like a flower of the tall-
stemmed species, her black head and insolent, childish face hanging a little
to one side; her slender height in itself was striking" (37). Having "white
teeth" that are crooked, a "childish face" that is not innocent but "insolent,"
and perhaps most significantly, being "striking" but too tall, as we are told
on many other occasions, Alpena also contrasts with the other members of
her community, the Bar, by virtue of her independent manners and forth-
right assessment of others. In some sense, Alpena enacts a kind of gender
cross-dressing in her behavior that, like Huck's literal transvestism, enables
the author to challenge gender and genre norms.

In particular, Alpena laughs too much, enjoying a joke at others'
expense. For instance, when an itinerant peddler transforms the haircut of
the narrator, Alf, into an exercise in artistic license—"he had not so much
shorn me as he had curled and elaborated me into some lost, lingering flow-

er of the romantic ages" (36–37)—Alpena derives immense pleasure from this unexpected transformation: "Alpena had laughed to the point of physical pain every time she had looked at me since the event" (37). The pleasure of excess hallmarks Alpena's responses, and this excess of humor, in particular, marks her as a bad girl. Writing about contemporary America in terms that resonate in the novel, Regina Barreca distinguishes between "Good Girls" and "Bad Girls" on the basis of their responses to, and involvement with, humor. For Good Girls she points out that "laughing out loud was out of the question."[20] Furthermore, of the Bad Girl she observes, "their ability to joke was seen as [paradoxical] evidence of both their sexual awareness and their lack of femininity. . . . But Good or Bad, women have been labeled as 'unfunny,' as less likely to laugh than their male counterparts" (6). Significantly, one of Alpena's characteristic modes is laughter, which Barreca suggests is "active and initiating." This mode contrasts with the more "passive and receptive" mode of the sentimental heroine that she performs elsewhere.[21] In laughing at Alf's discomfiture, however, Alpena negates another stereotype forwarded by Barreca herself: "women do not often laugh at the genuine misfortune of others. . . . Women are more likely to attempt to console than laugh at anyone who can be considered a victim" (12). Alpena herself acknowledges that she has only "a little bit of a heart" (37), for her humor consists as much in making fun of others as in (like Dorna) enacting humorous behavior herself. As with Greene's portrait of Dorna, we get another glimpse of the woman's perspective that Twain encodes indirectly and somewhat more conventionally in the invocation of sentimental narrative.

Deliberately confusing the painted lady and the sentimental woman—as well as the woman and the girl—Greene underscores the ambiguous quality of Alpena's character by emphasizing that she is an orphan, but this ambiguity reflects the possibility of Greene's ambivalence about creating an unconventional woman character for her readers. Even though *Flood-Tide* was written well into the era of the New Woman—or perhaps because it was—the novel reflects the author's uneasiness with a departure from feminine norms. When one of the local people blames Alpena for bewitching several men at the Bar, Greene's description of Alpena's response is telling: "the blackness of the girl's eyes gave a wicked gleam; her hair was smoothed from her forehead like a nun's" (75); here and elsewhere, others wistfully wish that Alpena "had a mother" (75). On the other hand, we might regard such descriptions as the author's deliberate invocation of cultural norms in order to (humorously, as Walker suggests) dismantle them. One thing is clear, however: Greene's perspective is far more elusive than Twain's.

Alpena's paradoxical "badness" emerges engagingly in a humorous scene that allies her with both Eve and witchcraft. Captain Abram Shale muses, "The's somethin' about Alpeny when she kittens up to anybody . . . with them white teeth o' hern just a mite twisted, ye know, an' hell an' thunder hid down in her eyes, makes me think of a play 't I seen a long ago away off down in Salem" (57), a play that reenacts the temptation of Adam:

> "Wal', then, Eve, o' course she began tryin' to git Adam ter eat that apple. He said no. 'Le's go an' git some prunes,' he says, 'or somethin' 't they ain't no cuss on.' Eve said she'd ruther go with her stommick plumb empty 'n eat prunes, or in fact anythin' else 'ceptin' them pertickaler greenin' apples, an' she got to foolin' 'round him an' fingerin' the button-hole on his coat—"
> "I thought Adam didn't have any coat."
> "Sartin, but it wouldn't 'a' done to present him that way, ye know." (59)

"Wicked" and a "nun," a kitten with "hell an' thunder hid down in her eyes," Alpena seems to mirror the painted lady, whose mother was Eve. Acknowledging her own wildness in a later scene, Alpena again assumes the bad girl's prerogative of joking. When Tyrolese Dunbar, the wealthy villain who woos Alpena, affirms that she may be "of excellent family," she asserts, "I hope I'm the daughter of a wild Indian and a smuggler—a jail-bird—a terror of some sort"; later in the same scene, as she is plucking daisy petals and playing "rich man, poor man," she jokes "'Indian chief!' I'm to marry an Indian chief." Finally, she uses this child's game to figure how many children she will have: "Forty-four. I'm to have forty-four children.' Alpena leaned against a tree and screamed with laughter" (229). Underscoring her impurity and her unsuitability as the sentimental heroine, to Tyrolese's declaration that she is "a tall harp set up there against the tree for the wind to blow upon," she affirms, "I am a human being . . . you are not my young man" (229; ellipsis in original). Here, in contrast to "bad girl" Huck who creates himself as a sentimental heroine, Alpena (and Greene) wittily counters Tyrolese's intention to corset her into this shape. Invoking an audience that wished to achieve the status of "human being" rather than heroine, Greene assigns Alpena a speaking subjectivity.

Yet, this subjectivity is tenuous, as the scene that follows suggests. During a wild dancing party that turns ugly, male rowdies take control of the gathering and force Alpena to dance with them one by one in a symbolic gang rape.[22] The description of Alpena in the scene zigzags back and forth from strong woman to bad girl to sentimental heroine. The climax of the scene arrives not with a violation of an already bad girl or a dramatic rescue by her gallant lover but with the arrival of a stronger force, Mrs. Temple, the "Bookwriter" whom, we learn ultimately, is Alpena's mother: "the stately woman, alone, from her walk through the unfamiliar night, clad in some shimmering gray cloth, pure and foreign to all this coarse-hued scene, swept toward Alpena with a magnificent instinct" (240). Here Greene apparently jettisons humor and enacts a complex movement toward the sentimental as embodied in Mrs. Temple, for Alpena at first mistakes her mother for Infra, the novel's paragon of sentimental power, as the language of the passage suggests. The transformation of Infra into Mrs. Temple evokes the sentimental connection between mother and daughter that is particularly potent for Alpena, the ostensible orphan; nevertheless, it modulates the sentimentality because Mrs. Temple is a strong woman "alone" who has an identity apart from a man.

More significantly, Mrs. Temple represents an avatar of Greene, herself the "Bookwriter." The portrait of Mrs. Temple is not overtly humorous here (though it is elsewhere), but at the narrative level, Greene has a joke on those who expect or hope Alpena to be rescued by masculine or sentimental means, pointing instead to her own power as the "mother" of the text, the "authority" to whom even the rowdies must defer. In spite of many intervening scenes that conjure the sentimental heroine and test its outlines on Alpena, it is this authority that ultimately prevails. The author kills Infra, the sentimental heroine; equally conveniently, she kills the local man who truly loves Alpena.[23] At the end of the novel, we are left with Alpena and Mrs. Temple as the center around which all the other stories revolve, and we discover that Alpena, "one of the most flattered and favored of an old aristocracy," "has never married—who was our beauty of the Bar—though it has sometimes been announced in select circles that she would marry, and she has entertained certain high proposals with Madonna-like thoughtfulness for a little while—no longer" (348–49). Alpena's heart has been given already, we are told, to "the sweet woman beside her, Mrs. Temple" (348).

Evoking the conventions of motherly love once again, Greene exceeds those conventions here—as she has done in her portrait of Dinny and Dorna Gleeson—to intimate finally that the connection between women, at the level of character and between author and readers, is central to female happiness and self-sufficiency. The last portrait the sentimental narrator gives us of Alpena is telling: "I saw again the small black head so queenly poised, the perfect features yet tender with human sensuousness. The black eyes had kept their mad dreams" (349). In this context, the narrator's highly charged sentimental and religious language of the closing provides a decoy for the novel's central concern, and it highlights Greene's dispersed humor, which she signals by closing the novel with the Bar greeting, used for both solemn *and* comic occasions, "Here is hoping!"

As Eileen Gillooly acknowledges, the "recognition of women's humor . . . which is frequently the major (and, in some, the only) site of [their] gender politics and moral outrage—is crucial in assessing the significance of these [humorous] texts" (483). While the sentimental mode, characteristically affiliated with the feminine—and in literary criticism, with the female—appears to conflict with the humorous mode that is historically associated in much criticism with a masculine perspective, we see in both Twain and Greene their overlap and complex interaction. While Twain's satire of sentimentalism has become a commonplace, the embeddedness of *Adventures of Huckleberry Finn* in the sentimental tradition, and Twain's affirmation of it at moments in the novel, has until recently been neglected. Twain frequently conjoins sentimentalism and humor in ways that suggest not only the ungendered quality of genre per se but also the problematics of artificially separating them, even in the language of this exploration.[24]

In this context, the ending of *Adventures of Huckleberry Finn* is ambiguous indeed. Skandera-Trombley argues that "Huck's plight resembles that of the sentimental heroines, but his choices are even more limited than theirs. Clemens's solution to the problem (of the self in opposition to society) may well have been having Huck choose as the subject for his story what he cannot rejoin in the usual sense—society. In his telling, therefore, Huck does effect a kind of return" (34–35). At the same time, the comic impulse—together with the adventure story—parallels the sentimental narrative that Skandera-Trombley constructs here, as Twain concludes the novel: "so there ain't nothing more to write about, and I am rotten glad of it, because if I'd 'a' knowed what a trouble it was to make a book I wouldn't 'a' tacked it, and ain't a-going to no more" (374). What we see plainly in Twain is the presence of a more concentrated and male-centered authorial consciousness that uses genre—humor as well as sentimentalism—more effectively than character as a means of connecting with its female readers.

Greene's combination of humorous and sentimental modes in *Flood-Tide* is more intense than the same combination in *Adventures of Huckleberry Finn,* and her own perspective is less immediately available than Twain's. Dispersing her voice throughout (at least) three narratives that sometimes compete and sometimes converge, and by using sentimentalism and humor both concurrently and sequentially, Greene undercuts a singular representation of characters and of the narrative itself. This aesthetic, apparently unorganized and random, "violat[ing] the rules of ordinary fiction at every turn," is precisely the "point," as the novel deconstructs readers' affiliation of gender with genre in a way that is different in shape than Twain's but similar in effect. It invites us to collude in dispersing authoritative perspectives and their allied valorizations. An important marker of this invitation is Greene's creation of both Dorna and Alpena, both of whom act, though differentially, as mediators between the "good" and "bad" images of Infra and Margaret, respectively. Dorna's voice is *both* the mother's and the comic's, while Alpena is *both* Eve and Madonna. For readers, especially the female reader, the categorical figures of Infra and Margaret break down under the pressure of these ambiguous portraits. Ultimately, Greene's text makes different demands of its readers, especially its female readers, than Twain's because it requires readers to take its humor and its sentimentality both seriously *and* comically. If Mrs. Temple is a revered figure as a mother, Greene intimates her own "Bookwriter's" control of the text, and of the various boys and girls who inhabit it, placing them, with readers, "under pet'coat gov'ment."

Notes

1. S. L. Clemens to Miss S. P. McLean, Hartford, 12 December 1881, Alderman Library, University of Virginia.

2. "'Cape Cod Folks' and its Author," *Book News* 12:134 (1893), 37; Karen Oakes, "Legacy Profile; Sarah Pratt McLean Greene," *Legacy* 11 (1994), 55–64.

3. Reviews of *Cape Cod Folks*, from the opening pages of Greene's second novel: Sally Pratt McLean, *Towhead: The Story of a Girl* (Boston: A. Williams, 1883).

4. Mark Twain, *Mark Twain-Howells Letters: The Correspondence of Samuel L. Clemens and William D. Howells*, vol. 2, ed. Henry Nash Smith and William M. Gibson (Cambridge: Belknap-Harvard University Press, 1960), 769.

5. Kate Sanborn, *The Wit of Women*, 2d ed. (New York: Funk and Wagnalls, 1885), 69.

6. Sarah P. McLean Greene, *Flood-Tide* (New York: Harper & Brothers, 1901), 172–73.

7. *Outlook* (3 September 1898), 89. Similarly, the *Boston Sunday Times* reviewer observed, "We rather doubt the justice or policy of ranking the work as a novel, for it is really a triumph of character sketching, with novelistic developments" (*Towhead* jacket notes; see n. 3 above).

Scholarly examination of sentimentalism is by now well established—from Ann Douglas's *The Feminization of American Culture,* Nina Baym's *Women's Fiction,* Jane Tompkins's *Sensational Designs,* and Cheryl Walker's *The Nightingale's Burden,* to Shirley Samuels's *The Culture of Sentiment* and Suzanne Clark's *Sentimental Modernism.* Here I explore how sentimentalism interacts with other genres to produce unexpected consequences in both male and female writing.

8. Nancy Walker, "Wit, Sentimentality, and the Image of Women in the Nineteenth Century," *American Studies* 22:2 (1981), 6. More recently, in *A Very Serious Thing: Women's Humor and American Culture,* Walker argues that "by the mid-nineteenth century . . . the 'cult of domesticity' was so firmly entrenched that womanly wit had difficulty maneuvering around the image of ideal womanhood—an image that denigrated woman's intellect in favor of her emotional and intuitive nature." See Walker, *A Very Serious Thing: Women's Humor and American Culture* (Minneapolis: University of Minnesota Press, 1988), 27. A further difficulty for women resides in the humorist's stance, which according to Walker is often one of superiority; she observes, "Women in American culture, however, have only rarely been granted or felt free to claim the sort of superiority required by this concept of the humorist" *(A Very Serious Thing,* 25). But Walker's assumptions about race and class are evident here, since, for example, many Native American women would not share this perspective. See Lois Rudnick, "Women's Humor and American Culture," *American Quarterly* 42:4 (1990), 670–77. For another discussion of the differential uses of race and class in American women's humor, see my earlier essay "'I like a woman to be a woman': Theorizing Gender in the Humor of Stowe and Greene," *Studies in American Humor* 3:3 (1996), 14–38.

9. Linda A. Morris, *Women's Humor in the Age of Gentility: The Life and Works of Frances Miriam Whicher* (Syracuse, NY: Syracuse University Press, 1992), 12.

10. Peter Stoneley, *Mark Twain and the Feminine Aesthetic* (Cambridge: Cambridge University Press, 1992).

11. Gregg Camfield, *Sentimental Twain* (Philadelphia: University of Pennsylvania Press, 1994).

12. Laura Skandera-Trombley, *Mark Twain in the Company of Women* (Philadelphia: University of Pennsylvania Press, 1994), 31.

13. As Walker and Eileen Gillooly both acknowledge, defining humor is virtually impossible; but as the latter observes, "female humor may be intercategorical, but it is not undifferentiated. . . . And clearly not all forms of humor have equal status or purpose in every text." Gillooly, "Review Essay, Women and Humor," *Feminist Studies* 17 (1991), 476.

14. John W. Crowley, *The Mask of Fiction, Essays on W. D. Howells* (Amherst: University of Massachusetts Press, 1989).

15. Mark Twain, *Adventures of Huckleberry Finn* (New York: Pocket Books, 1973), 21.

16. Skandera-Trombley suggests that Judith Loftus can be considered a bad girl. I disagree, for she seems to be merely acting vicariously, with no real agency of her own. Furthermore, the space allotted her in the novel is very small. She does provide an indication, however, of Twain's awareness of the cultural construction of gender roles (see Skandera-Trombley, 34).

17. The girl who comes closest to doing so in the story, Sophie Grangerford, dooms her family; her father, Buck, and her other brothers are killed in the story of her elopement. Ironically, this restlessness erupts out of the milder and more passive of the two sisters whom Huck conjures as sentimental heroines, suggesting Twain's fear that when conventional women act independently—even when enacting other conventions—their families suffer radically. We might also view the Mary Jane episode as another example of a girl being involved in an adventure; but Mary Jane has the experience only by proxy, and unwillingly, via the duke, the king, and Huck.

18. Marjorie Garber, *Vested Interests: Cross-Dressing and Cultural Anxiety* (London: Penguin, 1993), 50. Garber discusses cross-dressing in Twain at some length (288–90), but she only references *Adventures of Huckleberry Finn*. Garber's argument contains resonances I do not have space to discuss here. Most notably, since cross-dressing indicates a category crisis, we might look at the categories Twain finds anxiety-provoking—namely, those not only of gender but also of race and sexuality (see nn. 9, 16, 17).

19. Discussing the crisis of confidence in matters of authenticity and the fear of falsity in white middle-class nineteenth-century culture, Karen Halttunen presents the spectacle of the "painted lady" and the "confidence man" as ones to be assiduously avoided. Halttunen, *Confidence Men and Painted Ladies: A Study of Middle-Class Culture in America, 1830–1870* (New Haven: Yale University Press, 1982).

20. Regina Barreca, *They Used to Call me Snow White . . . but I Drifted: Women's Strategic Use of Humor* (New York: Penguin, 1991), 6.

21. Barreca cites psychologist Rose Laub Coser on this distinction between passive and active, receptive and initiating (7).

22. Worth noting is that the "wild man" in this scene, the uncivilized villain, is portrayed as the "Indian chief" that Alpena unwittingly imagines in the preceding scene; here, Greene reflects the racism of her time.

23. Greene also renders the bad woman, Margaret Langthorne, forever lonely in a meaningless marriage to Tyrolese Dunbar, who is disabled in a sentimental-humorous scene.

24. I am grateful to Henry B. Wonham, MLA panel respondent to an earlier version of this chapter, for this insight. Wonham, "Response," "Mark Twain and Other Authors," Modern Language Association Convention, 27 December 1994, San Diego, CA.

Dimensions of Major Authors as Humorists

Making Fun of the Critics:
Edith Wharton's Anticipation of the
Postmodern Academic Romance

Michele S. Ware

In "Raiders of the Lost Archives," an irreverent 1993 essay, Adam Begley explores the phenomenon of what he calls the "Postmodern Postdoctoral Romance" in contemporary literature (36). His analysis of A. S. Byatt's *Possession,* Umberto Eco's *Foucault's Pendulum,* and Louise Erdrich and Michael Dorris's *The Crown of Columbus,* among others, points to a preoccupation of a number of writers in the last decades of the twentieth century with the status of the scholar and critic in contemporary culture. Begley suggests that these novels are part of a collective enterprise to reclaim "the scholar/ hero triumphant" (37) in an age when scholarship is taking something of a beating on the popular front. But the enterprise Begley imagines to be a product of postmodern skepticism—that is, the critical rethinking of the position and power of the scholar/critic—was anticipated by Edith Wharton as early as 1910 in her short story "The Legend" and in a 1926 story, "The Temperate Zone." While it is something of a stretch to think of Edith Wharton as a humorist (so much of her work is so resolutely tragic and renunciatory), her short stories are richly satiric. Like Mark Twain, Wharton wrote at times with "a pen warmed up in Hell." And like Twain, she did not suffer fools gladly. "The Legend" and her other stories dealing with the critical impulse demonstrate her candid, humorous, and often quite vicious portrayal of the passions of scholars, critics, and other dilettantes.

Wharton's stories share a number of characteristics with the postmodern academic romance: the quest motif, where the often bumbling scholar/critic searches for someone or something lost or suggested in the world of art and literature; the portrayal of the scholar/critic as hero, stumbling at first in his or her search but ultimately successful; and the need, as Begley puts it, "to bridge the gap between contemporary sensibility and some other past or distant frame of mind" (38), in other words, to come to terms with history. Like Byatt, Eco, Erdrich, Dorris, and others, Wharton, too, emphasizes the passionate and often comical desire for possession that is the basis of all critical or scholarly activity. Yet Wharton is in a particularly awkward position, occupying as she does the place of both writer and critic; because she was herself an avid scholar and reviewer, she is both the desired one and the one who desires possession of another. In "The Legend," Wharton constructs a paradigm of artistic creation and scholarly interpretation that is marked by ambiguity and comedy, articulating her own skepticism and ambivalence about literary acclaim, authorial power, and the motivations of the scholar/critic.

The mystery of connection and the thrill of the chase, both characteristics of the postmodern academic romance, are especially strong in this story. Told from the scholar/critic's point of view, "The Legend" clearly endorses the creative act of interpretation yet provides Wharton with opportunities for satire as well, most notably in the characterization of a pompous, self-important, self-proclaimed intelligentsia. In this story's moments of light comedy, Wharton emphasizes the ludicrous nature of the critic's fears and the projection of his own ambition and desire onto the characters least likely to comprehend them. But "The Legend" is more tragicomic than comic; although his interpretive powers are admirable, the critic's desire for mastery over his subject is overwhelmingly selfish, even parasitic in nature. Perhaps more than any of her stories about critics, "The Legend" illustrates Wharton's ambiguous portrayal of the scholar/critic, her persistent exploration of the tangled and contradictory motives behind critical or scholarly activity.

"The Legend" is one of Wharton's most fragmented and haunting stories. In six different narrative sections she illuminates a mystery; yet she solves the mystery in the first paragraph of the story. What is ostensibly a tale about a missing person becomes something quite different—and identifying what the story is about is the real mystery Wharton expects her readers to solve. In terms of its plot, "The Legend" is fairly straightforward: John Pellerin returns to New York after twenty-five years' self-imposed exile. As a young philosopher and writer, he had been ignored and misunderstood, so he chose to disappear. In the ensuing years, Pellerin isolated himself on the other side of the earth, well away from civilization. He allowed the rumor of his death to filter back to society. Returning in the guise of Mr. Winterman, he finds his youthful ideas entrenched in the popular institution of "Pellerinism," with its various interpreters and "Custodians of the Sacred Books" (2:107). When he makes an attempt to reenter the literary world as Winterman, he is rejected as a second-rate imitator of Pellerin. After sitting through a lecture on the meaning of Pellerinism, Winterman disappears again, presumably for good.

The narrator of "The Legend" is Arthur Bernald, a drama critic for a New York newspaper and a literary man, the early-twentieth-century equivalent of today's academic. Bernald discovers Mr. Winterman at the home of his friend, Dr. Bob Wade, who has taken Winterman under his wing. Both Dr. Wade and Bernald immediately recognize the man's unusual qualities. As Dr. Wade notes, "He's worked a lot with his hands, but that's not what they were made for. I should say they were extraordinarily delicate conductors of sensation" (2:94). At their first meeting, Bernald realizes that Winterman is someone very special. Even Winterman's silent presence strongly affects those around him: "[Bernald] reflected afterward that there must have been a mysterious fertilizing quality in the stranger's silence: it had brooded over their talk like a rain cloud over a dry country" (2:95). Although it takes some time, Bernald finally discovers that Winterman *is* Pellerin. Ironically, Dr. Wade's younger brother, Howland, is the prime "Interpreter" of Pellerinism to the world. He pronounces Winterman's literary and philosophical efforts "frightfully crude," dismissing him as derivative, a kind of diluted Pellerin (2:110). It is Howland Wade's lecture on the meaning of Pellerinism that precipitates Pellerin's final disappearance. Certainly Wharton is having broadly comic fun in naming this premier critic, suggesting that what he does best is to "howl and wade" through the works of a better writer and thinker.

"The Legend" is a rather strange mixture of tragic despair and biting satire. Wharton attacks the self-important, self-proclaimed "emancipated" members of the Uplift Club—Howland Wade's literary circle (2:106). And her characterization of Howland Wade's parasitic appropriation of Pellerin is especially caustic:

It might have been supposed that one of the beauties of Pellerin's hidden life and mysterious taking off would have been to guard him from the fingering of anecdote; but biographers like Howland Wade are born to rise above such obstacles. He might be vague or inaccurate when dealing with the few recorded events of his subject's life; but when he left fact for conjecture no one had a firmer footing. Whole chapters in his volume were constructed in the conditional mood and made up of hypothetical detail; and in talk, by the very law of process, hypothesis became affirmation, and he was ready to tell you confidentially the exact circumstances of Pellerin's death, and of the "distressing incident" leading up to it. (2:98)

Wharton satirizes the so-called literati of New York and their pretentious gatherings and lectures with extraordinary nastiness. Her own distrust of popular acclaim, her fear of biographers, and her suspicions about the incompetence of critics are fully articulated in this story.

If we consider this story as solely "about" John Pellerin's return from the dead and his disappointed return to oblivion, "The Legend" is, as Cynthia Griffin Wolff argues, one of Wharton's "harsher" tales (155). But this story is not about the defeat of a literary figure. There is something extraordinary about John Pellerin's return—his youthful rage has softened, and he demonstrates no contempt for the silly people who have distorted his ideas. Of course he is disappointed, but he has as well a stoic air of acceptance and strength about him. The aging Pellerin recognizes what happens when an author's work enters the public arena, and he is still willing for the work to find its own way. Wharton modeled Pellerin on Henry James, I suspect because she partly believed James had lost his audience and had been brutalized by the popular reception of his work, or rather by the lack of a popular reception. But she never admitted that. As she explained in a letter to Morton Fullerton, it was James's serenity that she wished to embody in her character: "I . . . thought of him when I described the man in 'The Legend' as so sensitive to human contacts & yet so *secure* from them" (202). Pellerin's final disappearance, then, is an act of courage, of self-sufficiency, and of self-preservation. By leaving, Pellerin remains inviolate. Pellerin's story isn't harsh at all.

If, on the other hand, we consider this to be Bernald's story, then "The Legend" becomes far more interesting and far more complicated. The ending doesn't provide readers with a definite sense of closure but with an invitation back into the story for something we may have missed. What we discover is that Bernald himself is a potential violator of Pellerin, that he is no better than Howland Wade. Bernald possesses a suffocating desire to engulf Pellerin as his own precious find. In a way, "The Legend" is a story of obsessive love, with Bernald in pursuit of a beloved ideal. Pellerin has been his hero, the focus of his own literary ambitions, and Bernald has a chance, finally, to possess him. Wharton likens Bernald's pursuit of Pellerin to a courtship, in fact a rather comic courtship, forestalled by all sorts of interruptions and false starts. From their very first meeting, Bernald is inordinately excited to have Pellerin all to himself: "'Now I'll be with him alone!' thought Bernald, with a throb like a lover's" (2:96).

Bernald's anticipation of intimacy is repeatedly thwarted by the inopportune appearance of others. As he imagines what awaits him, his thoughts turn to his more literary frustrations. Obsessed with his own still-born manuscript on Pellerin, he has developed a long-standing (though silent and secret) rivalry with Howland Wade: "'If he'd only kept his beastly pink hands off Pellerin,' Bernald sighed, thinking for the hundredth time of the thick manuscript condemned to perpetual incarceration in his own desk by the publication of Howland's 'definitive' work on the great man" (2:98). Bernald's contempt for Howland Wade is only slightly stronger than his professional jealousy. But when he finally gets Winterman alone for a short walk through the woods (before the discovery of his true identity), Bernald is transported:

> The walk through the woods remained in Bernald's memory as an enchanted hour. He used the word literally, as descriptive of the way in which Winterman's contact changed the face of things, or perhaps restored them to their deeper meanings. And the scenes they traversed—one of those little untended woods that still, in America, fringe the tawdry skirts of civilization—acquired, as the background to Winterman, the hush of a spot aware of transcendent visitings. Did he talk, or did he make Bernald talk? The young man never knew. He recalled only a sense of lightness and liberation, as if the hard walls of individuality had melted, and he were merged in the poet's deeper interfusion, yet without losing the least sharp edge of self. (2:99–100)

In short, Bernald falls more deeply in love. When Pellerin's real identity is revealed (only to Bernald), the two men talk until dawn in perfect communion, perfect intimacy. Pellerin shares his new ideas with his admirer, and he reads Bernald's manuscript while Bernald stares out over the ocean, slowly watching the sun come up.

But even that perfect meeting of minds is marred by jealousy and anger when Bernald thinks of the reception of Pellerin's work in progress: "In a brief flash of retrospection Bernald saw the earlier books dwindle and fall into their place as mere precursors of this fuller revelation; then, with a leap of anger, he pictured Howland Wade's pink hands on the new treasure, and his prophetic feet upon the lecture platform" (2:104). Bernald can't bear to have Howland Wade touch his treasure, and his profound jealousy makes him go to great lengths to protect his relationship with Pellerin.

The sexual implications of Bernald's lust for possession are clear. In "The Legend," as in several of her stories, Wharton links homosexual or bisexual desire to a hidden moral corruption. In "The Eyes," for example, the main character's immoral emotional parasitism (victimizing a woman and a man) is explicitly tied to his bisexuality and his sexual predation. In "The Triumph of Night," "Her Son," and "A Bottle of Perrier," homosexual attraction is less explicitly but still clearly linked to captivity, crime, fear, and mental or moral instability. In "The Legend," Bernald's yearning for Pellerin represents for Wharton the immoral, selfish, and parasitic qualities of criticism and interpretation. Bernald can laugh at the "Interpreter," Howland Wade, but he can't recognize his own complicity in the interpretive activities that surround Pellerin.

We see the full force of Bernald's desire in the climax of the story, when Howland Wade dismisses Winterman's work as derivative of Pellerin. Bernald is exultant, not only because Wade makes such a fool of himself but also because his rejection of the real Pellerin justifies and confirms Bernald's vision of himself as the true interpreter of Pellerin:

> Bernald sat silent, divided between the satisfaction of seeing the Interpreter rush upon his fate, and the despair of knowing that the state of mind he represented was indestructible. Then both emotions were swept away on a wave of pure joy, as he reflected that now, at last, Howland Wade had given him back John Pellerin. The possession was one he did not mean to part with lightly; and the dread of its being torn from him constrained him to extraordinary precautions. (2:104–5)

Mentally rubbing his hands together, Bernald is overcome with the humor of seeing Howland Wade lecture unknowingly on Pellerinism to Pellerin, and only once does he think of his idol's response. Bernald briefly has "the sense of being a party to something not wholly honorable" (2:108), yet he quickly dismisses his qualms and enjoys the ironic show, imagining his and Pellerin's intimate talk after the lecture and dinner are over. Here Wharton reveals the full selfishness of Bernald's delusion:

> The vision of Pellerin and his Interpreter, face to face at last, had a Titanic grandeur that dwarfed all other comedy. "And I shall hear of it presently; in an hour or two he'll be telling me about it. And that hour will be all mine—mine and his!" The dizziness of the thought made it difficult for Bernald to preserve the balance of the supper plates he was distributing. Life had for him at that moment the completeness which seems to defy disintegration. (2:109)

Although he is clearly a voyeur in this scene, what Bernald doesn't see is the pain Pellerin must be in, watching and listening to the professional purveyors of Pellerinism and knowing the industry his own work had become, supporting a group of self-important fools. Bernald leaves the party and goes home to prepare himself for their tête-à-tête: he lights the fire, positions a favorite chair nearby, gets out a pipe for his friend, and sits down to await Pellerin's arrival, "with the reverent care of a celebrant awaiting the descent of his deity" (2:112). But Pellerin never arrives, and Bernald never sees or hears from him again.

It is not unusual to find writers making fun of critics; criticism has long been considered a laughable—even pernicious—profession. Offhand, I can think of half a dozen authors who have at one time or another blasted the parasitic incompetence of literary critics. Wharton herself indulged in this activity frequently. It is unusual, however, to find an articulation of the reclamation of interpretation, the redemption of the scholar/critic. This is the enterprise Adam Begley identifies as the hallmark of the postmodern academic romance. Yet Wharton's story "The Legend" ends with the scholar/ hero triumphant too, chastened but redeemed. What appears to be a story about a literary figure's encounter with the vicissitudes of worldly acclaim becomes instead a kind of initiation story for his disciple. Pellerin's disappearance isn't the end of the story. We see Bernald a year later, still suffering from the loss of what was most precious to him. But in the passage of that year, Bernald seems to have come to terms with the loss of Pellerin, to have grown and learned and finally understood the example Pellerin provided. Loss is a great gift, according to Wharton, bringing with it self-knowledge and the courage to change. The process she describes in "The Legend" is a familiar one to Wharton's readers—redemption through renunciation. In this case, Bernald has to recognize how intrusive and selfish his relationship with Pellerin had become. And he has to renounce his desire for possession in order to be completely redeemed. Wharton doesn't suggest that there is no place for criticism, or that all critics are pernicious. On the contrary, this story reclaims the act of interpretation. It is clear, for example, that Bernald, in fact, does understand Pellerin's work in a way no one else does, that he is, in effect, the true "Interpreter" of Pellerin. But Bernald lacks awareness of his own motivations; he simply can't see his own similarity to the Howland Wades of the critical world—until he loses John Pellerin. Bernald's awakening self-knowledge and his humility in the face of such knowledge constitute his redemption.

Wharton had a healthy, skeptical attitude toward her own critical reception, and she laughed at the sometimes conflicting views of her fiction.

Yet at the same time, she adopted the role of literary critic with enthusiasm, writing reviews and essays on the work of other writers with a forceful critical eye. Wharton's criticism is sensitive and generous, but she is not afraid to take a writer to task for artistic failure. Perhaps most important, her critical writing argues for an awareness on the part of the critic, an integrity that includes an acknowledgment of the critic's underlying motivations in approaching a literary text or a literary figure. The desire for possession is an appetite that must be recognized and controlled, subsumed to the higher calling of scholarly activity. And unless the critic can make an accommodation between responsibility and desire, the criticism will be necessarily flawed. In "The Legend," when Pellerin comments on his critical reception and the institution of Pellerinism, we can hear Wharton's warning to critics: "I knew then how it frees an idea to be ignored; how apprehension circumscribes and deforms it" (2:102). She recognized the risks of criticism from two very different perspectives, and she offers in this story a way to reconcile the seemingly irreconcilable impulses of critical desire and authorial autonomy.

I realize my own complicity here in my desire to possess Wharton and be her interpreter. And I feel her slipping out of my grasp, threatening, like Pellerin, to disappear forever. Wharton has been much used by critics, and the critical battles that continue to be fought over her resemble, ironically, the jockeying for position she described with such comedy and contempt in "The Legend." Of course, it sounds very old fashioned to say that critics have a responsibility when they put pen to paper, that critics always exist in a moral relation to what they critique. But this is what the postmodern academic romance argues, usually in a rather humorous way. Specifically, the contemporary postmodern novelists who redeem academic endeavors do so through comedy. Perhaps they recognize the supreme difficulty of articulating the urgency and importance of scholarly exploration in a more serious vein. Yet while they make us laugh, they also show us how to be responsible critics. Edith Wharton saw this need long ago and antici-pated their mission by portraying the development, education, and redemp-tion of the critic in "The Legend"—her own version of the scholar/hero, silly in the extreme, shaken by loss, but finally triumphant.

Works Cited

Begley, Adam. "Raiders of the Lost Archives." *Lingua Franca* (July/August 1993), 36–40.

Lewis, R. W. B., and Nancy Lewis, eds. *The Letters of Edith Wharton.* 1988.
    Reprint, New York: Collier Books, 1989.
Wharton, Edith. *The Collected Short Stories of Edith Wharton.* Ed. R. W. B.
    Lewis. 2 vols. New York: Charles Scribner's Sons, 1968.
Wolff, Cynthia Griffin. *A Feast of Words: The Triumph of Edith Wharton.*
    New York: Oxford University Press, 1977.

The Comstock Matrix of Twain's Humor

Lawrence I. Berkove

To fully appreciate the Comstock as a matrix of Twain's humor, one must recognize that on the Comstock, lying was a high art. This meant not only tall tales—although they certainly were part of the matrix—as well as clever hoaxes or practical jokes played on naïfs and unsuspecting greenhorns, but also outright lying. It was practically a daily feature of Comstock existence. Today, society might be shocked by it, but such were the temptations of the Comstock, and such were the stakes that, while lying was not exactly countenanced, it was understood as a necessary evil, and clever lying was even admired. Fred H. Hart, the editor of the *Austin Reveille,* published in 1878 the *Sazerac Lying Club,* a collection of his newspaper articles about an imaginary organization. The book cannot be better summed up than by his own introduction: "This purports to be a book on lies and lying, but it does not treat of the lies of politicians, stock-brokers, newspaper men, authors, and others, who lie for money; neither does it touch on the untruths of scandal, mischief, or malice, but only on those lies which amuse, instruct, and elevate, without harm" (8). The *Sazerac Lying Club* was a very successful book that quickly ran into additional editions. Unfortunately for him, however, Hart really believed in telling only elevating and harmless lies. In 1880, shortly after he became editor of the *Territorial Enterprise,* he opposed the election of the silver king James G. Fair for United States senator, calling Fair by his richly earned nickname, "Slippery Jim." Hart told the truth, but he forgot that Fair's partner, John W. Mackay, was half owner of his paper, and so Hart's job lasted only three months.

Twain's emergence into professional status, therefore, began in a distinctive matrix, and it may help in appreciating his humor to know something about the lies and liars that flourished on the Comstock during its brief heyday—a period of about only twenty years. The years after his departure also deserve consideration because there is some evidence that through newspaper exchanges as well as letters and visits from Comstock friends, Twain kept at least in occasional touch with what was happening there, and so his early instruction in artistic lying was thereby reinforced.[1]

160

One of Twain's earliest and most notable mentors was William Wright, better known as Dan De Quille, his colleague on the *Territorial Enterprise* and his sometime roommate. De Quille's humor tended to be mild and without the sharp edge we associate with Twain's, but he did not take second place in ingenuity to anybody. De Quille excelled at two kinds of humor: obviously absurd but witty "stretchers"; and "quaints," his term for the short but more subtle flights of drollery he was fond of passing off as news stories in his regular newspaper columns.

Several practically unknown but interesting quaints are worth recalling. De Quille once told of a man who discovered several acres of petrified animals in the Wind River range of Wyoming. According to the quaint, the man also discovered a process by which he could change the stone back into the original meat, and he expected before long to have birds and reptiles of the Silurian period walking about and on exhibition in menageries.[2] In another quaint, De Quille deceptively attributed the following pet fancier information to the *Boston Post:* "A regulation black-and-tan poodle, to be worth $100, must have a head about the size of a black walnut; eyes that stand outside of their sockets; a tail about the size of a lead pencil, and legs so attenuated that the animal falls over on his back every time he lifts his head to bark."[3] This item was widely copied all over the country. Twain came up with something like it in his lecture comment about a "long, low dog" —apparently a dachshund—he encountered on a train that he thought would have been more "structurally sound" if it had had six legs instead of four.

A third notable quaint, tucked in among the items in an 1877 De Quille column of local news, was this report:

> Not long since a member of the Austin Sazerac Lying Club straightened out, and was to all appearances dead. The club turned out in full regalia to bury him. When the grave was reached, the man awoke from his death-like trance and clamored to be let out of his coffin, swearing he was not dead. The faces of the brethren beamed with satisfaction. "He's a good one—a most worthy member, and true to the last," said they, as they planted him in his narrow home.

A squib in the *Enterprise* subsequently reported that De Quille had been elected as a member of the Sazerac Lying Club on the basis of this stretcher, and included, solemnly, another stretcher: "He is the first newspaper man ever admitted to the club" (*Territorial Enterprise,* 13 October 1877).

Characteristically, De Quille's quaints consisted of something preposterous or impossible that was so convincingly supported with plausible details that readers found themselves believing it despite their better judgment. An editor of the *American Naturalist* magazine, for instance, responded to a tongue-in-cheek description of a "mountain alligator" with a request for the skeleton and skull of one of them.[4] Because De Quille seldom gave warning of what he was about, his readers had to be on their toes to detect these subtle hoaxes. One excellent example is this gem of misleading understatement:

> A. B. Flowers of Alexandria, La., writes to the *Scientific American* that the statement made in a recent article on this subject, to the effect that no one has ever witnessed a case of spontaneous combustion in the human body, is a mistake, as he was himself, with several others, an eye-witness to a case of the kind. The person who was the victim was a hard drinker, and was sitting by the fire surrounded by Christmas guests, when suddenly flowers of a blueish tint gushed from his mouth and nostrils, and he was soon a corpse. The body he states, remained extremely warm for a much longer period than usual. (*Territorial Enterprise*, 15 February 1870)

The matter-of-fact style, the plausible situation (the ignition of a hard drinker sitting by a fire), the vividness of detail, and the ascription of the information to a respected journal combine to disarm skepticism. (Note, however, that De Quille says only that A. B. Flowers *wrote* to the *Scientific American*, not that the letter was *published* in it.) Even closer to the edge of believability is De Quille's account of eyeless fish that were discovered "in the water now flooding both the Savage and Hale and Norcross mines." The fish were described as three to four inches in length and blood red in color. "The temperature of the water in which they are found is 128 degrees Fahrenheit—almost scalding hot. When the fish were taken out of the hot water . . . and placed in a bucket of cold water, for the purpose of being brought to the surface, they died almost instantly. The cold water at once chilled their life blood." This quaint inspired curiosity from merely credulous readers and outrage from equally credulous but also financially sensitive mine owners. This latter group was afraid that De Quille's mention of water flooding the mines—a commonplace occurrence on the Comstock—might drive off potential purchasers of stock.[5] Among the merely credulous was a member of the United States Centennial Exposition commission who requested De Quille to preserve some of the fish in alcohol and mail them to him—"All charges will be paid, send C.O.D."—so the specimens could be added to the collections of the Centennial and the Smithsonian.[6]

In 1865, three years after Twain's notorious 1862 hoax, "The Petrified Man," De Quille followed up with his own straight-faced account, entitled "A Silver Man," of a corpse found in a cave whose chemical action had mineralized the body into silver. So convincing was De Quille that he was able to pull off the same joke on the same audience, but without the hostility Twain had experienced.[7] De Quille's most successful quaint, however, was a two-part hoax about "solar armor," begun 2 July 1874. According to the first part, an inventor concocted a device that protected its wearer against "the fierce heat of the sun in crossing deserts and burning alkali plains." It was essentially a rubberized suit with a portable air conditioner. The inventor tested it by attempting to cross Death Valley. He did not make it across; his body was discovered the next day twenty miles out. "He was dead and frozen stiff. His beard was covered with frost and—though the noonday sun poured down its fiercest rays—an icicle over a foot in length hung from his nose. There he had perished miserably because his armor had worked but too well, and because it was laced up behind where he could not reach the fastenings."

This story quickly spread across the country. The *Scientific American* noted the story on July 25, but, most important, it was reported in the *London Daily Telegraph* on August 3. One of the editors of that paper expressed a wish for more details, and the word got back to De Quille from a Comstock engineer who subscribed to the *Telegraph*. Obligingly, De Quille wrote a sequel that listed in convincing detail the sort of chemicals the inventor supposedly used and what had gone wrong.[8] The hoax has to be read to fully appreciate its delicate artistry, but suffice it to say that both parts were written so as to impart the same impression of accurate and dependable reporting that we today associate with our newspapers.

Rollin Mallory Daggett was an associate of Twain's on the *Enterprise*. He was particularly adept at writing pugnacious editorials and was most likely the friend who helped Twain write the fiery challenge to a duel that precipitated his abrupt departure from the Comstock. In later years, after Daggett had mellowed somewhat, he related in his memories one of the most audacious legal prevarications in Comstock history:

> As I prefer to deal with pleasantries of the past rather than
> with its flagrant misdemeanors, it will be perceived that I
> employ a somewhat gentle phrase in designating a period
> in the judicial history of the Comstock when judges were

corrupted, the verdicts of juries were purchased and troublesome witnesses were killed or spirited out of the Territory: when mining records were tampered with, and witnesses before testifying were drilled in perjuries like squads of raw recruits. Sometimes, to increase the value of their rascally services, these drilled witnesses would overreach themselves. I will present a single example.

In 1862 the owners of the Yellow Jacket mine, in Gold Hill, swallowed two locations immediately in front of their east line, belonging to the Union and Princess corporations. The Yellow Jacket location, which was the earliest of the three by some days, was made too far up the hill to cover the Comstock fissures, and the owners did not discover their mistake until the real vein was developed by the two companies adjoining. They then sought to rectify it by floating their original boundary lines 200 or 300 feet farther down the hill. It was a difficult undertaking, but Comstock courts and juries were accommodating in those days, and it was successfully accomplished.

Several of their witnesses testified that they had seen the original location notice of the Yellow Jacket tacked to a nut-pine stump well down the hills and within the boundaries of the adverse claimants. Finally their principal witness took the stand. He seemed to know all about the Yellow Jacket location, and knew that the nut-pine stump referred to by the other witnesses marked the southeast corner of the original claim of the Yellow Jacket. He saw the notice the day after it was put there. He worked in a tunnel in Crown Point ravine and passed it half a dozen times a day for more than three consecutive months. He had read it frequently, perhaps twenty times, and remembered its phraseology perfectly, and the names of the locators, and glibly recited both to the jury. Such testimony seemed to be unanswerable.

"Take the witness," said A. W. Baldwin with a smile of triumph, addressing General Charles H. S. Williams, the leading counsel for the Union.

"Only a single question," replied the general, adjusting his spectacles and slowly removing a scrap of weather-worn paper from a clip. "Only a single question," he repeated, handing the scrap to the witness through an officer of the court. "Look at that piece of paper you hold in your hand," continued the general, addressing the witness, "and examine it closely."

The witness raised the paper to his flushed and troubled face, and for a full minute stared at it vacantly, while every voice was hushed and every eye in the court-room was turned upon him.

"Well, sir," resumed the general to the witness, "now that you have carefully examined the paper in your hand, I ask you to read to the jury what you find written upon it, and tell them whether or not it is the same that you have sworn you read so often while passing to and from your work in Crown Point Ravine."

The witness looked imploringly at his counsel, but as they were ignorant of the character of the paper they could convey to him no instruction. At length, crushing the paper in his hand, with his eyes to the floor he hesitatingly said:

"I—I—I can't read or write."

The effect was dramatic. The self-convicted perjurer was not ordered into custody. The Judge took a glass of water, and the most of the jurors did not seem to observe that there was anything inconsistent in the testimony of the witness. They were in the box to fix the boundary at that nut-pine stump and they did it.

"Nothing further," said the general, setting back in his chair with a satisfied smile. Another witness was called, and the case was proceeded with as if nothing unusual had occurred. Wise men took another look at the jury and went out and sold their Union and Princess shares for what they would bring. (*San Francisco Morning Call,* 10 September 1893)

Although Twain's account of "The Great Land-Slide Case" in *Roughing It* had its origin in a real event, that real event was a practical joke, a mock trial. Daggett's narrative, however, was of a real trial—which Twain likely knew about—whose implications were so serious that Daggett waited thirty years to write about it. Daggett does not condone a judicial system so corrupt that it countenanced outright, even clumsy, lying, but from his humorous tone it is apparent he recalls with some fondness this perverse anecdote of Comstock history.

Jim Townsend—the "Truthful James" of Bret Harte's famous poem, who is better known as "Lying Jim"—was one of the great liars of the Comstock. Twain briefly mentions him in *Roughing It,* but he deserves to be better known. His genius at invention was legendary in his own time, but nothing compares to his most outstanding achievement: an almost epic lie. A swindler named Butterfield went to England to sell shares in so-called mining properties near Lundy, California. In order to make his case convincing he hired Townsend to write and publish a newspaper in the nearly deserted region in which the supposedly lucrative activities of the mines would be chronicled. Townsend did better than that. He single-handedly resurrected a defunct local newspaper known as the *Homer Mining Index* and created a bustling town, peopled it with distinct personalities, and for months without a single subscriber or paid advertiser ran regular and detailed reports of its imaginary church and social events and scandals, composed imaginary advertisements, and manufactured statistics on equally imaginary mining activities. Copies of the paper were then sent to England to con potential investors. Eventually the scam was exposed, but Townsend escaped jail. A sort of scamplike Colonel Beriah Sellers in *The Gilded Age,* Townsend was not believed on the Comstock but was nevertheless regarded affectionately.[9]

Slightly less elaborate but equally ambitious was the Arizona diamond hoax of 1872. A go-getter named William Lent formed the Colorado Diamond Company to sell shares in an Arizona property he claimed had diamonds on it and induced some reputable people, including the Civil War hero General George McClellan, to lend their names to it. In a special sense, Lent told the truth. There *were* diamonds on the property: he had planted them there. Joe Goodman, editor of the *Enterprise,* learned of the scheme, recognized it for what it was, and in print called the company "a gang of swindlers." Lent sued Goodman for libel. The reply of the *Enterprise* to the suit fights fire with fire, but the lies it tells are transparent, although gorgeous. The reply is a classically elegant achievement of journalistic irony. After reprinting the entire offensive article, which laid out the evidence that points to the conclusion that Lent and his associates were swindlers, the editorial concludes:

> Upon a careful perusal of this article we discover that there is certain personal roughness in connection with the mention of Mr. Lent, which is doubtless the incentive to the suit against this paper. The leading grievance of Mr. Lent probably consists in the fact that the *Enterprise* was the first journal on the coast to refer to the incorporation

of the Colorado Diamond company as a gang of swindlers. In the absence of Mr. Goodman we [deem] it a duty to disavow, in his behalf, an intention of associating the name of Mr. Lent with any scheme in which there was a suspicion of fraud or wrongdoing. Familiar, as we are, with Mr. Goodman's habits of thought, we are satisfied that he is the victim, in this instance, of some terrible typographical blunder. It is probable that the writer intended to say that Mr. Lent was the "victim" rather than the "purchaser" of the diamonds from Ritter, Leverson & Co., for it is unreasonable that his name should have been associated in the mind of the writer with anything bearing the remotest resemblance to sharp practice or dishonesty. All acquainted with Mr. Lent know him to be incapable of a dishonest action. He is a model of virtue and integrity, and God-fearing mothers point to him as an example for their children. No mother contemplates with composure the possible death of her son upon the gallows, and in the career of Mr. Lent a means of escaping that unhappy fate is discerned, no matter how merciless may be the exactions of violated law. Mr. Lent a swindler? Wm. M. Lent a party to fraud of any kind! Bill Lent a corrupt and dishonest man! Perish the thought, and with it the recollection that it has ever been entertained. His character is as pure as the lily of the Sierras, which grows amidst perpetual snows and dies with the breath of summer. Mr. Lent is well known in California and Nevada, and within the large circle of his acquaintance he is everywhere beloved and respected as a man of irreproachable integrity and self-sacrifice. His ways are ways of pleasantness, and all his paths are peace. In the article quoted above we observe through the mist that will intrude between our eyes and the great injustice, that Mr. Lent is certainly referred to as a swindler, with the grosser intimation that he is little better than a thief. It is wonderful that this thing should have crept into print. And now, with the solemnity with which the resolutions of reproach were expunged from the journals of the United States Senate years ago, we deliberately draw our pencil across the obnoxious sentence referring to Mr. Lent as a swindler or the confederate of swindlers. Around it we draw the black lines of our ceaseless regret, and blot the letters

> with the drops of our repentance. With this explanation, if
> Mr. Lent still refuses to dismiss his suit, we shall be con-
> strained to believe that he is stirred to the litigation by
> malice, and prepare to meet the outraged and injured gen-
> tleman with such weapons as law and public sentiment
> afford.[10]

The suit against Goodman was never pursued because, fortuitously, the
diamond hoax was exposed quite independently and definitively by the
geologist Clarence King. Lent survived the exposure and turned his sharp
talents to shrewd speculation in mining stocks. When Lent died, many years
later, an enormously wealthy man, Goodman was no longer on the Comstock; all details of how Lent had accumulated his wealth had been
forgotten, and a memoirist was able to say, "I never heard of any one who
had [resentment] toward Mr. Lent."[11] The author of the *Enterprise* editorial
correctly gauged his audience, therefore, when he chose to be ironically
humorous instead of outraged by Lent's shameless audacity in pressing suit
against Goodman.

It is not suggested that any, let alone all, of these lies directly
influenced Twain. Rather, they are presented here simply as introductions
to an insufficiently known aspect of the Comstock matrix from which he
developed and to some of Twain's Comstock mentors and competitors.
Twain was rightly identified by Pascal Covici as a master of the hoax,[12] and
none of Twain's books is as rich in hoaxes as *Roughing It*. This cannot be
accidental, for the apple falls close to the tree. It is important to keep in
mind, however, that Twain's most artistic and powerful hoaxes are not those
easily detected but those that take in their readers. Even in *Roughing It*, not
all of the hoaxes are funny, and as Twain's career advanced, he increasingly
presented deeply serious issues within the structure of subtle and sometimes
grim hoaxes. The Comstock was the place where Twain saw firsthand and on
a daily basis the snares and delusions of the world, where he could not help
but study the techniques of expert hoaxers, and where he began to practice
the lessons he learned—and to master them—sometimes with exuberant
humor but always with skillful irony. How well he succeeded we are still
discovering, but as good as he is, from the Comstock perspective he might
be more accurately regarded as primus inter pares—first among equals.

Notes

1. For more information on Joe Goodman's continuing influence on Mark Twain, see my discussion in "'Assaying in Nevada': Twain's Wrong Turn in the Right Direction," 68–69.

2. Undated and unidentified clipping, William Wright Papers, carton no. 2, PG-246, Bancroft Library, University of California, Berkeley, CA.

3. Anonymous letter to De Quille, dated Virginia [City], 9 September [1875?], Morris Family Collection of Dan De Quille, State Historical Society of Iowa, Iowa City.

4. The original "mountain alligator" hoax item from the *Territorial Enterprise* is now lost, but the letter, dated 18 September 1888 and mailed from Philadelphia by Professor E. D. Cope, is in the William Wright Papers collection at the Bancroft Library.

5. The complete hoax, entitled "Eyeless Fish That Live in Hot Water," can be found in De Quille's *The Fighting Horse of the Stanislaus,* 1, 20.

6. The letter, written by a Mr. Donaldson, dated 7 March 1876, and mailed from Philadelphia, is in the William Wright Papers collection at the Bancroft Library.

7. See "A Silver Man," in *The Fighting Horse of the Stanislaus,* 3–8.

8. For both parts, see "Solar Armor," in *The Fighting Horse of the Stanislaus,* 14–19.

9. A brief survey of Townsend's career, and some of his collected writings, can be found in Dwyer and Lingenfelter, *Lying on the Eastern Slope.*

10. The original article was printed in the *Virginia City [NV] Territorial Enterprise* on 27 February 1873. It is reprinted in Berkove, "Life After Twain," 27–28.

11. Goodwin, *As I Remember Them,* 98–99.

12. Covici, *Mark Twain's Humor.* See also Covici's entries on "Hoax" and "Humor" in the *Mark Twain Encyclopedia.*

Works Cited

Berkove, Lawrence I. "'Assaying in Nevada': Twain's Wrong Turn in the Right Direction." *American Literary Realism* 27:3 (spring 1995), 64–80.

———. "Life After Twain: The Later Careers of the *Enterprise* Staff." *Mark Twain Journal* 29:1 (spring 1991), 22–28.

Covici, Pascal, Jr. *Mark Twain's Humor: The Image of a World.* Dallas: Southern Methodist University Press, 1962.

De Quille, Dan. *The Fighting Horse of the Stanislaus: Stories & Essays by Dan De Quille.* Edited and with an introduction by Lawrence I. Berkove. Iowa City: University of Iowa Press, 1995.

Dwyer, Richard A., and Richard E. Lingenfelter. *Lying on the Eastern Slope: James Townsend's Comic Journalism on the Mining Frontier.* Miami: Florida International University Press, 1984.

Goodwin, Charles C. *As I Remember Them.* Salt Lake City: Salt Lake Commercial Club, 1913.

Hart, Fred. *The Sazerac Lying Club.* San Francisco: Samuel Carson, 1878.

Le Master, J. R., and James D. Wilson, eds. *Mark Twain Encyclopedia.* New York: Garland, 1993.

Mark Twain's Fingerprints
in *Pudd'nhead Wilson*

Louis J. Budd

Far more than most novels, Mark Twain's *The Tragedy of Pudd'n-head Wilson* (1894) is a prototypical artifact. Most obviously, it can be used to classify and to judge the critics themselves. We can infer their basic values or tastes from what they find in the text—the "Faulknerian aspects" of its "rhetoric," for instance. We can judge their standard of responsibility by the degree to which they account for the total text instead of using only the passages that fit a thesis or ignoring the context of tone. Above individual critics we can build a progressive display of theories, from the ethical-mimetic principles of the late nineteenth century to the newest turn of meta-criticism. Or we can trace the course of Twain's reputation, which had to reach major status on other grounds before *Pudd'nhead Wilson* could attract serious, sophisticated interest. When Twain next rose to the status of a unique, quintessential spokesman for his nation, then the novel appeared to embody the sociocultural perceptions that intrigued the critic's own cohort at that time.

If (like Twain himself) we consider books as a commodity, *Pudd'n-head Wilson* can exemplify the growth of a mini-industry after World War II when college departments of English accepted and then enlarged the canon of writing produced in the United States. At the same time, an upsurge in quality paperbacks created a demand for lively introductions that promised still another feast. *Pudd'nhead Wilson* got important boosts of that kind from F. R. Leavis (1956), Langston Hughes (1959), and Malcolm Bradbury (1969). Concurrently, career publishing by academics boomed, bringing two problems. First, because tomahawk criticism—that is, making the main enterprise a detailed, ad hominem attack on published opinions—has appealed less and less as the corporate ideal has prospered, academics searched for "original" discoveries or insights. By 1975 a veteran Twainian could declare that "criticism of *Pudd'nhead Wilson* seems to have come to a dead end" (Gerber, 21), meaning that all imaginable approaches were bristling with scouts. Second, taking a positive viewpoint inexorably modulates into a case for great achievements, for the canonizing of another masterpiece. A 1987 three-day conference held at the University of California at Santa Cruz and devoted entirely to *Pudd'nhead Wilson* amounted to at the very least a beatification. Its interdisciplinary approach was polished into a weighty, reverential book, slightly counterbalanced by one essay taking the position of a devil's advocate (Gillman and Robinson).

Pudd'nhead Wilson also furnishes a fine exhibit or, better, an arena for the still rising debate about intentionality in all its circuits—biographical, psychic, professional, formalist, and thematic. Most simply there can be no doubt that Twain both wanted and needed big royalties. By 1891 he had to dismantle his beloved but expensive household in Nook Farm, and up through 1894 he increasingly worried about the prospect of utter disgrace (a fate that does envelop Roxy's son in the novel—from here on referred to as Tom Driscoll rather than Valet de Chambre). Soon after starting on the first version of what became *Pudd'nhead Wilson,* Twain assured his copublisher (in effect, his agent) that "it will be a book that will *sell* mighty well. . . . *I* believe there's a 'boom' in it" (Hill, 319). In revamping drastically he kept angling for mass appeal, boasting to his agent in July 1893 that he had "stripped" his manuscript "for flight" while adding material (the finger-printing) that was "virgin ground—absolutely *fresh,* and mighty curious and interesting to everybody" (Hill, 355). The next month, mailing the manuscript from abroad, he breathed relief: "It'll furnish me hash for a while I reckon" (Hill, 359). Perhaps an adaptation for the stage already lay in the back of his mind; up front he had always counted on serializing the book in one of the best-paying magazines.

Under the garishness and superlatives, any biographical accounting for Twain can get complicated. Now and then insistent on self-defeating behavior, he could have aimed for pure art when he could worst afford it. Or, floundering emotionally, he could have aimed for self-distraction above all (as he would do more and more). Or the working through of his psychic needs could have seized control of the manuscript. Or he could have coldly decided to produce another potboiler like *The American Claimant* (1892) or *Tom Sawyer Abroad* (1894). Ideally, an author can earn riches by composing a masterpiece that the high-culture establishment at once promotes reverently (though bookstore sales never brought enough royalties by Twain's standard). Whatever the inner calculus, Twain's stated motives focused on furnishing some kind of entertainment. In his first mention of the project, he described it as a "howling farce" centered on Siamese twins (Hill, 319), and he stated his firm intention to sign the book with his trademark-name rather than toying with anonymity, as he soon did with *Personal Recollections of Joan of Arc* (1896). Nobody who started on the actual book could doubt its broadly amusing side, immediately flaunted in "A Whisper to the Reader," or the plentiful, cartoonlike illustrations (which the title page describes as "Marginal," without intending a pun). On a first reading anyway, the opening seven chapters confirmed those elements. As for the gloomy "Conclusion," the book as published in 1894 went on (though only in its American edition) to include "the Comedy / Those Extraordinary Twins," which self-indulgently proclaimed itself a jumble of failed ideas for a romp. No fingerprinting sleuth was needed to verify Mark Twain, a broad and often reckless humorist, named on the cover, as the trueborn author of the book, rather than the false names on the title page. A leading actor-producer quickly saw material that could succeed as a popular play without changing the main plot.[1]

Even when most anxious to restrain his humor (as with *Joan of Arc*) Twain could stay dead serious for only so long. Indeed, his admirers and enemies agree about his irrepressible impulse toward broad burlesque and low comedy. These elements plainly push into *Pudd'nhead Wilson,* and Twain himself (in "Those Extraordinary Twins") would comment that the "exchange of the children had been flippantly and farcically described." Who can find subtlety or plausibility in the kick that "lifted Tom clear over the footlights" (chap. 11), in the near misses at the duel (Roxy's skinned nose, the Judge's clipped hair), or in taking out insurance against enthusiastic firemen instead of fires? *Pudd'nhead Wilson* often reminds us that we are reading a humorist so irrepressible as to compose a burlesque *Hamlet* or, a few weeks before his death in probably his final stretch of writing, compose a mocking set of rules for approaching St. Peter at heaven's gate.

But another side of the Twainian equation is that his humor continually swerved toward touches that could chill laughter into tension. An anonymous contemporary reviewer praised the "brightness and grotesqueness and funniness" (*Critic,* 11 May 1895, p. 338–39). While the irony of action often approaches burlesque—Roxy blackening her face for a disguise—it can suddenly puzzle, can depress more than it amuses us (perhaps in the instance just given). In other words, Twain the incorrigible jester could not stay dead humorous for very long either. The narrator's most frequent voice in *Pudd'nhead Wilson* is ironic—again, even comically so but often tightening into astringency. The maxims at the head of chapters, occasionally broad fun, have a firm cynical impact when absorbed collectively. Furthermore, though the firmness and bent of Twain's intention are vague on this detail, he did decide to lead off his title with "The Tragedy of." After all, most people, including those hooked on low comedy, find only tragedy in chattel slavery.

Impatient readers should avoid *Pudd'nhead Wilson.* It's an "on the other hand" case that deserves the statue of Nataraja, the Hindu god of the dance, or one of Emmeline Grangerford's portraits for its logo. If we decide for tragedy as its genre, we grow emotionally dissatisfied, even after allowing for Shakespearean, comic relief. This dissatisfaction holds true even in France, where—as Roger Asselineau observes—Twain's humor "does not travel well." Following the text open-mindedly, David E. E. Sloane finds that Twain's career as a literary comedian fitfully reasserts itself, especially in the episodes where David Wilson reprises Twain's transcendent showmen and in the prolonged, climactic trial, tuned much more for comedy along with melodrama than for tragedy. The verdict finally has to rest on the quality of tone. A pratfall—though not by that name, to be sure—can arouse grief or horror when slanted effectively. In our time "serious" literature treats the crumbling of identity in ways that arouse pity or grief. But the good person disoriented by confusion and toppled into self-doubt has served comedy for millennia, and its scriptwriters still fall back on the classic line, "Will somebody please tell me what's going on?"

Twain, at the more intellectualized range of his impulses toward humor, could not resist toying with, destabilizing, distorting any idea or attitude. Thus, appraising the comic element in *Pudd'nhead Wilson* hinges on three questions. First, is the humor forced or inspired? Twain's best humor, flooding out of his psyche, has made him perhaps immortal. But the humor he pumped up on demand works little better than that of many a hack, and some of it clouds *Pudd'nhead Wilson*. Second, if we grant that a comic impulse was vital here, what were its targets? Not the system of slavery nor, obviously, the compounded wrongs done to Chambers (that is, the legitimate Tom Driscoll) but at least two of Twain's long-standing charges against human nature: the drive to rationalize away one's selfish actions (as Tom does so egregiously) and the herd instinct (the thread of the town's fickleness toward the outsider it nicknames Pudd'nhead). Third, in searching for tragic themes and welding them into some overarching pattern, do we dwarf or ignore the presence of the narrating persona, a wittier showman, a far more skeptical, irreverent, cosmopolitan, and transcendent outsider than David Wilson himself?

Entertainment can bypass comedy to aim for pure melodrama, which can nevertheless amuse us through its own devices. We enjoy its massive ironies of event, its pat reversals, its triumphs of reason through the unmasking of villainy, and also its deceptions when used righteously. Twain took a childish delight in disguises, crucial to the plotting of *Puddn'head Wilson*. But blatant, solemn melodrama also abounds, keyed by the titles of chapters—"Tom Stares at Ruin," "The Judge Utters Dire Prophecy," "The Murderer Chuckles," or "Doom." It erupts full force in chapter 8 with Roxy's penniless return to Dawson's Landing; in an extended, packed chapter 18, Roxy, suddenly infallible at reading minds, keeps outsmarting the villain. "Sold down the river!" becomes a contrapuntal dirge. In an old-fashioned kind of gender equality, men totter from emotion as easily as women (and Judge Driscoll "sank forward in a swoon" on hearing that Tom had ignored the code duello) (chap. 12). The changeling plot climaxes in a trial scene that soon, according to the *New York Times* review, played as "one of the most effective that has been put on the stage here for many years" (*New York Times,* 16 April 1895, p. 5). The audience was spared the conventional love plot, which Twain started (and indeed failed to edit out completely), only because Tom, legally black, cannot woo Rowena without offending even a postbellum, 1890s readership, which knows his secret.

To admire *Pudd'nhead Wilson,* readers must ignore the mimetic tradition, defined by Twain's crony William Dean Howells as fidelity to experience and probability of motive acted out by rounded characters. Even the often effective melodrama cannot distract our skepticism from Tom's success with female disguises or his burning the props unnoticed, right after the murder, in the "haunted house" three hundred yards from the scene of the crime (chap. 19). Any scoffer can compile a list of wonderfully convenient or else sloppily crafted twists of events. Very improbably for the era and the place, the Capello twins take a stroll at eleven P.M. just so they can rush into the victim's house and then wait to become the accused. On ordinary days they behave so improbably that one critic decides that—like Huck Finn's duke and dauphin—they are imposters, maybe not even Italian (Williams, 39).

Significantly, the melodrama blurs several values long important to Twain. The graces of character that his plotting demands for the "best" families (and, somewhat, the twins) undercut his contempt for aristocracies by birth; dueling, which he had ridiculed elsewhere for both personal and social reasons, recovers some of its dignity. Most important of all, in order to have Roxy storm theatrically, Twain magnified Tom's one thirty-second of Negro blood into an argument for racism. Reviewing the play, young Willa Cather judged that Roxy's emphasis on that fraction of heredity identified a "right enough" cause of Tom's behavior (Curtin, 477–78). John C. Gerber, kindly disposed toward Twain, tries to cover all such problems with the umbrella of "fabulation," which, like the old tradition of the romance, allows a loose-jointed liberty with the texture of typical experience.

Nevertheless, an approach to intentionality at the working level has to doubt how well *Pudd'nhead Wilson* achieved the inner coherence that the Western literary tradition has come to expect from any genre. Misleadingly, it elicited one of Twain's most memorable fits of caring about detail when he saw that a copyeditor, who hailed from Oxford University, had "small-poxed" the final manuscript with changes. Twain reported to his wife, "I said I didn't care if he was an Archangel imported from Heaven, he couldn't puke his ignorant impudence over *my* punctuation," and "I couldn't sit in the *presence* of a proof-sheet where that blatherskite had left his tracks" (Wecter, 273). But painstaking study has showed that Twain first wrote the twins section (chap. 11 onward); then, months later, the climactic chapters that came before; and still later, the bulk of the opening chapters. After finishing, he did not carefully revise the earlier manuscripts to adjust for the saliency of the themes and problems introduced during the final stage of inscription, nor did he even bother—any craftsman might complain—to wipe all his thumbprints from the supposedly polished surface.

Hershel Parker has pursued the manuscripts to their most damning implications.[2] Going far deeper than the surface flaws—in the published book the twins, Siamese in the early draft, do not always have separated bodies; at the end, Tom is sold as a slave by the estate of Percy Driscoll, who (at the end of chap. 4) had in fact sold the rights to the true Chambers a month before dying—Parker accuses Twain of such carelessness that no thematic approach can bridge all the gaps. Centering on probability of character, Parker explains—condemningly—why Tom, stunned and revolted to learn that he's legally a Negro, soon slides back into his cocksure and abrasive way of interacting with the townspeople. However, Parker has failed to intimidate the latest critics, who "read the incoherence in Twain's narrative not as aesthetic failure but as political symptom, the irruption into this narrative ... of materials from the nineteenth-century political unconscious" (Gillman and Robinson, vii).

Before Parker's indictment, several main lines of analysis, all familiar to readers of Twain's previous work, had already exfoliated.[3] The plot of *Puddn'head Wilson* centers on the Old South with its system of slavery buttressed by racism. Roxy's experiences in Arkansas (chap. 18) graphically encapsulate that system in action out in the cotton field. Earlier, readers encountered troubling scenes of Roxy as a household servant in town. She also embodies miscegenation—not just the hypocritical existence of it but the attitudes toward the mulattoes it generated, compounded in generations of forbidden sex until a "black" and a "white" baby are born so nearly identical that only their mother-nurse can tell them apart. Twain then complicates any clear moral position by having Roxy blame Tom's baseness on "de nigger in you" (chap. 14). The only comfortable way out of this embarrassment is to praise Twain for grasping another evil of slavery—that is, its success at often managing to have the victim internalize the values and prejudices of the master class. Such a tactic allows one to deny that Roxy's slur has Twain's support. Less cogently we can argue that Roxy blames not African blood but genes tainted by treatment as a slave. In any case, this crux should not blur the fact that just when romanticizing the Old South reached its peak in popular fiction during the 1890s, *Pudd'nhead Wilson* acted out a dark rebuttal, underlined by references to the democratic ideals on which the United States had been founded.

Twain's interpreters know that before he learned to question the justice of the slavery he grew up with, he began to agonize over the efficacy of free will, increasingly believing that the verdict falls on the side of determinism. Sometimes he invoked heredity, although more abstractly than Roxy; with much greater zest he invoked an innate selfishness, which Tom can easily be seen to exemplify at its most stubborn degree. Most often he invoked "training"—the formative pressure of society, exerted imperceptibly through the consensus on major values but drilled in scowlingly or jeeringly by the persons who deal with us face to face. "Training is everything," as Twain's maxim for chapter 5 declares almost jokingly, but the principle was central to *A Connecticut Yankee in King Arthur's Court* (1889) and, still more starkly, to *What Is Man?* (1906). Of course Twain's contemporaries agonized even more viscerally than we over the nature-nurture equation. One reviewer decided that the career of the "rightful heir . . . seems to teach the greater force of education and habit than blood or heredity," yet "the more minutely detailed behavior of his substitute" appears "to prove the opposite." But Twain's contemporaries agonized less rigorously than we about fiction, and that reviewer could round off: "Perhaps the author would have smiled in his cynical way had he supposed that any attempt would be made at deductions of this nature, when his object, primarily at least, was to entertain" (*Public Opinion,* 14 February 1895, p. 117).

Nevertheless, the action of *Pudd'nhead Wilson* climaxes with a searing mismatch between the fates of the changelings, an imbalance that few critics have managed to adjust under one theory with anybody else's agreement. If training as a slave misshapes Chambers, the dignity of freedom should have given us a somewhat upright Tom, even as a master-class white; if heredity carried the indelible flaw—the birthmark of evil in Tom—Chambers should have grown up into a natural gentleman potentially worthy of the aristocratic F.F.V.s in his lineage. A solution for these dilemmas would depend on explaining Tom and Chambers in terms of different kinds of training, on using different levels of abstraction in accounting for the shaping force of society. One excellent critic, who escapes them by heeding Ahab-Melville's "Hark ye yet again—the little lower layer," argues, "In the end, there is only the realization that man is tricked by God or Providence and his own sinful nature into thinking that through choice (Roxy) or through the saving grace of ironic humor (Pudd'nhead) he could change destiny and reform the world and himself" (Brodwin, 176). On sea or land it was all a dark necessity. Still, two critics, as learned as they are sophisticated, have persisted in cutting deeper, down into the political, scientific, and legal marrow of the 1890s; the long underestimating of Twain's mind and range of knowledge has ended (Sundquist; Thomas).

Lately, moving with a trend in the enveloping culture, critics have played variations on the theme of appearance versus reality. At the simplest level they expound the detective plot as baring the evil that hides beneath bland routine. This plot reverberates also with social hypocrisy, sounded en masse by the discord between the idyll of Dawson's Landing as it basks domestically during the opening paragraphs and its cruel substructure. Closer to specific individuals, the narrative lights up the gulf between worth assigned by the color of the skin and that assigned by the qualities beneath it. Together, the irony of being misjudged for as long as twenty-three years, the disguises that work, a double life led between the small town that is home and the wicked city, concealed motherhood, nearly identical babies, and unsuspected changelings have encouraged a series of critics to stress "the way in which the realities of life . . . have been hidden beneath multiple layerings of fictions, deceptions, counterfeitings, and imitations until these patterns have been legitimized as habit" (Wood, 376–77). Anyone familiar with the record of Twain's mind can accept this list and the principles uniting it as firmly characteristic. Its spirit has been summoned first as a defense, then as a positive case for that once belittled, final quarter of *Adventures of Huckleberry Finn*. Nevertheless, *Pudd'nhead Wilson* serves as the centerpiece for the most ambitious analysis of how Twain's mind played with or was played by shifts, slippages, and inversions of identity (Gillman).

Only recently has discussion focused on David Wilson, who is of course the title character. Twain himself helped cause the delay. After a zigzag of stated intentions he later wrote to his wife, "I have never thought of Pudd'nhead as a character, but only as a piece of machinery—a button or a crank or a lever, with a useful function to perform in a machine, but with no dignity above that. I think we all so regarded him at home" (Wecter, 291). As a candidate for a political office, which actually has little function as a "crank" in the plot, Wilson can serve to exemplify the democratic process at the grassroots. As a lawyer, he invites scrutiny of legal authority, of its function and fairness. As someone badly underestimated by the populace, he questions the authority of communal judgment or, less abstractly, the soundness of opinions reached casually and then passed along by the crowd. Earlier critics developed such perspectives to praise Wilson as the outsider who tolerates his crude nickname, patiently if unwittingly prepares himself to save the community from its worst blunders, and wins civic leadership while accepting his triumph modestly or even gratefully. Lately that struggle for acceptance has aroused trendy objections that he perseveres toward a shoddy goal, that he lets himself get co-opted, and that his climactic popularity and power clinch the defeat of winning the favor of a society that deserves cold rejection instead. If so, Twain, who loved applause and dazzling prominence, was either going against his grain or reprimanding himself too.

Poststructuralism and Hershel Parker have incongruously joined to produce a deconstruction of Twain far more drastic than either the demotion of Wilson to a true Pudd'nhead or the argument that ambivalence about the South in which Twain was reared left fault lines in every draft. Highly subtle critics have concentrated on the fissures in the text as a gate for deeper probes, with thanks or even credit to Twain for leaving the fissures so wide. An explorer heeding Derrida's advice to press "beyond the closure" soon found that the novel presents "with startling clarity both the traces of erasure of previous writing and the suppression of unacknowledgable material."[4] Finding anticipations of not only Derrida but Nietzsche, Heidegger, and Foucault, an imposingly packed explication rises from the principle that "both for formal and polemical purposes, *Pudd'nhead Wilson* relies on a necessarily contradictory structure" (Rowe, 148). The unintended irony here is that a manuscript cobbled together by a harried author is attracting such sophisticated study, like a pileup of several automobiles being disentangled by agents for competing insurance firms. If one assumes Twain had aimed primarily for a humorous entertainment, then one incurs the anti-intentional irony that the mishaps, the irrationalities of behavior, the posturings, and the skating past sensible questions before they can be asked—all standard features of comedy—are darkened into frowning ponderosity.

Frustrating to modernists, Twain's notebooks comment on his writings in plain, stoutly pre-Jamesian terms. While in the heat of rebuilding from a knockabout farce about Siamese twins, he declared simply that he was cutting the manuscript down to three main characters. Besides Wilson and Roxy, he of course named Tom Driscoll, whom every interpreter must align with the concepts of race and determinism so clearly raised (if finally muddied) by the plot. But nobody has found complexity, resonance, or even believability in Tom as a human being. Besides murdering a kind foster-father, he insists on continually being the deep-dyed villain, especially toward Roxy, who keeps telling us this is so because Twain could not work within the Turgenev-Howells-James ideal of letting characters do all the revealing of themselves. Tom also enjoys his insistent cruelty to Chambers, whose own psychic weather is curiously, maybe studiously, ignored. Although his attitude toward Tom must have grown helplessly, massively bitter, his feelings for Roxy could have grown intricate because she probably gave him confusing signals. Actually, Twain chose to stay so vague about their relationship that we do not learn what kind of ties the daily pattern of slavery permitted or tolerated between them once Chambers was old enough to work like a man.

Most critics admire Roxy as a technically polished character as well as a brave individual. Overstating out of relief, some praise her as Twain's best attempt at portraying a sexually vibrant woman.[5] In another dubious compliment, especially so considering the times, reviewers in 1894–95 judged her compelling as a black mother. A survey of sixty preceding novels whose plot involved miscegenation concludes that she differed from the stereotyped mulatto, if only because she takes no pride in blackness (Kinney). Whereas one carefully sifted case claims great dignity for her both as a mother and a black, a rival sifting proves that Twain debased her with many touches, starting with her unlikely, field-hand dialect and her petty thieving.[6] The easiest mistake is to fail to realize that Twain, like many a contemporary in the age of Jim Crow, could abhor slavery yet condescend—comically, paternally, or both—toward blacks as a race. Again we come back to the infinite dividedness of his narrative, which keeps ahead of a transfixing analysis like Zeno's tortoise when pursued even by Achilles. Roxy does make self-respecting, bold moves, yet she will suddenly disappoint us, as when she demands whisky: "She tilted it up and took a drink. Her eyes sparkled with satisfaction, and she tucked the bottle under her shawl, saying, 'It's prime. I'll take it along'" (chap. 8). One would-be admirer concedes that her personality can change with "bewildering speed" (Pettit, 149).

In the daily routine Roxy was a "doting fool of a mother" (chap. 4), compounding her mistakes because Tom is her legal master, not just her own child, and also because she wants to avoid crises that might bring on closer scrutiny. She once asserts, heredity aside, that she is "sponsible" for his mean behavior (chap. 18). Likewise, Judge Driscoll broods that he has "indulged" Tom "to his hurt, instead of training him up severely" (chap. 14). Eventually, Wilson, by then a respected voice of wisdom, expatiates on how foolishly an elderly couple can spoil a foster child (chap. 19). The larger point is that varying levels of Twain's ideas poured into *Pudd'nhead Wilson.* We don't have to project Tom solely in terms of heredity or else major social forces. Although male-dominated criticism has taken little interest in the rearing of children as a theme, Twain devoted much time and effort to a family with three daughters who entered maturity during the early 1890s. In 1885 he jotted in his notebook, "Write a pamphlet about the government of children." Instead he published a letter advising a father who had mishandled a balky toddler (Salsbury, 206–8). His fierce conscience asked him regularly whether his conduct toward his daughters met Victorian principles of rearing by precept and parental example.

Reading *Pudd'nhead Wilson* with alertness to any idea, however mundane, will reveal that Twain's kaleidoscopic, churning interests kept bursting into the main flow of the narrative. Sporadically persuaded by some notion about diet, he digresses: "Tom got all the delicacies, Chambers got mush and milk, and clabber without sugar. In consequence, Tom was a sickly child and Chambers wasn't" (chap. 4). Rowena's name reminds us that Twain once went so far as to blame the Civil War on the Southern passion for the romances of Sir Walter Scott. Because "her heart gave a great bound, her nostrils expanded, and fine light played in her eyes" on hearing the twins say that they come from the "old Florentine nobility" (chap. 6), we realize that the animus behind *A Connecticut Yankee* (1889) still held perceptible warmth, and we recall that throughout the 1890s Twain helped criticize fashionable circles in the United States for acting giddy over any European who claimed to have a hereditary title. More substantively, we hear rumblings of Twain's sardonicism toward Sunday school orthodoxy, as in his clowning about the slaves' pilfering: "even the colored deacon [an anachronism?] himself could not resist a ham when Providence showed him in a dream, or otherwise, where such a thing hung lonesome and longed for someone to love" (chap. 2). Perhaps uselessly if not harmfully for thematic focus, Judge Driscoll strides forth as a freethinker during one paragraph. Although Twain was totally alert to the hypocrisy of professing Christianity while owning human beings, his tone implies that a merciful God would not allow the larger sin to happen and even that the subjugation of slaves by a master mirrors the relationship between a Calvinistic God and humankind. Finally, on a level well below divine or earthly justice, *Pudd'nhead Wilson* reflects, and is partly shaped by, Twain's fascination with any line of expertise. Professionals such as physicians and lawyers generally tower above the masses for their personal qualities, not just their skills. He was especially fascinated by technology put to practical use, such as using fingerprints as a tool of detection.

Whether shipping for aesthetic whales or minnows, approaches to *Pudd'nhead Wilson,* even in the age of metacriticism, quickly drift into thematizing seas again. One critic, renouncing literalist naïveté about content, promises to concentrate on structure and, after backsliding grievously, does discover a "double narrative action, which may be diagrammed by two intersecting curves" (Wood, 378–79). Lexical approaches through formalism have discovered that Twain unifies the text with a chain of legal metaphors or else a gamut of major and minor references to "dog," "cur," etc. (Briden; Fisher). In fact, starting with Wilson's failed joke, that list grows surprisingly long. Still, the meaning, the referential effects of the narrative, overpower emphasis on Twain's artistry, a result he never protested in other instances.

The maxims from "*Pudd'nhead Wilson's* Calendar" have raised their own narrowed debate. Attempts to fit them to the events or tone of the particular chapter they precede will fail in too many places, while attempts to fit them reciprocally to Wilson's ongoing personality work better. Still, in their range of values, interests, moods, and wit they match best the Twainian persona who is inscribing the entire text. Incidentally, the maxims had a separate popularity that lingers today. Although one critic (Rowe) associates them with a late Nietzschean attitude toward logocentrism, they had plenty of models among literary comedians, especially those who developed a regular column in the newspapers.

Beyond the purely aesthetic—the pleasures of narrative achieved as symmetry through language—what can *Pudd'nhead Wilson* continue to offer? First, it will always serve to document the Old South, all the more interestingly because, along with *The Adventures of Tom Sawyer* (1876) and *Adventures of Huckleberry Finn* (1885), it forms a triptych from a gifted eyewitness. Second, as a novel it projects a net of vicarious experiences that are by now foreign to its readers, including those who have lived through a later phase of the American small town. Third, as entertainment, which too many intellectuals pretend to disdain, it does emanate from a great humorist who remains beguiling even when he ranges below the peaks of his talent. Fourth, it comprises a prolonged visit with a persona developed over decades—since 1863, if the first signature of his pen name marks the baseline. *Pudd'nhead Wilson* has its lode of Twainian qualities, muted or skewed but authentic. Whichever of those qualities it may slight, the novel does display the weavings of his restlessly ironic mind. Whatever its failures, it transmits enough of Twain's spirit to make it worth our time and empathetic effort. The text bears his fingerprints—unique, indelible, revelatory, always incipiently comic. Twain intended such violence against complacency, injustice, and failures of perception; this violence needs to be tracked it to its source.

Finally, *Pudd'nhead Wilson* constructs an inviting framework for our own, subjectively favored meditations on matters that, although basic, change in urgency along the watershed between generations. Recently, Twain's narrative has helped to focus or else to deconstruct our concern with identity, with the fixing or the exposure of the true self—that is, the psyche's fingerprints. As the New Historicists force us back to the fact that we cannot ignore the social and political accountability of literature, *Pudd'nhead Wilson* will prove more hospitable than Dawson's Landing did to young David Wilson. If they are anywhere near right about it, Twain was a polymath who achieved dazzling, profound, and premonitory insights.

Notes

1. *New York Herald* (16 April 1895, p. 10) gives an act-by-act summary. Schirer holds the most authoritative details about the career of the stage version.

2. Actually the history of composition is far more tangled than I suggest here; Parker has been sorting out that history for at least ten years.

3. Perhaps this point is detailed best by Rowlette (84).

4. Smith, 22–23; Carton (92) concludes that the "fundamental disunity" of the novel achieves the "repeated structural imitation of the dividedness that its represented society covets."

5. See Butcher, 225; Kaplan (342) labels Roxy as "the one mature and explicitly sexual women in all his fiction."

6. Chellis and Butcher, respectively. Rowe (161) decides that Roxy may "approximate" Nietzsche's "extra-moral sense of freedom when she rebels against the social order, but she succumbs in the end to the sentimental delusion of maternal instincts." Much more compelling and poignant is the argument that motherhood as a slave thrusts Roxy into a double bind (Porter).

Works Cited

Asselineau, Roger. "Quelques réflexions inspirées par la lecture de *American Humor in France* de James C. Austin." *Thalia* 2 (1979), 45–49.

Briden, Earl F. "Idiots First, Then Juries: Legal Metaphors in Mark Twain's *Pudd'nhead Wilson*." *Texas Studies in Literature and Language* 20 (1978), 169–80.

Brodwin, Stanley. "Blackness and the Adamic Myth in Mark Twain's *Pudd'nhead Wilson*." *Texas Studies in Literature and Language* 15 (1973–74), 167–76.

Butcher, Philip. "Mark Twain Sells Roxy Down the River." *CLA Journal* 8 (1965), 225–33.

Carton, Evan. "*Pudd'nhead Wilson* and the Fiction of Law and Custom." In Eric J. Sundquist, ed., *American Realism: New Essays*. Baltimore: Johns Hopkins University Press, 1982, 82–94.

Chellis, Barbara A. "Those Extraordinary Twins: Negroes and Whites." *American Quarterly* 21 (1969), 100–12.

Curtin, William M., ed. *The World and the Parish, Vol. One: Willa Cather's Articles and Reviews,* 1893–1902. Lincoln: University of Nebraska Press, 1970, 477–78.

Fisher, Marvin, and Michael Elliott. "*Pudd'nhead Wilson:* Half a Dog Is Worse Than None." *Southern Review,* n.s., 8 (1972), 533–47.

Gerber, John C. "*Pudd'nhead Wilson* as Fabulation." *Studies in American Humor* 2 (1975), 21–31.

Gillman, Susan. *Dark Twins: Imposture and Identity in Mark Twain's America.* Chicago: University of Chicago Press, 1989.

Gillman, Susan, and Forrest G. Robinson, eds. *Mark Twain's* "Pudd'nhead Wilson"*: Race, Conflict, and Culture.* Durham: Duke University Press, 1990.

Hill, Hamlin, ed. *Mark Twain's Letters to His Publishers 1867–1894.* Berkeley: University of California Press, 1967.

Kaplan, Justin. *Mr. Clemens and Mark Twain: A Biography.* New York: Simon and Schuster, 1966.

Kinney, James. "Nurture Not Nature: *Pudd'nhead Wilson.*" *Amalgamation: Race, Sex, and Rhetoric in the Nineteenth-Century Novel.* Westport, CT: Greenwood, 1985, 215–24.

Parker, Hershel. "*Pudd'nhead Wilson:* Jack-leg Author, Unreadable Text, and Sense-Making Critics." *Flawed Texts and Verbal Icons: Literary Authority in American Fiction.* Evanston, IL: Northwestern University Press, 1984, 115–45.

Pettit, Arthur G. *Mark Twain and the South.* Lexington: University Press of Kentucky, 1974.

Porter, Carolyn. "Roxana's Plot." In Gillman and Robinson, 121–36.

Rowe, John Carlos. "Trumping the Trick of Truth: The Extra-Moral Sense of Twain's *Pudd'nhead Wilson.*" *Through the Custom-House: Nineteenth-Century American Fiction and Modern Theory.* Baltimore: Johns Hopkins University Press, 1982, 139–67.

Rowlette, Robert. *Twain's "Pudd'nhead Wilson": The Development and Design.* Bowling Green, OH: Bowling Green University Popular Press, 1971.

Salsbury, Edith Colgate, ed. *Susy and Mark Twain.* New York: Harper, 1965.

Schirer, Thomas. *Mark Twain and the Theatre.* Nuremberg: Hans Carl, 1984.

Sloane, David E. E. *Mark Twain as a Literary Comedian.* Baton Rouge: Louisiana State University Press, 1979.

Smith, Allan Gardner. "*Pudd'nhead Wilson:* Neurotic Text." *Dutch Quarterly Review* 11 (1981), 22–33.

Sundquist, Eric J. "Mark Twain and Homer Plessy" [1988]. In Gillman and Robinson, 46–72 [reprint].

Thomas, Brook. "Tragedies of Race, Training, Birth, and Communities of Competent Pudd'nheads." *American Literary History* 1 (1989), 754–85.

Twain, Mark. *Pudd'nhead Wilson.* 1894. Introduction by Langston Hughes. New York: Bantam, 1959. [Though more easily available, this text has less authority than the Norton Critical Edition (Sidney E. Berger, ed. [1980]), which will be superseded eventually by the text from the Mark Twain Project. Two other well-known paperback editions exist: one with an introduction by F. R. Leavis (New York: Grove, 1956) and the other with an introduction by Malcolm Bradbury (Harmondsworth, Eng.: Penguin, 1969).]

Wecter, Dixon, ed. *The Love Letters of Mark Twain.* New York: Harper, 1949.

Williams, Murial B. "The Unmasking of Meaning: A Study of the Twins in *Pudd'nhead Wilson. Mississippi Quarterly* 33 (1979–80), 39–53.

Wood, Barry. "Narrative Action and Structural Symmetry in *Pudd'nhead Wilson.*" Critical edition of *Pudd'nhead Wilson and Those Extraordinary Twins.* Ed. Sidney E. Berger. New York: Norton, 1980, 370–81.

Eddie Didn't Do Stand-up:
Some Keys to Poe's Humor

David Tomlinson

Poor Eddie Poe suffers from a humor gap. He did not create this gap, and it was more an accident of death than of birth. Rufus W. Griswold, Poe's literary executor, had more than a casual role in creating it. Whatever and whoever were the causes, the fact remains that from Poe's death in 1849 until 1931, when James Southall Wilson rediscovered some humorous elements in Poe's early writing, no one except T. O. Mabbott paid any attention to that side of the prodigious literary artist. This absence of recognition is part of a larger tendency by critics to avoid discussing humor, even though many of our major authors, including Hawthorne, Melville, and Henry James, are notable practitioners. Even Theodore Dreiser, seldom noted for his jocularity, was an ironist capable of lifting a passage from George Ade to describe the drummer Drouet in *Sister Carrie*. The irony of John Dos Passos is similarly hard for critics to acknowledge, especially when it is delivered straight-faced, as in the description in *U.S.A.* where Janey is separated from her Negro friend Pearl and counseled by her mother to respect colored people but never associate with them on an equal basis. The grotesque scene carries its own intrinsic message, but like Poe's humor, it is enveloped in the conventions of an ugly milieu, in this case that of social realism rather than gothic style, with the former just as enveloping as the latter.

The image of Poe forged during that eighty-two-year gap has helped militate against a more balanced view in which humor plays an integral part. While others established that humor does exist in Poe's writing, as does Donald Stauffer in his fine study of Poe's "merry" moods, I shall demonstrate here both that his efforts to create humor spanned his entire career and that his humor was sardonic, not lighthearted. Perhaps the easiest way to establish the character of Poe's humor is to compare him to the comedians we know best in the late twentieth century: the stand-ups. In doing so, I am not arguing that stand-up comedy as we know it existed in Poe's day. What we can see by using this *via negativa* is how far Poe's humor is from that light-hearted banter we accept as part of daily life. To begin, it helps to establish what stand-ups do. There is no mystery about the term "stand-up": it refers to the posture most such comedians assume when giving their acts. They stand in front of their audiences, ready to catapult their listeners into laughter. Most often they use the tools of verbal humor to do their job, painting ludicrous word pictures that convulse listeners.

What subject matter do they use? They *can* use anything in the world, but most use themselves. Rodney Dangerfield made a career out of stating that he got no respect and then giving innumerable examples. Louie Anderson, like a host of male and female heavyweights, uses his size to evoke laughter. A few, like Bob Newhart, reveal their quirks in skits rather than merely telling us straight out what those quirks are. Then there is also the physical comedy. Gallagher and his ilk smash watermelons and reduce indestructible furniture to kindling. David Letterman has full paint cans tossed seven stories to splatter in the streets below. Others volunteer to juggle eggs and, being unable to juggle at all, drop every one. We do not laugh just because someone breaks eggs or talks about his own liberal poundage; but when these things are put in the right context, we laugh uproariously. Good stand-up artists show their virtuosity by getting us to laugh at the most unlaughable situations.

Poe differed from the stand-ups in a variety of ways, both in personality and in material. Although often depicted as a timid man, Poe did face audiences—but as a lecturer not a humorist. In the reviews of his lectures, sometimes listeners noted beauty of expression, the singsong pattern of his reading, the dignity he exuded as a poet; but no one ever accused him of humor. Unlike the stand-up comedians, Poe did not use his own faults to evoke humor. Nor did he react well when others pointed to perceived failings. At Charlottesville in 1826, after Poe had read a lengthy story of his to friends, they—according to Thomas Good Tucker, who was present—"spoke lightly of its merits, and jokingly told him that his hero's name, 'Gaffy' occurred too often" (Sherley, 431). After this chance occurrence, they began to call him "Gaffy" Poe, a name that stuck. The immediate criticism caused the young Poe to throw the story immediately into the fire before his friends could stop him. Tucker remembered that the lost tale "was intensely amusing, entirely free from his usual sombre coloring and sad conclusions" (Sherley, 431). In person, Poe neither sought nor was able to create the right atmosphere for humor. He could not, like the stand-ups, walk into a room and have people rollicking. He could, however, command their attention. He might have been a Charlie Chaplin character, but without the funny walk or amusing movements.

In writing, however, Poe's attempts at humor abound. He dealt with at least three types of humor in writing, none of which necessarily causes laughter: satire, the hoax, and the grotesque. Whereas Mark Twain, the best-known humorist of the nineteenth century, also uses these same forms, he does so in an entirely different way, one that makes his audience laugh. For Poe, these techniques were instruments of wit and therefore served to show an incisive mind rather than provide a way to laugh. As a consequence, then, he did not try to make his humor accessible to all. Only those whose insightfulness allowed them to see the wit he used would be entertained by it. Others, often those he satirized, missed it entirely, and when it was called to their attention, they would sometimes react with great anger, seeing Poe's derision as unfair criticism. One has only to read "Berenice," with its grotesque dentistry as a conclusion, to realize that for Poe, gothic horror and parody were borderless transparencies that significantly overlapped each other.

Because Poe's humor is not self-deprecating, because it is not—as most stand-up humor is—easily accessible, and because it is not underwritten by a man who looks funny, both readers and scholars, like some of those targets of the humor, tended to discount its existence at all. Looking at Poe and his work from three different perspectives can help us feel comfortable in proclaiming that the humor exists, that its tone is biting, and that Poe used such humor from the beginning of his writing career until its end in 1849.

The historical perspective allows us to look at observations by Poe and his contemporaries about the nature of his writing. While these evidences of Poe's humorous side have been around for a century and a half or more, most of us are just becoming aware of them in our effort to recover something of the lost Poe. Not only did the young Poe read a humorous tale to his classmates at the University of Virginia, but once he arrived at West Point in 1830, he also regaled the cadets there with a work he composed consisting of satiric verses: "One of the first things of the kind that he perpetrated was a diatribe in which all of the officers of the Academy, from Colonel Thayer down, were duly if not favorably noticed" (Gibson, 755). While we do not have the entire work, the single extant verse suggests a work like Alexander Pope's *The Dunciad*. And indeed, it is helpful to think of most of Poe's humor in that vein.

The plans for "The Tales of the Folio Club"—discussed by Poe as early as 1833 but alluded to again and again until his September 1836 letter to Harrison Hall—give us the earliest glimpse of the writer as satirist. In the letter he lays out the plan for seventeen members of the club to read tales at their monthly meeting. According to Poe, not only were the tales of a "bizarre and generally whimsical character" but the criticisms of the members of each tale were "intended as a burlesque upon criticism generally" (Ostrom, 1:103–4).

One of the tales presumably in the collection was "Berenice," which the *Southern Literary Messenger* published in March 1835. By the end of April, Poe gave the owner of that journal his view of both the nature of popular publishing and what must be included in successful magazines:

> The history of all Magazines shows plainly that those which have attained celebrity were indebted for it to articles *similar in nature—to Berenice*—although, I grant you, far superior in style and execution. I say similar in *nature*. You ask me in what does this nature consist? In the ludicrous heightened into the grotesque: the fearful coloured into the horrible: the witty exaggerated into the burlesque: the singular wrought out into the strange and mystical. (Ostrom, 1:57–58).

The statement is as near an artist's credo about the necessity of humor as we have from Poe. Others recognized that he practiced what he preached. When "Lionizing" came out in the May 1835 issue of the *Messenger,* the editor Edward Spearhawk called it "an inimitable piece of wit and satire" (Thomas and Jackson, 155). Apparently Poe himself got into the act, noting his own powers of humor for the *Baltimore Republican,* in which he said that "Lionizing" was "a piece of burlesque, which displays much reading, a lively humor, and an ability to afford amusement or instruction" (Thomas and Jackson, 157). James Kirke Paulding also noted the high comedy of the piece in a letter to the magazine's publisher (Jackson, "Letter," 41).

When "Hans Phaal, A Tale" graced the magazine's pages, it was described by the the Charleston, South Carolina, *Daily Courier* as "one of the most exquisite specimens of blended humor and science that we have ever perused" (Thomas and Jackson, 160, 162). At the same time the *Baltimore Republican* was calling it "a capital burlesque upon ballooning" (Thomas and Jackson, 160). Other tales like "Loss of Breath," "Bon-Bon," and even "Politian" received reviews from New York, Washington, Richmond, and Charleston that note their natures as burlesques or extravaganzas or their adventures into graphic humor.

In writing John Pendleton Kennedy on 11 February 1836, Poe explains his intentions in producing such material:

You are nearly, but not altogether right in relation to the satire of some of my Tales. Most of them were *intended* for half banter, half satire—although I might not have fully acknowledged this to be their aim even to myself. "Lionizing" and "Loss of Breath" were satires properly speaking—at least so meant—the one of the rage for Lions and the facility of becoming one—the other of the extravagancies of Blackwood. (Ostrom, 1:83–84).

That Kennedy recognized satire when he saw it should be no surprise. Like many Southern writers of the time, he claimed the eighteenth century English satirists—Addison, Steele, Johnson, Dryden, Pope, and Swift—as literary progenitors. Closer to home, he, like Poe, had seen the spirit of such satire kept alive by William Wirt. Kennedy himself had been a partner in the *Red Book,* an irregular Baltimore publication that made fun of individuals and institutions in the 1820s. While his *Swallow Barn* was satire in its most gentle form, in 1840 he gave vent to sharper feelings in *Quodlibet,* a political tract to which he did not attach his name as author. All these rollicking works had some of the difficulties of in-jokes—that is, the references they made to external conditions required the habitual vocabulary of a particular group if they were to be entirely understood.

Did Poe's satires have all the difficulties of in-jokes too? At least prospective publishers thought so. In a 3 March 1836 letter to Thomas White, publisher of the *Southern Literary Messenger,* James Kirke Paulding said the Harpers had decided not to publish Poe's stories in book form. They felt the obscurity of reference would keep readers from "enjoying the fine satire they convey" (Aderman, 174). Poe expected his audience to be as knowledgeable as he was about literary matters and to catch passing references. The Harpers were afraid that this elitism would keep the works from being popular enough to become profitable in book form. But, if the public were bound to miss the jokes, why could the public not be satirized? They would not even realize they were the focus of the fun. It was a point that had not escaped Poe.

He took the public in at every turn. "Hans Pfaal," "The Balloon Hoax," and *Arthur Gordon Pym* all fooled portions of his audience. Only the cognoscenti recognized the jokes. Although the fact *Pym* was a hoax escaped the *Morning Courier,* the *New York Gazette,* and Poe's favorite dunderhead, Lewis Gaylord Clark, Horace Greeley's paper, the *New-Yorker,* recognized the novel's understated manner and its presentation of the wildest fictions as truth. Richard Locke, a hoaxer himself, while denying his own hand in *Pym,* recognized both its nature and Poe's work. Outraged at Poe's attempt,

William E. Burton said in his *Gentleman's Magazine,* "A more impudent attempt at humbugging the public has never been exercised" (Thomas and Jackson, 254). Americans were not the only ones who failed to recognize when they were being had. George Putnam quoted Mr. D. Appleton as saying that in England, "the grave peculiarity of the title and of the narrative misled many of the critics as well as ourselves, and whole columns of these new 'discoveries,' including the hieroglyphics (!) [*sic*] found on the rocks, were copied by many of the English country papers as sober historical truth" (Thomas and Jackson, 255).

Not all who read Poe's tales found them humorous or even witty, however. When Lea and Blanchard published *Tales of the Grotesque and Arabesque* in December 1839, the *Boston Notion* found them wild, "without anything of elevated fancy or fine humor to redeem them (Thomas and Jackson, 282). Where straitlaced Bostonians saw no humor, Morton McMichael, who reviewed the *Tales* for *Godey's Ladies' Book,* noted that Poe "possesses a fine perception of the ludicrous, and his humorous stories are instinct with the principle of mirth" (Thomas and Jackson, 285). The *Southern Literary Messenger* even listed two tales it said were specimens "of the author's power of humor, 'The Man that was used Up,' and 'Why the Little Frenchman wears his hand in a Sling'" (Thomas and Jackson, 285).

By 1843 Poe was not only publishing solutions to puzzles and crafting mysteries that excited the imagination, he was showing off that ripping humor that made him both admired and hated. Reviewing a pamphlet containing "The Murders in the Rue Morgue" and "The Man That Was Used Up," George Lippard noted that the stories developed "the analytic talent of the gifted author, as well as his powers of cutting and sarcastic humor" (Thomas and Jackson, 430). That same autumn, Poe continued in the comic vein by publishing "Raising the Wind; or, Diddling Considered as One of the Exact Sciences" in the *Saturday Courier,* recently identified by Kent Ljungquist as a parody on lecturers Poe had known for over a decade. The next year, the put-ons "The Spectacles" and "The Balloon Hoax" appeared, as did "Mesmeric Revelation," which deceived people on this continent and in Europe.

Poe displayed throughout his career a spirit of satire and derision in his work that would have made Swift proud. His biting humor not only found a place in fiction but created mostly animosity when he used it in his six-part series on the New York literati in *Godey's Ladies' Book* in 1846. The last of Poe's attempts at extravagance and humor did not appear until 1849, the year of his death. "Von Kempelen and His Discovery," a hoax on the gold rush of 1849, and the humorous sketch "X-ing a Paragrab" both appeared in that final year. The historical perspective on Poe's humor, then,

informs us of its pervasiveness. Poe used that satiric edge consistently from
the beginning of his career to the end, never failing to wield it as a weapon
as well as a vehicle for entertainment.

In conjunction with a look at the historical perspective, the critical
perspective on Poe needs to be revisited. It may be that the critical perspective of Poe that Rufus Wilmot Griswold and others set in the mid-nineteenth century has helped block our view of Poe's humor, but if we can partially blame that kind of literary criticism for obscuring Poe the satirist and
hoaxer, we can also thank another brand of criticism for leading a charge to
uncover those gifts in this century.

Perhaps the easiest measure of the success of that movement is the
inclusion of Poe in *The Oxford Book of Humorous Prose*. While admitting
that "Poe was hardly a key figure in the development of humorous prose in
the United States," editor Frank Muir recognizes a body of humorous work
in the Poe canon. The first critic this century to note Poe's humor was
James Southall Wilson, who saw the parodic intention of the plans of the
Folio Club in 1931 (Wilson, 217). In recent years, however, there has been
an avalanche of material on humor in Poe. In 1983 David Galloway made
a collection of what he called comedies and satires and persuaded Penguin
Books to publish *The Other Poe*. In his critical introduction, Galloway says
the nineteen pieces that comprise the collection are not the only ones be-
traying Poe's satiric outlook. In the same year *The Other Poe* appeared,
Dennis Eddings published *The Naiad Voice: Essays on Poe's Satiric Hoaxing*.
He includes fifteen essays (by as many authors), which claim to find some
kind of humor or hoaxing in pieces as diverse as "Ligeia," "The Assignation,"
"The Imp of the Perverse," "The Angel of the Odd," "Hans Pfaal," *Arthur
Gordon Pym*, "Tarr and Fether," and "The Island of the Fay." Others have
independently suggested irony in "Eiros and Charmion," bugaboo in "The
Man That Was Used Up," satiric vampirism in "Berenice," and hoaxing in
"The Masque of the Red Death." By listing a number of critical materials,
I do not mean to endorse them as a group; but when added to the testimony
of history, the critical perspective verifies the perception of a pervasive humor in Poe's work. *A Companion to Poe Studies*, edited by Eric W. Carlson
and published in 1996, contains Stuart and Susan F. Levine's "Comic Satires
and Grotesques: 1836–1849," which covers the period encompassing Poe's
effective literary career. Their bibliography enumerates over thirty items.
Notably, a whole other class of fiction—the balloon hoaxes, the scientific
hoax of Von Kempelen and M. Valdemar, and "Melonta Tauta," the science
fantasy—appear in a different article in the same book ("The Scientific Fiction and the Landscape Sketches," by David E. E. Sloane and Michael J. Pettengell), while "Hop-Frog" is dealt with in yet a third category. Clearly, criti-

cal interest in Poe's humor can be identified as a standing category for the analysis of his canon.

Finally, the psychological perspective can be added to the historical and critical approaches to help achieve a triangulation of Eddie the stand-up. Since Marie Bonaparte, there has been no shortage of material viewing Poe from a psychological perspective. There are, however, few attempts to look at the psychological causes of humor in Poe's work. One such work, Paul Lewis's article "Poe's Humor: A Psychological Analysis," provides important insight to understanding the nature of the humor and its relationship to the overwhelming horror in some of Poe's work. Lewis claims, appropriately it seems to me, that to see Poe only as an elitist whose jokes could not be grasped by a general audience is to sell him short. He does not deny this elitist side of Poe, but he sees a "broader, more universal, less intellectual humor that screams out from the center of Poe's work" (532).

Lewis's contention is that humor and fear have a special relationship in Poe's tales. Humor, taken to its limits, leads readers to fear. "Over and over, when humor fails, we are left with images of fear: the raven's shadow, the howling cat, the putrescent corpse, or the fallen house" (Lewis, 535). This change occurs, he contends, in "The Premature Burial," "Hop Frog," "The Black Cat," "Ligeia," "Facts in the Case of M. Valdemar," and *Arthur Gordon Pym.* In "The Black Cat" and "Ligeia," Lewis argues that our first impressions of the narrators are half comic. "We are led gradually away from this humor into an expanding horror of men driven to acts of obscene cruelty" (Lewis, 537). The confrontation between humor and horror occurs differently in "Hop Frog," where cruelty and joking commingle. "What happens in this tale is not just that cruel jokers are destroyed by a cruel joke but that joking itself gives way to horror, as the extreme cruelty of the joke destroys its ability to continue functioning as a joke" (Lewis, 536). The appeal of Lewis's psychological insight is that it rings true. Fear and humor are inextricably linked. One can see this in hospitals and funeral parlors, in the grim humor with which people pass the time while a threat of a devastating storm or a flood nears. Watching the evening news almost any day will allow informal verification of it. What he says about Poe, then, is not that we need to examine Poe's psyche but that we need to take more seriously Poe's understanding of how the psyches of his readers would operate.

Our investigation of Eddie in light of the stand-up tradition and in light of critical, historical, and psychological insights leads to five summary observations about his status as a humorist. First, Poe's humor was not the lighthearted banter or physical comedy experiences most often found on television or in comedy clubs. Second, the tone of Poe's humor in which he laughs at or fools his characters or his audience is more like that of Allen

Funt with his *Candid Camera* than that of the stand-ups. It is more *laughing at* people than leading them to laugh along with him. This habit of holding individuals and groups up to derision can explain some of the hostile reactions Poe's reviews and portraits of literati received. It undoubtedly explains some of the spleen Rufus Griswold displayed when he wrote about Poe. Third, the humor in Poe's work is not wholly or even primarily the work of inventive twentieth-century critics. Poe himself and those who read his work noticed the satire and the biting nature of his reviews. Fourth, what critics have done is begin to trace the threads of humor in Poe's works so that students can examine them more closely. Finally, through psychological work, commentators have also begun to examine reactions to Poe's writing. These reactions point to a potent mixture of horror and humor that keeps drawing new readership in every generation.

Works Cited

Aderman, Ralph M., ed. *The Letters of James Kirke Paulding.* Madison: University of Wisconsin Press, 1962.

Blythe, Hal, and Charlie Sweet. "Poe's Satiric Use of Vampirism in 'Berenice.'" *Poe Studies* 14 (1981), 23–24.

Carlson, Eric W., ed. *A Companion to Poe Studies.* Westport, CT: Greenwood, 1996.

Eddings, Dennis W. *The Naiad Voice: Essays on Poe's Satiric Hoaxing.* Port Washington, NY: Associated Faculty Press, 1983.

Fisher, Benjamin Franklin, IV. "Poe, Blackwood's, and 'The Murders in the Rue Morgue.'" *American Notes & Queries* 12 (1974), 109–11.

Gibson, T. W. "Poe at West Point." *Harper's Monthly* 35 (1867), 754–56.

Jackson, David K. "A Poe Hoax Comes Before the U.S. Senate." *Poe Studies* 7 (1974), 47–48.

———. "An Uncollected Letter of James Kirke Paulding." *Poe Studies* 15 (1982), 41.

Kemp, Anthony. "The Greek Joke in Poe's 'Bon-Bon.'" *American Literature* 56 (1984), 580–83.

Kock, Christian. "The Irony of Oxygen in Poe's 'Eiros and Charmion.'" *Studies in Short Fiction* 22 (1985), 317–21.

Levine, Stuart, and Susan F. "Comic Satires and Grotesques: 1839–1849." In *A Companion to Poe Studies,* ed. Eric W. Carlson. Westport, CT: Greenwood, 1996, 129–18.

Lewis, Paul. "Poe's Humor: A Psychological Analysis." *Studies in Short Fiction* 26 (1989), 531–46.

Ljungquist, Kent P. "'Raising More Wind': Another Source for Poe's 'Diddling' and Its Possible Folio Club Context." *Essays in Arts and Sciences* 26 (October 1997), 59–70.

Mabbott, T. O. "On Poe's 'Tales of the Folio Club.'" *Sewanee Review* 36 (1928), 171–76.

Mead, Joan Tyler. "Poe's 'The Man That Was Used Up': Another Bugaboo Campaign." *Short Studies in Fiction* 23 (1986), 281–86.

Ostrom, John Ward, ed. *The Letters of Edgar Allan Poe.* 2 vols. 1948. Reprint, with supplement, New York: Gordian, 1966.

Poe, Edgar Allan. *The Other Poe: Comedies and Satires.* Edited and with an introduction by David Galloway. New York: Penguin Books, 1983.

Pitcher, Edward W. R. "'To Die Laughing': Poe's Allusion to Sir Thomas More in 'The Assignation.'" *Studies in Short Fiction* 23 (1986), 197–200.

Richard, Claude. "The Tales of the Folio Club and the Vocation of Edgar Allan Poe as Humorist," trans. Mark L. Mitchell. *University of Mississippi Studies in English* 8 (1990), 185–98.

Ruddick, Nicholas. "The Hoax of the Red Death: Poe as Allegorist." *Sphinx* 4 (1985), 268–76.

Sherley, Douglas. "Old Oddity Papers, IV: Edgar Allan Poe While a Student at the University of Virginia." *Virginia University Magazine* 19 (1880), 376–81, 426–45.

Sloane, David E. E., and Michael J. Pettengell. "The Science Fiction and Landscape Sketches." *A Companion to Poe Studies,* ed. Eric W. Carlson. Westport, CT: Greenwood, 1996, 257–75.

Stauffer, Donald Barlow. *The Merry Mood: Poe's Uses of Humor.* Baltimore: Enoch Pratt Free Library & The Edgar Allan Poe Society, 1982. [This is a twenty-three-page pamphlet.]

Thomas, Dwight, and David K. Jackson. *The Poe Log: A Documentary Life of Edgar Allan Poe, 1809–1849.* Boston: G. K. Hall, 1987.

Toner, Jennifer DiLalla. "The 'Remarkable Effect' of 'Silly Words': Dialect and Signature in 'The Gold Bug.'" *Arizona Quarterly* 49 (1990), 1–20.

Foreign Language
and American Humor

Mark Twain and the Funny Magic
of the German Language

Holger Kersten

"Conſtantinopolitaniſcherdudelſackspfeifenmachersgeſellſchaftl"

"Nihiliſtendynamittheaterkäſtchensſprengungsattentatsver-
ſuchungen!"

"Transvaaltruppentropentransporttrampelthiertrei-
bertrauungsthränentragödie!"

"Mekkamuſelmannenmaſſenmenchenmörder-
mohrenmuttermarmormonumentenmacher!"

These are the magic words that Hank Morgan, Mark Twain's Connecticut Yankee in King Arthur's Court, uses in a pivotal scene of the
novel.[1] They represent the key elements of a carefully calculated performance with which Twain's Yankee tries to impress his Arthurian audience.
With his knowledge of nineteenth-century entertainment, Morgan is well
versed in the art of manipulating his gullible spectators. Using Latin chants,
imposing gestures, and real as well as verbal fireworks, he transforms what
is in reality a minor repair job into a breathtaking miracle. He is very much
aware of the effects he wants to produce and has a keen sense of the importance of this moment. With the intention of establishing himself more thoroughly as the kingdom's most powerful magician, he leaves nothing to coincidence.

199

It is before this backdrop that the selection of the German language for his magical incantations becomes highly significant. Magical incantations are characterized by unusual words, preferably from a language other than the vernacular. The utterances require no obvious meaning, but their effect is enhanced by a resonant quality of the words, which heightens the feeling of mystery that the magician wants to convey. Traditionally, Latin or Hebrew, in combination with unidentifiable words, formed the basis for magical spells. Twain, however, found it more appropriate to use German, a language with which he was more familiar than any other—except English—because, in one form or another, he had been exposed to it throughout his life. By the time *A Connecticut Yankee* was published, he was able to exploit the language with great skill.

Ever since the appearance of *A Tramp Abroad,* with its appendix on "The Awful German Language," critics have commented on the hilarious aspects of Twain's preoccupation with German. Paying attention only to his ironic observations, they concluded that the writer saw the language as nothing but ridiculous and inefficient. The chapter preceding the Yankee's use of the German words seems to confirm this view. Commenting on his companion Sandy's interminably long sentences, Hank Morgan refers to her as "the Mother of the German Language" (212):

> She had exactly the German way: whatever was in her mind
> to be delivered, whether a mere remark, or a sermon, or a
> cyclopedia, or the history of a war, she would get it into a
> single sentence or die. Whenever the literary German dives
> into a sentence, that is the last you are going to see of him
> till he emerges on the other side of the Atlantic with the
> verb in his mouth. (213)

Even though this may seem funny to readers, Hank Morgan does not see it as a reason for laughter. He is impressed by it and unconsciously takes "the very attitude of reverence," an experience that, only a little later, makes him use this powerful instrument himself. Morgan's natural speech, contrasting so vividly with that of Arthurian England, had bedazzled Sandy, prompting her to call it "golden phrases of high mystery" and "great and mellow-sounding miracles of speech." Yet he decides that his show of force requires a more powerful tool: only the "devastating syllables" borrowed from the German language can produce the effect he envisions.

Hank's verbal explosions operate on two levels. In the context of the narrative, they serve to depict him as a magician in possession of the most potent magic formulas. As his listeners hear the words, they simultaneously witness the miracle and are convinced of the immense power this magician wields. Modern readers may be susceptible to the power of sound in the rhythmical litanies of religious groups, in dialogue chants used by prisoners or slaves, in language games played by children, or in the persuasive cadences of political speech making. While they can obviously never be as awed as the Arthurian masses, they are quite likely a little astonished at the sight of these verbal monstrosities that are so hard to decipher. It is not only the incredible length of the words that makes the reading so difficult but also the fact they are set in "black letter" type, as gothic German script is often called. This device very effectively underscores their magical quality, especially since the mystique of language has for a long time been based on the belief that cryptic writing contains special powers that can only be understood by the initiated.

However, intimidation is not the only reaction that this performance produces. There can be no doubt that the interminable words provoke a humorous response in readers because they have the features of an amusing stimulus: they have a funny look and, presumably, a funny sound. Unintelligible words and phrases have always had their place in human speech and may represent a desire to exploit the acoustic potential of language. Even without a specific meaning they appeal to readers because of their nonsensical qualities, which often translate into comical effects. Most important, however, Hank Morgan's words work so efficiently because they provide an intertextual link to Twain's comments on the German language in *A Tramp Abroad*. In this way they constitute an implicit reference to the stereotypes about the language and its speakers that have been prevalent among Americans for a long time. While readers definitely experience a humorous moment with the incantation, Hank Morgan, too, seems to enjoy himself thoroughly in this specific situation. From the way he dramatizes this spectacle, it is obvious he feels great about showing up his antagonist Merlin and impressing the ignorant people of the strange world he has been thrown into. "It was a great night, an immense night," he says at the end of his performance. "There was reputation in it. I could hardly get to sleep for glorying over it" (224).

In his enjoyment of his own calculated delivery of German words, Hank Morgan resembles a curious character in Mark Twain's *Roughing It:* Mr. Ballou. Both characters delight in the mere sound of the words they use and completely disregard their actual meaning:

> What Mr. Ballou customarily meant, when he used a long
> word, was a secret between himself and his Maker. . . . His
> one striking peculiarity was his Partingtonian fashion of

loving and using big words for their own sakes, and independent of any bearing they might have upon the thought
he was purposing to convey. . . . If a word was long and
grand and resonant, that was sufficient to win the old man's
love, and he would drop that word into the most out-of-
the-way place in a sentence or a subject, and be as pleased
with it as if it were perfectly luminous with meaning.[2]

As a matter of fact, this characterization does not only bring to mind Hank
Morgan. It bears a resemblance to Twain himself and to his fascination with
long German words—an interest that reached its first climax during his initial
sojourn in Germany, in 1878. In the same way other tourists collect bric-a-
brac, Twain seems to have intently collected the curiosities of the German
language—a fact to which his 1878 notebooks, as well as *A Tramp Abroad*'s
appendix, bear ample witness.[3] In this connection, it is notable that his
fondness for long words was not restricted to German alone. In his analysis
of Twain's vocabulary, Robert Ramsay observed a general predilection for
compounds and word combinations, and he claims it was this fondness that
predestined him "to fall in love with the German language."[4]

At the time he was working on *A Connecticut Yankee*, German
matters were again very much on Twain's mind: he organized a German class
that, in 1887, almost ten years after his family's trip to Germany, met at regular intervals at his house. This activity is reflected in the numerous occurrences of German in his notebooks of that period and in the short three-act
play "Meisterschaft," which grew out of the class.[5] He toyed with the idea of
writing a play about the Franco-German War and on several occasions gave
lectures and readings using material from *A Tramp Abroad*.[6]

Among the many observations Twain records in the appendix of *A
Tramp Abroad*, one observation has not received the attention it deserves,
although it is necessary for a complete and adequate appraisal of his views.
"The *sound* of the words is correct," he claims in the section on the virtues
of the German language; "it interprets the meanings with truth and exact-
ness; and so the ear is informed, and through the ear, the heart" (616). In
relation to all the playful criticism Twain heaps on the language, this
statement seems short and insignificant. But it is important to keep in mind
that Twain's publisher wanted *A Tramp Abroad* to be a funny book—a true
successor to *The Innocents Abroad*. Since positive statements lend themselves
less well to humorous intentions than ironic remarks, it is hardly surprising
that Twain worked his grievances against the German language for all they
were worth while allowing only minimal space to praising remarks. Twain

himself, however, seems to have believed entirely in what he said about the strong points of German. He explained,

> There are some German words which are singularly and powerfully effective. For instance, those which describe low-ly, peaceful, and affectionate home life; those which deal with love . . . those which deal with outdoor Nature . . . in a word those which deal with any and all forms of rest, re-pose, and peace; . . . and lastly and chiefly, in those words which express pathos, is the language surpassingly rich and effective. There are German songs which can make a stran-ger to the language cry. (615)

Within this characterization is a very strong personal tone, which manifests in the way Twain used the German language in his family circle. German had been part of the family experience ever since his wife Olivia began German lessons in 1871.[7] Three years later, when their second daughter Clara was born, the Clemenses hired a German nursemaid for her and their oldest child, two-year-old Susy,[8] and before the Clemens family left for their first European sojourn in 1878, they intensified their studies of the complex-ities of the language with the help of a new German nursemaid.[9] After their return from Europe, they tried to conserve as many of their language skills as possible by conducting some family communications in German. Olivia gave her children language lessons and included even little Jean: their third daughter, who was born after the family's return from Germany. Twain wrote a short poem in a mixture of German and English: "O du lieb' Kidit-chen / Du bist ganz bewitchin."[10] Twain once gave his wife a bouquet of roses accompanied by a note on which was written in German, "Liebes Geschenk on die Mamma."[11] In letters to family members he also used German words and phrases, many of them expressing affection. The fact that German was often used to express emotions found its supreme expression after Olivia Clemens's death: Twain ordered a German epigraph engraved on his wife's tombstone, which read, "Gott sei dir gnädig, O meine Wonne!"[12]

The magical quality German held for the entire Clemens family is best illustrated by the word "unberufen," whose meaning Twain recorded in his 1878 notebook: "Unberufen! & knock *under* the table or other wood 3 times—the superstition being that the evil spirits hear you say 'What fine weather it is!' They will immediately change it unless you ward it off [with] the invocation 'Unberufen!'"[13] What may at the time have appeared to Twain as a silly superstition eventually developed into a powerful formula the family used repeatedly during times of illness, especially shortly before Olivia died.[14]

But the magic of the German language worked for him in less touching and innocent ways too. It was, in a certain respect, Twain's secret code. In a humorous episode in *A Tramp Abroad,* Twain's fictitious travel companion, Harris, attempting to shield his partner—who was talking about what he called "pretty private matters"—from eavesdroppers, recommends: "Speak in German—these Germans may understand English."[15] In real life Twain did in fact sometimes resort to German to express something unsuitable for the times and the society he lived in. Swearing, for example, was one of the things that both his wife and a motherly friend objected to, and he tried to accommodate them.[16] Later, during his sojourn in Germany, he noticed how uninhibitedly Germans used swearwords in ordinary conversation, and he seems to have enjoyed this freedom of expression.

In his essay "The Awful German Language," Twain downplays the matter, claiming that German swearwords have "plenty of meaning, but the *sounds* are so mild and ineffectual that German ladies can use them without sin."[17] In the context of an incident from his home life, however, it becomes clear that this was Twain's own personal perception—one not necessarily shared by his wife, Olivia. In his *Autobiography* he remembers Jean's German nurse Eliza, who was "loaded to the eyebrows" with profanities.[18] It is quite obvious that he enjoyed the verbal outbreaks of the girl very much: "It grieves me," Twain writes, "that I have forgotten those vigorous remarks. I long hoarded them in my memory as a treasure."[19] Susy, in her biography of her father, records the expressions "O heilige Maria Mutter Jesus!" and "Ach Gott!"—the latter of which apparently became one of Jean's favorite oaths, that is, until her mother found out and prevailed on her daughter to abandon the custom.[20] But Twain himself did recall one of the German girl's curses and print it in his *Autobiography.* According to Twain, Eliza had a lot of trouble combing the children's hair and relieved her frustration with the help of strong language: "And when finally she was through with her triple job she always fired up and exploded her thanks toward the sky, where they belonged, in this form: 'Gott sei Dank! Ich bin schon fertig mit'm Gott verdammtes [*sic*] Haar!'"[21]

While these examples appear relatively harmless today, modern readers might think differently about those German words Twain recorded for their phonetic quality. Noting "Hamburg-Amerikanische Packet*fahrt* Actien Gesellschaft," he did not save the expression primarily for his collection of long words. The fact that he italicized *fahrt* makes it very clear he was interested in the effect it had on the English ear. Maybe it is not surprising that Twain paid special attention to words of this kind, for it was only two years before that he had written *1601,* the notorious piece of bawdry entirely based on similar vulgarities.[22] Apparently, the fact he was exposed to an atmosphere that seemed less concerned with moral propriety than his own culture reminded him of the limitations a nineteenth-century American writer had to face: "By far The [*sic*] *very* funniest things that ever happened or were ever said, are unprintable (in our day)," he complained in a notebook entry of May 1878. He then jotted down a few phrases to remind himself of three humorous incidents that came to his mind in this connection. Two lack a clear reference to their raunchy nature, but the third contains a German sentence that may have been the key to a story he had in mind: "Er ist in ihr aftern" (He [or, it] is in her posterior). Since the note on page 280 follows the words "The Burning Shame" on the previous page, Twain may have used the German language to conceal the point of the story.[23] For some reason Twain decided to cancel the sentence, but it reappears in its original form at the end of the year in another list of supposedly humorous but risqué topics.[24]

Many years later, when working on *A Connecticut Yankee,* Twain used bawdy material written in German. "Aus seinem After kommt ein grellendes poo-o-o-o!" (From his rear comes a hard Poo-o-o-o!), he jotted down in August 1887, and at the end of the month he repeats the sly wordplay on the German words "Fahrt" and "Konnt" that he had first noted shortly before his 1878 sojourn in Heidelberg.[25] Twain rationalized his interest in scatology by pointing to great literary predecessors like Rabelais and Boccaccio,[26] and in a letter to his friend William Dean Howells, Twain complained about the "sad, sad false delicacy" that made impossible what he considered one of the best things in literature—namely, obscene stories.[27] Yet he used the device of hiding racy allusion behind the smokescreen of the German language before he had even published his first book: in an 1866 contribution to the San Francisco *Golden Era,* Twain reported on a spiritualist séance in which a German participant addressed the presumed spirit in one long word that was supposed to represent a question: "Finzig stollen, linsowftterowlickterhairowfterfrowleinerubackfolderol?"[28] Twain knew that by appealing to the stereotypical conception his readers had of the German language and its endless words, he could amuse his audience; thus he created this word of fifty-three characters. But this was only part of the joke; the other part, a sly sexual reference, was concealed under a confusing spelling and reserved for the delectation of those of his readers who had a solid familiarity with German. Separated into its components, the fabricated word reveals its true identity as a line from a bawdy song or poem: "Links auf der Au liegt der Herr auf der Frau" (To the left, on the meadow, the gentleman lies on top of the woman).

Thus one can conclude that the "Awful German Language" was not so awful to Mark Twain after all. No one would deny that German was a source of frustration to him that fueled his humorous assaults, although to interpret his ironic comments as an attempt to denigrate Germany or its people would be an exaggeration. Yet it is also clear that this frustration does not represent his only reaction to the language, and may not even indicate his predominant feelings toward it. German was also an inspiration and a source of enjoyment for him. Much like Hank Morgan unlocking the dried-up fountain, Twain used the German language as a magic instrument. It put in his hands a topic that occupied him for a long period of his life and yielded one of his most popular essays; it enriched his and his family's ways of expressing themselves in a very personal way; and finally, it served him as a code for his interest in forbidden words and topics.

Notes

1. Mark Twain, *A Connecticut Yankee in King Arthur's Court,* ed. Bernard L. Stein (Berkeley: University of California Press, 1983), 221–22. Subsequent references to this and other works by Twain are given parenthetically in the text.

2. Mark Twain, *Roughing It,* ed. Harriet E. Smith and Edgar M. Branch (Berkeley: University of California Press, 1993), 180–81.

3. *Mark Twain's Notebooks & Journals, Vol. 2 (1877–1883)* [N&J2], ed. Frederick Anderson, Lin Salamo, and Bernard L. Stein (Berkeley: University of California Press, 1975), 82, 96, 98, 103, 109, 110; Mark Twain, *A Tramp Abroad* [TA] (Hartford, CT: American Publishing Company, 1888), 612.

4. Robert L. Ramsay, *A Mark Twain Lexicon* (Columbia: University of Missouri Press, 1938), lxvii, lxxix.

5. E. Hudson Long, *Mark Twain Handbook* (New York: Hendricks House, 1957), 213.

6. *Mark Twain's Notebooks & Journals, Vol. 3 (1883–1891)* [N&J3], ed. Robert Pack Browning, Michael B. Frank, and Lin Salamo (Berkeley: University of California Press, 1979), 369, 372, 392, 396, 433, 437, 444, 446.

7. Olivia Clemens to Samuel L. Clemens, 30 December 1871, Mark Twain Papers, University of California, Berkeley [MTP].

8. Samuel L. Clemens to Mary E. (Mollie) Clemens, 11 January 1874 [MTP]; Albert B. Paine, *Mark Twain: A Biography. The Personal and Literary Life of Samuel Langhorne Clemens* [MTB] (New York: Harper and Brothers, 1912), 509.

9. *N&J2*, 43; Justin Kaplan, *Mr. Clemens and Mark Twain* (New York: Simon and Schuster, 1983), 212.

10. *MTB*, 822, 824.

11. Susy Clemens, *Papa: An Intimate Biography of Mark Twain by His Thirteen-Year Old Daughter Susy*, ed. Charles Neider (Garden City, NY: Doubleday, 1985), 127; and *Mark Twain's Autobiography [MTA]*, ed. Albert Bigelow Paine (New York: Harper and Brothers, 1924), 167.

12. ("God be merciful to you, Oh, my joy!") *MTB*, 1223.

13. *N&J2*, 66.

14. *MTB*, 1082, 1216–17.

15. *TA*, 103 (chap. 11); cf. *N&J2*, 130.

16. *Mark Twain's Letters, Vol. 1 (1853–1866)*, ed. Edgar M. Branch, Michael B. Frank, and Kenneth M. Sanderson (Berkeley: University of California Press, 1988), 122, 134.

17. *TA*, 617 (appendix D).

18. Clemens does not identify the German nurse by name, but in Paine's biography she is called Eliza *(MTB*, 775).

19. *MTA*, 168.

20. Susy Clemens, *Papa*, 129.

21. [Thank God! I'm done with the goddamn hair!] Clemens decided not to translate this outburst *(MTA*, 169).

22. Mark Twain, *Date 1601, Conversation as It Was by the Social Fireside in the Time of the Tudors*, ed. Franklin J. Meine (Chicago: n.p., 1939; reprint, New York: Lyle Stuart, 1961).

23. For more information on the issue of "The Burning Shame," see Walter Kokernot, "'The Burning Shame' Broadside," *Mark Twain Journal* 29:2 (fall 1991), 33–35.

24. *N&J2*, 87, 280.

25. *N&J3*, 302, 310; cf. *N&J2*, 58.

26. *N&J2*, 87, 303.

27. Samuel L. Clemens to William D. Howells, 19 September [1877], *Selected Mark Twain–Howells Letters, 1872–1910*, ed. Frederick Anderson, William M. Gibson, and Henry Nash Smith (New York: Atheneum, 1968), 101.

28. Mark Twain, "Mark Twain a Committee Man," *San Francisco Golden Era*, 11 February 1866, p. 5, col. 6.

Works Cited

Aron, Albert W. "Mark Twain and Germany." *Monatshefte für deutsche Sprache und Pädagogik* (1925), 65–80.

Clemens, Susy. *Papa: An Intimate Biography of Mark Twain by His Thirteen-Year Old Daughter Susy.* Ed. Charles Neider. Garden City, NY: Doubleday, 1985.

Cracroft, Richard H. "'Exactly the German Way': Mark Twain's Comic Strategies with 'The Awful German Language.'" *Thalia: Studies in Literary Humor* 13:1–2 (1993), 11–21.

Crystal, David. "The Magic of Language." In *The Cambridge Encyclopedia of Language,* ed. David Crystal. Cambridge: Cambridge University Press, 1987, 8–12.

Hemminghaus, Edgar. *Mark Twain in Germany.* New York: Columbia University Press, 1939.

———. "Mark Twain's German Provenience." *Modern Language Quarterly* 6 (1945), 459–78.

Hibler, Leo von. "Mark Twain und die deutsche Sprache." *Anglia: Zeitschrift für englische Philologie* 65 (1940), 459–78.

Klett, Ada M. "'Meisterschaft' or The True State of Mark Twain's German." *American German Review* 7 (1940), 10–11.

Kokernot, Walter. "'The Burning Shame' Broadside." *Mark Twain Journal* 29:2 (fall 1991), 33–35.

Krumpelmann, John T. *Mark Twain and the German Language.* (L.S.U. Studies, Humanities, no. 3). Baton Rouge: Louisiana State University Press, [1953].

McIntosh, C. "Magic." In *The Encyclopedia of Language and Linguistics,* ed. R. E. Asher. Oxford: Pergamon Press, 1994.

Mitchell, Lee Clark. "Verbally *Roughing It:* The West of Words." *Nineteenth Century Literature* 44:1 (1989), 67–92.

Paine, Albert B. *Mark Twain: A Biography. The Personal and Literary Life of Samuel Langhorne Clemens.* New York: Harper and Brothers, 1912.

Ramsay, Robert L. *A Mark Twain Lexicon.* Columbia: University of Missouri, 1938.

Schultz, John Richie. "New Letters of Mark Twain." *American Literature* 8 (1936), 47–51.

Sewell, David R. *Mark Twain's Languages: Discourse, Dialogue, and Linguistic Variety.* Berkeley: University of California Press, 1987.

Twain, Mark. *A Connecticut Yankee in King Arthur's Court.* Ed. Bernard L. Stein. Berkeley: University of California Press, 1983.

———. *Date 1601, Conversation as It Was by the Social Fireside in the Time of the Tudors.* Ed. Franklin J. Meine. Chicago: n.p., 1939; reprint, New York: Lyle Stuart, 1961.

———. *Mark Twain's Autobiography.* Ed. Albert Bigelow Paine. New York: Harper and Brothers, 1924.

——. *Mark Twain's Letters, Vol. 1 (1853–1866).* Ed. Edgar M. Branch, Michael B. Frank, and Kenneth M. Sanderson. Berkeley: University of California Press, 1988.

——. *Mark Twain's Notebooks & Journals, Vol. 2 (1877–1883).* Ed. Frederick Anderson, Lin Salamo, and Bernard L. Stein. Berkeley: University of California Press, 1975.

——. *Mark Twain's Notebooks & Journals, Vol. 3 (1883–1891).* Ed. Robert Pack Browning, Michael B. Frank, and Lin Salamo. Berkeley: University of California Press, 1979.

——. *Roughing It.* Ed. Harriet E. Smith and Edgar M. Branch. Berkeley: University of California Press, 1993.

——. *Selected Mark Twain–Howells Letters, 1872–1910.* Ed. Frederick Anderson, William M. Gibson, and Henry Nash Smith. New York: Atheneum, 1968.

——. *A Tramp Abroad.* Hartford, CT, 1888.

Wecter, Dixon. "Mark Twain as Translator from the German." *American Literature* 13 (1941/42), 257–63.

Weishert, John J. "Once Again: Mark Twain and German." *Mark Twain Journal* 12 (summer 1965), 16.

Huck Finn on His Best Behavior:
The Problem of Translation

James R. Papp

One November day soon after arriving in Bratislava, I was trying to find something interesting for my first-year English majors to grapple with and discovered the Raftsman Passage hibernating in a United States Information Service anthology. I xeroxed it, gave my students a little introduction, and told them to be ready to talk about it the following week. One of them recalled seeing a Slovak translation of this passage, xeroxed the translation, and distributed it to the rest of his group. Consequently, the following week I found them prepared to talk about not the passage itself but an echo of it. We compromised by agreeing to talk about neither the text in English nor the Slovak translation but about how the former had been transformed into the latter. I describe the latter as an echo because the Raftsman Passage is one of Twain's richest celebrations of frontier idiom and rhetoric, and the translation had drained most of the blood from it by transferring it into standard, grammatical, respectable literary Slovak.

This mediocre (though not unusually bad) translation, the original text itself and the way the text came up for discussion illustrate four crucial points about translation that those of us studying our domestic literature don't often realize:

(1) Translation is the common form through which literature becomes world literature.

(2) Nonnative speakers reading an English text in English bring to it their own linguistic perspectives. This is even more true for those readers seeing it through the glass of a translation they have previously read.

(3) A translated text—whether well or badly done—is an aesthetic object distinct from the original version read by domestic readers. As a result, an international literary work is a different thing from the national work of literature whose name it shares: it needs to be looked at differently.

(4) Finally, all this laborious linguistic translation is accompanied by an instantaneous cultural translation. An international work of literature adds something new to its readers' conceptions, but it can only do this by first being fitted into their preconceptions. A work completely foreign to their experiences communicates information but not understanding.

The transformation of *Adventures of Huckleberry Finn* into world literature, in this case into the Slovak language, is particularly illustrative because in the novel, Twain is aiming precisely at the portrayal of a peculiar time, place, and institution. He directs the portrayal at readers with a (more or less) shared language but (more or less) unshared moral and social philosophy; and he relies on not just the chunks of the language code but how the chunks are assembled and used by different people. It is also illustrative because Slovak society is so distant from the peculiar institution of slavery, and the Slovak language, particularly in literary form, is ill-equipped to reproduce the effect of the American language. The result—*Dobrodružstvá Huckleberryho Finna*—is necessarily a very distinct work from *Adventures of Huckleberry Finn*. Twain's original text is so demanding of some sort of accommodation from the target language of translation that if it were ever translated to anything like its potential, it would affect the strictures of the target language itself. Not so informal, not so much of an outcast, not so unintentionally piquant in his observations, Huck is on his best behavior in literary Slovak. But if he stuck around long enough, he would have (we can only hope) a bad influence on it.

Before looking at two Slovak translations of *Adventures of Huckleberry Finn,* I want to sketch out some of the problems translators grapple with and the solutions they find. Ideally, a translation changes the code while retaining the meaning. At a certain level—the level of shared words or concepts—this is reasonably simple. There are always certain objects, actions, and ideas common to both the source culture and cultures, even between the source and target languages. Especially in the modern global village, new concepts often flow from one language to another with little or no change in appearance. Slovak, for a thousand years something of a backwater language in the Hungarian empire, has been very receptive to loaned words: one verb form that accommodates borrowings has made possible *relaxovať* and *telefonavať;* describing their employment abroad for the summer or the next year, students use *babysitovať* (to work as an au pair in America) or *aupairovať* (to work as an au pair in Europe); a less savory export, found in *Dobrodružstvá Huckleberryho Finna,* is *lynčovať* (to lynch). Pure word-for-word equivalents offer no problems for the translator, excepting the pitfall inherent in words that keep their form but mutate in meaning (for example, the Slovak adjective *komfortný* is closer to "luxurious" than "comfortable").

Concept-for-concept equivalents are also a problem. The Slovak word for "mother" is *matka,* yet I have never heard a native speaker of Slovak use that word. As a Slavic language, Slovak is heavily dependent on diminutives, and "mother" is always diminutive—a *mama* or *mamička*—whether she is mine or yours or somebody else's. Another problem is concepts that are yoked together into one word in one language but not the other, including metaphors and puns. A colleague of mine was having trouble translating a modern Slovak fairy story into English because it balanced entirely on a pun in *stolička,* which means both "chair" and "molar." She wanted to skip that story. The author (an excellent translator of English children's poetry into Slovak who was quite ready to invent substitutions where need be) didn't see it as a problem. So my colleague was reduced to writing a long and (appropriately) tongue-in-cheek introduction to the story, explaining the lost pun.

The last major problem I want to mention, and the one dominating *Adventures of Huckleberry Finn,* occurs when the meaning is encoded not simply in the word or the grammar but the particular form the word or grammar takes. "Ain't" at a basic level means "am not" or "is not," but it also sends a message about the speaker who uses it, especially if we happen to be speakers who don't use this contraction and thus are objectively aware of its usage. This level of encoding is so important in *Adventures of Huckleberry Finn* that Twain even includes an "Explanatory" about it right after his famous "Notice." Readers supposing "that all these characters were trying to talk alike and not succeeding" would underestimate not only the author but the book.

To deal with these problems, translators work between two poles— one source oriented, the other target oriented. Should they be as faithful as possible to the forms of the original text, trying to give foreign readers a direct experience of them (though in a different language)—for instance, literally translating idioms even though they don't carry the same meaning or force in the new language? Or should translators try to reproduce the effect the text has on domestic readers, using the idioms of the target language that their readers are comfortable with and "understand," not only in a literal but an emotional sense? (As an acquaintance of mine who translated Saul Bellow's *Herzog* said, "First I translated it into Slovak, and then I translated it from Slovak into good Slovak.") The translations of *Adventures of Huckleberry Finn* I discuss here, Alfonz Bednár's of 1971 and Otakar Kořínek's of 1985, are somewhat at a loss on how to answer this question. (Significantly, both leave out the "Explanatory": they don't want to get into the issue of language at all.)

Slovak may be a good language for communicating different levels of affectionate informality, but it is terrible at communicating nonstandard deviation in speech. Its spelling (apart from very recent slang borrowings like *babysitovať*) is phonetic, and its six noun cases—unlike those of English—are fully preserved, so it is not subject to two of the most common errors that occur in English: spelling and declension. Its slang consists largely of diminutives, shortenings, and elisions, rather than rhetorical inventions. Literary Slovak represents dialect in dialogue but resists it in narrative. One hears different versions of the extent of its own Slovak dialect variants, but in a country of only five million people, variations seem slight by European standards. Standard Slovak, developed some 150 years ago from the dialect of Central Slovakia, was intended to be as neutral as possible. Slovaks understand each other (which not all European co-nationals do). Slovak and Czech, even Slovak and Serbo-Croat, are mutually understandable, for that matter.

Much of *Adventures of Huckleberry Finn* depends on a comparison between the deviation of sound and the deviation of sense, and this aspect is largely abandoned in *Dobrodružstvá Huckleberryho Finna*. Yet the later translation shows some improvement, which suggests that a future translation might be even better.

The first thing in both translations that strikes American readers is that Huck addresses readers in the formal voice, which in Slovak is used with strangers and betters. English dropped the informal second person some centuries ago; theoretically we speak to everyone in the formal. Yet grammatical formality—or distance—is a strange concept to connect with the otherwise irreproachably informal Huck. Both translations retain the rambling, hypotactic nature of Huck's speech (though rambling hypotaxis is such a common element of Slovak rhetoric, especially among academics, it is hard to determine what effect this produces on Slovak readers). The second thing that is striking (if not surprising) to American readers is the use of more or less standard Slovak for Huck's voice. In the earlier translation, by Bednár, Huck's sentences are grammatical and his words correctly spelled, and indeed the idiom is pretty standard, with little use of slang or unusual words or images. Literary Slovak does not have much use for such things.

This may be because literary Slovak is not particularly old. The century and a half since Ľudovit Štúr's regularization has allowed less time for a struggle to develop between spoken and written forms than has occurred in the use of English. Or it may be because the Slovak language is centrally controlled (by the Slovak Academy of Sciences) and spoken by a relatively small number of people who live in a somewhat compact area, value their distinction from neighboring ethnic groups, and see literature as a means of preserving their national culture rather than criticizing and questioning it.

Finally, the problems of correctness are different in Slovak than in English. Slovak contains fewer words; conjugations, though in several forms, are regular. As mentioned, spelling is phonetic, and the forms that cause trouble for speakers in specific areas of English because of their general disappearance (like pronoun declensions, for instance) are retained throughout Slovak. The eighteenth-century Latinate reforms of English (such as the stamping out of the intensive double negative) have no Slovak equivalent. Whereas an American might speak what we recognize as "uneducated English," an uneducated Slovak would simply speak his regional dialect. Uneducated Slovak is not possible in the same way uneducated English is, and having Americans speaking a particular nonstandard Slovak regional dialect in a translation would simply strike Slovaks as odd. Moreover, while a dialogue in dialect is one thing, a whole narration in dialect, or with slang, may represent something else in a country where, although people are often quite rude (especially if they work in service industries), they are rude in the formal voice.

Neither translator communicates very well Huck's uneducated and nonstandard linguistic personality. "She learned me" becomes "She taught me." "Drownded" is "drowned." Subjects have their correct number in the verb. Huck's characteristic double negatives have no effect because Slovak retains double negations. The later translator, Kořínek, does work harder against the obstacles, yet his efforts are limited. As in the original he misspells "civilize," but the most he can bring himself to do is to add an *s* before the *c* of *civilizovat*, rather than replace the *c* entirely.

Kořínek also includes more verbal panache that Huck actually has. "Miss Watson, a tolerable slim old maid, with goggles on" becomes "a pretty bony old maid with spectacles," rather than simply Bednár's "thin." "Honest injun" doesn't translate into Slovak, but Kořínek quickly follows it with a comparable Slovak idiomatic phrase, using the Slovak word for lying— *cigánit'* —that is based on the word for gypsy, much like our "to gyp." Kořínek's voice of Huck may be no less grammatically correct than Bednár's, but at least it is less formal and more idiomatic. In fact Bednár practices formalisms that are strange even for Slovak, sometimes rendering "Pap" as "my father" (*otec*) rather than the diminutive *tatko*. This may be a symptom of the kind of neutral, technical language that easily pops up in unskillful translations. Although it might not be appropriate to make Huck a regional Slovak, there is no reason to make him prissily correct.

Naturally those parts of Huck's speech that represent his regional accent are more or less meaningless to Slovak readers (or were before

Southern evangelical groups began sending missionaries to Slovakia as English teachers) and are dropped by both translators. "A-rab," for instance, becomes "Arab." Perhaps something would have been communicated by a source-based reproduction of these idioms, perhaps not. Certainly there is no sign of a target-based attempt to reproduce a regional accent by using, for example, village Slovak of some eastern region. Not at least with Huck and the other white characters in the book. Kořínek does insert mild misspellings into Jim's speech to suggest nonstandard pronunciation—"Who" (*kto*) becomes *kdo; Šalamún* (Solomon) becomes *Šalarmún*—and even a little nonstandard grammar, though nothing on the scale of the original. Such idioms as "dog my cats," literally *pesovaj moje mačky,* would be entirely puzzling to Slovaks. Yet are they any less puzzling to mainstream American readers?

Kořínek's choice is problematic because no linguistic outsiders exist in Bednár's translation, and in the later translation Jim is the only linguistic outsider. So while Jim mispronounces "Solomon" in the later translation, Aunt Sally's neighbor renders "Nebuchadnezzar" correctly in both translations. This parable of outsiders struggling with official versus real morality is thus still possible to figure out in the world literature *Adventures of Huckleberry Finn,* but without the linguistic frame, the message is not delivered with the same force and concision.

The very nature of American society, with its constant degradation of the formal language—matching its practical degradation of formal morality—is to some extent impossible to communicate in Slovak. How should one translate the transitional "Yes'm" and "No'm"? Both translators opt for the formal "Yes, madam" or "Yes ma'am." "Shucks," which is left out of the earlier translation, is rendered as the charming *tresky-plesky* (from onomatopoeic words for a bang and a flap) in the later. But the crucial resonance of the word "nigger" is missing in the Slovak *černoch,* or "black man"; to find a word with similar implications, one would have to search through local contexts, looking, for instance, at the difference between "Gypsy" and "Romany," a symptom of Slovakia's own equivalent to American racism and segregation. In a target-based translation, perhaps that would be the only possible way to recreate the same moral complication and emotional impact *Adventures of Huckleberry Finn* offers an American audience.

If Huck, his relations and neighbors, the people he meets along the way, and even knaves like the duke and the dauphin do not have their moral fluidity reflected in linguistic turmoil, and if the educated representatives of morality and leadership are not linguistically (and often ironically) distinguished from the rest of the rabble, do these translations at least retain another voice, that of Twain's knowing one behind the relative innocence and

gullibility of Huck? In some regards, Twain as author is a sort of Tom Sawyer to Huck's narrator: both Twain and Tom are cleverer but with more artistic and less practical ends in view. Slovak is capable of carrying some of
Twain's ironies but falls short with others, either not having available the
same double meanings in the same words or simply not having as many
words to represent shades in concepts. The confusion between orgies and
obsequies in the original is transformed to *orgie* and *obrady* (orgies and cere-
monies) in Bednár's translation and *orgie* and *liturgie* in Kořínek's. After the
rats are let loose by little Thomas Franklin Benjamin Jefferson Elexander
Phelps, Aunt Sally, instead of standing on the top of the bed "raising Cain,"
is "shouting with her whole throat" in Bednár's version and making "thunder
and lightning" in Kořínek's. The rats, instead of "doing what they could to
keep off the dull times for her," in both versions follow the idiom of
"wishing to shorten a long time for her." Again, the second translator shows
more skill by replacing an English pun with a Slovak-Hungarian one, in the
duke's name. In the earlier translation, "Bridgewater" is rendered as is, and
"Bilgewater," as the dauphin calls him, would be meaningless for a Slovak
audience. (Bednár also drops the pun of "dolphin" and "dauphin," though it
would be the same in Slovak.) Kořínek transforms "Bridgewater" into
"Buckingham," which the dauphin mispronounces as "Bugrišham," *bugriš*
being a quite rare word signifying a large, somewhat stout person. Both
rename the subject of Emmeline Grangerford's "Ode to Stephen Dowling
Bots, Dec'd"—Kořínek taking "bots" literally and rewriting it as "Stephen
Mucha" (Stephen Fly), and Bednár more obscurely calling him "Stephen
Dolomita," *dolomita* meaning "dolomite" in English. (Here I think each
misses the point, which is the ridiculous rhythm of the name to American
ears.)

Other transformations are not so successful. Huck's concise
summary of *Pilgrim's Progress*, "The statements was interesting, but tough,"
is rendered by Bednár as "It was very interesting, only not sufficiently
understandable" and (with a sense of the pun, but wanting perhaps to be too
clear) by Kořínek as "The reading was interesting, but tough for me, I didn't
understand everything." This I find peculiar because *tažký* in Slovak has a
similar double meaning as "tough" in English (both "heavy" and "difficult"),
and the genius of Twain in putting these words into Huck's mouth is in his
suggestion of the heavy obstreperousness of Bunyan lurking behind the mere
technical challenge. Another problematic rendition is the book's last line.
Bednár's response to Aunt Sally's promise (or threat) to "sivilize" Huck—"I've
already tried that"—is no more satisfying than Kořínek's "I've already experienced that." Neither can approach the naive adolescent poetry of "I been
there before."

Slovaks say that reading *Adventures of Huckleberry Finn* in English is a completely different experience than reading it in Slovak—a much more powerful one. From my brief look at these two translations, as well as the Raftsman Passage translation, I would agree that this is true. The Raftsman Passage of course is not included in either the 1971 or the 1985 translation I have been referring to. In the passage the two boasters and tall-tale tellers use standard Slovak—not only grammatical, but not particularly exaggerated, nor rhetorical and pseudo-Hebreo-Greco-Latinate in the mode of the Bible-thumping frontier preachers that the Child of Calamity and the Corpse-Maker might have used as their models. The term "corpse-maker" is rendered literally, with no reference to a war machine; such an interpretation takes away from the mechanistic power (and joke) of its epithets: "old original iron-jawed, brass-mounted, copper-bellied."

Most of my students read Czech or (if they can) Hungarian translations, claiming that these translations are more sophisticated, both because of the skill of the translators and because Czech is a more complex and literary language. Hungarian translations are especially useful because the language has a long and rich translation tradition and more idiomatic range than Slovak. The Slovak language has neither a long literary tradition nor the linguistic self-confidence to undercut itself in the way *Adventures of Huckleberry Finn* undercuts English. Slovaks, at least those of the older generations, look to literature as an expression of the best and tend to reject "bad language," claiming it makes a book nonliterary. (The vogue of Charles Bukowski among younger Slovaks may change that.)

Also relevant is the cultural issue of how *Adventures of Huckleberry Finn* has been treated critically in Slovakia. This is partly as a children's book, as can be seen from the illustrations of the 1971 edition, published by a children's publishing house. *The Adventures of Tom Sawyer* was first translated into Slovak in 1929; *Adventures of Huckleberry Finn* not until 1954 (Baštín, *Dejiny,* 257). Was it as a children's book that *The Adventures of Tom Sawyer*—before the Communist era—sold profitably? Would *Adventures of Huckleberry Finn* not have done as well commercially as an adult book? Or was it simply too difficult for a translator to handle properly? Curiously, it is to the Communist era that Slovaks owe both the translation of *Adventures of Huckleberry Finn* and its establishment in Slovak schools as a world classic. Or perhaps this is not so curious, for its official use under Communism was as a revelation of the cruelties and corruption of a capitalistic society. "Twain's humor served to point up errors in the American position of the individual in society when he was placed in a condition of hardship," according to a Slovak university textbook used under the old regime (Baštín, *A Short History,* 36–37). Likewise, a Czech textbook states that Twain was "one of the classic Americans who began in idealism to seek in their own country the standards of conduct which they were missing in Europe, yet in the end were forced to see the bitter truth about their country" (Oliveriusová, 24). Future translations, freed from these somewhat simplistic approaches, may be more sophisticated.

In fact there has been one post–Communism era translation, by Eliška Hulejová, undated but apparently published in 1991. Like the 1971 edition, it is packaged as a children's book. The illustrations show a mixture of gay nineties and roaring twenties clothing styles, and Huck himself is portrayed throughout as a somewhat pudgy lad wearing a sailor suit (no one could say that the market economy was a harbinger of good taste). This edition lacks both the "Explanatory" and the "Notice." In this translation Huck continues to address us in the formal voice. Hulejová uses Kořínek's *scivilizuje* but is so uncomfortable with it that she always puts it in quotation marks. The language is tolerably sprightly: Miss Watson is "a parched old maid," but no mention is made of her goggles. In addition, whole passages disappear, often the ones Americans would consider the most fun. In chapter 5, for instance, the conversation with Judge Thatcher is preserved, but the section concerning Jim and his hair ball is gone. Indeed, while Mark Twain's version has forty-two chapters, Hulejová's only has thirty-four. The Grangerfords are left out completely; so are Sherburn and Boggs, as well as anything unsavory, or interesting. As Slovaks often complain, under capitalism the price of everything has gone up (the Shakespearean Revival is now 50 cents instead of 25 cents), and you get less of it. The end of Communism has brought a new simplification of Huck.

Having examined the two complete translations, I believe Kořínek's, from 1985, is significantly superior to Bednár's (1971) work. Not simply a formal, technical, neutral rendition, Kořínek's attempts more accurately to portray the linguistic quirks of the original and to reproduce their aesthetic impact—to be both more source- *and* more target-oriented. Curiously, my perceptive and well-read student who supplied his colleagues with the translation of the Raftsman Passage and who loaned me both of these Slovak translations of *Adventures of Huckleberry Finn* prefers the earlier one. Perhaps this is because he is reading his language in the translations, and I am attempting to read my own. At any rate, the current translations of *Adventures of Huckleberry Finn* constitute a different book than Twain's original, and Slovak will need to become an older, more complex, and above all more inclusive (or decadent) literary language before its international and our national *Adventures of Huckleberry Finn* move closer together. When such a translation is done, which puts Huck and his world into an idiomatic Slovak context, this will not only deepen Slovak understanding of the American book but will have to make Slovaks *relaxovat* about their own language as well.

Works Cited

Baštín, Štefan, Jozef Olexa, and Zora Studená. *Dejiny anglickeja americkej literatúry* [A history of British and American literature]. Bratislava: Vydavateľ' stvo Obzor, 1993.

——. *A Short History of American Literature*. Bratislava: Univerzita Komenského, 1995.

Oliveriusová, Eva. *A Survey of American Literature*. Prague: Státní pedagogické nakladatelství, 1982.

Twain, Mark. *Dobrodružstvá Huckleberryho Finna*. Trans. Alfonz Bednár. Bratislava: Mladéletá, 1971.

——. *Dobrodružstvá Huckleberryho Finna*. Trans. Otakar Kořínek. Bratislava: Tatran, 1985.

——. *Huckleberry Finn*. Trans. Eliška Hulejová. Bratislava: Fortuna print, [1991?].

Linguistic Affinities:
Translating Bryce Echenique's
Lima Humor for Readers of English

Alita Kelley

(French and Spanish translations by Alita Kelley)

The influence of the writing of the United States of America on Spanish fiction during recent decades is readily admitted by critics and by the writers themselves. The debt to Faulkner is proclaimed proudly—Gabriel García Márquez calls him "my master" (90); Carlos Fuentes calls him "the only writer in the Western hemisphere who has faced up to [the] tragic proposition" (139) that history does not guarantee happiness or progress, while Jorge Luis Borges, whose postmodern humor antedates the concept of postmodernism by dating from the 1920s, once declared that the United States had turned "brutality into a literary virtue" (Vargas Llosa, 79). While Faulkner's work does not lack humor, criticism in Spanish not only neglects that aspect of his genius but whenever possible has chosen to ignore humor per se. One Hispanic critic has pointed out that two influential thinkers, Unamuno and Ortega y Gasset, could never forgive Cervantes for being a comic writer (Cueto, 37), and an expressed dislike of humor caused Peru's leading contemporary novelist, Mario Vargas Llosa, to continue insisting in his criticism (well-known to readers of Spanish) that the comic be seen as a falling off from literary greatness (Harss, 445–46)—even after he had published two acclaimed comic novels himself (Duncan, 135). The language that originated the modern novel does not lack humorous texts, and recent writers have been influenced by writing from the United States, but major problems exist when any text is translated into another language. The first novel by the Peruvian Alfredo Bryce Echenique will serve as an illustration of some of these problems.

The main protagonist of Bryce's *Un mundo para Julius* (A World for Julius) (1970) is a young boy who is eleven at the novel's end. Julius dotes on the stories of Mark Twain, whom he has read, no doubt, in Spanish translation, and when his adolescent brother gets drunk and starts destroying

Julius's room, the little boy's only comment is "my Mark Twains!" (468–69). The narrative voice in the novel shows the eventual influence of Mark Twain, and as late as the 1970s, when the book appeared, Bryce's narrator aroused critical interest by communicating in a regional and social dialect, instead of a standard written form of Spanish (Luchting, 17–18).

Translators of humorous texts are faced with two impossible acts—or "tasks," if one prefers Walter Benjamin's term, though the punning sense in the original German is unfortunately lost in English translation (de Man, 80). The first impossibility is the act of translation itself; the second is knowing whether something on the printed page is meant to be comic. The Scottish translation teacher Margaret Hart, referring to the semiotic theories of the phenomenologist Karl Bühler (453), has stressed that translators themselves, not realizing they are doing the impossible, do it anyway, while linguistic and representational schema go their separate ways (Innis, 34). Some years ago, I undertook to translate Bryce's first novel as part of a doctoral dissertation, ignorant of the fact that I was defying nature, since I had been earning a living as a commercial and technical translator for decades and had already published several literary translations. I became aware of the varying tenets of translation theory and the metaphysical niceties involved in the act while working on the critical part of my dissertation, after the translation itself was complete.

Along with translation theorist André Lefevere, I believe no intrinsic difference exists between literary and any other type of translation, and I have never felt a hierarchy in which practical, as opposed to literary translation, occupies a lower rung (Lefevere, Lecture). If a consensus ultimately arises on the value of a given translation, it can fall just as easily. As Lefevere says, "There is no court of appeal" (88). I do not believe that the person responsible for a translation, which I saw in a published text in South America, that has Emily Dickinson saying in Spanish that she never saw a Saracen and never saw the sea could cause as great an impact as another, fortunately caught in time, that was erroneously telling readers of the target language to test for an electric current with their thumbs.

The operation involved in all translation requires the translator to enable readers in the target language to understand, *insofar as is possible,* a text in the source language; but then, we must ask a Joycean "what about possible?" The cornerstone of possibility or impossibility of translation is an extension of the poststructural concept, arising from the arbitrary relation between signifier and signified, that the very nature of language itself makes absolute communication impossible, even when speaker and listener are using the same language. Some critics, including David Lodge, appear to feel that Bakhtin's theory of dialogism provides an answer to the poststructural dilemma (4, 90), but it is difficult to see why a continuous dialogic search for answers, with no assurance they will ever come, should be considered less bleak than absence of belief in either the possibility or the impossibility of absolute certainty. The fact that the deconstructive glass is half empty and the Bakhtinian glass is half full does not alter the drink one has left, and it was deconstructive theory that finally began to help reinstate the translator in English-speaking countries after almost two hundred years of academic banishment. Academic disciplines that use translations of foreign texts had been condemning the translator as performing an unworthy activity (Bassnett-McGuire, 4). The victim is finally being vindicated, since if she or he does not produce a "primary text" in the traditional concept of such, at least no one else can claim access to a direct linguistic pipeline to the infinite that allows them to produce one either (Eagleton, 73).

My selection of Bryce's first novel arose from my own surprise at its neglect: twenty years after its publication in Spanish, no English version had yet appeared. While I was working on the critical appreciation of the text, a translator signed a contract with a university press to publish the novel in English. Comparing translations can be an essential part of the recently recognized field (in some English-speaking universities) of translation theory. Such comparisons bring readers face to face with the second impossibility—knowing whether something on the printed page is meant to be comic.

I had laughed with almost every page of Bryce's text, but of the few articles of prior criticism—in Spanish, English, and French—that I found to exist as recently as 1992, none classified the text as comic. Only one critic refers to humor (Duncan, 120), and another mentions readers' occasional laughter (López-Baralt, 55). Nor is it certain that others who had translated the novel, into French and into English, had seen it as humorous. The first part of Bryce's text is called "The Original Palace," and the first sentence reads, "Julius nació en un palacio de la avenida Salaverry," which, word for word, translates as "Julius was born in a palace on Avenida Salaverry" (or "on Salaverry Avenue") (9). The French translator Albert Bensoussan, in a critical article, describes the residence as "a great palace, full of glorious memories of the past" (50), while the English version has Julius born, noncommittally, in "a mansion," and the structuralist critic Wolfgang Luchting equates the "original palace" with original sin (29).

Walter Nash, in *The Language of Humour,* states, "Humour nearly always supposes some piece of factual knowledge shared by humorist and audience" (4), but unfortunately, it is not necessary for the knowledge to be shared in order for words to be put into another language. Nash goes on to say that understanding a comic text requires readers to be "broadly informed," not only with scholarship but with things that might otherwise seem insignificant, "things that one ought to know before being allowed to board the Clapham omnibus" (4). A bus ride along the Descalzos–San Isidro route in Lima goes along Avenida Salaverry and is actually described, stop by stop, in one chapter of Bryce's novel (272–78). Readers who know Lima also know that the bus does not go by any palaces, much less ancient ones, and that Julius must have been born in a pretentious house typical of the Lima suburbia that came into being during the presidencies of Sánchez Cerro and Leguía. Such houses were built in the late 1920s or early 1930s—a time when, as the Peruvian critic Miguel Gutiérrez reminds us, the government first delivered Peru "to the rule of Yankee financial capital" (25). Readers learn of the relations of Julius's father's family with Sánchez Cerro (1894–1933) when mention is made, almost at the beginning of the novel, of the dinner set he gave them just before being assassinated (13). Many Lima readers will have used the word "palace" in the same sense as the narrator. My children and nephews, for instance, would tell one another to use the back door because "there's a palace reception going on." This usually meant that their grandmother was giving a bridge party.

The first line of Bryce's text sets the tone for the rest of the novel, but that tone can be represented only by oral inflection. To a person from Lima, the first sentence (in Spanish) says "Julius nació en un *palacio* de la Avenida Salaverry," with a pronounced plosive, accompanied probably by a facial gesture, and not the neutral statement "Julius *nació* en un palacio de la Avenida Salaverry" read by the translators. Since suprasegmentals do not appear on the printed page, there is no way to clarify the stress textually. How then should this first line be translated to balance two contextual focuses at the same time and fit words in English around a worldview that differs from that of the writer and his intended Lima readers? My translation, "Julius was born in one of those palaces you find on Avenida Salaverry," trusts that readers do not customarily think of palaces as existing in multiples. I cannot affirm, however, that I am right in my interpretation and that the other translators have misunderstood the narrator's intent. I have observed readers who were brought up in Lima laughing as they start the text, but translators who interpret the first sentence at face value cannot be faulted; it is, in de Man's terminology, "unreadable," and so, in this regard, "untranslatable."

The pioneer translation theorist Eugene Nida has dealt at length with the question of translatability. In Eugene Nida and Charles Taber's *The Theory and Practice of Translation,* which deals with Biblical translation, we are told that "Anything that can be said in one language can be said in another unless the form is an essential element of the message" (4). The text contains enlightening observations on the translation of rhetoric but not humor. They continue, "The writers of the Biblical books expected to be understood" (7), yet without familiarity with the way in which Bronze Age Hebrews bantered with each other, we can never know for sure whether Ecclesiastes has his tongue in his cheek, though we might suspect so.

Nida was an early advocate of relative, sociolinguistically based translation. Rather than aiming for an impossibly absolute linguistic equivalence, he points out that even in an ideal communicative situation where only one language is involved, at least 20 percent of meaning is lost ("Framework," 63). In the transference of nonlinguistic, linguistic, and metalinguistic codes that constitute the humor of a comic text, loss in translation is hardly surprising, yet texts are translated that cause laughter, at least in some readers. John Rutherford's English translation of Leopoldo Alas's *La Regenta* even provides equivalent malapropisms. A character given to them compares the voluptuous title character to the Venus del Nilo (instead of de Milo) (65), while in English she is described as a Venus de Melons (107). Interestingly, though, Rutherford does not attempt to translate the title of the novel, which, although it literally means "The Judge's Wife," implies something akin to "her with her nose in the air." Some wordplay will translate, some will not; there is no assurance that either will be communicated to all readers in both languages, or even in the source language alone.

Thematic clues in Bryce's novel open textual referents to broader interpretation and imply the narrator's tone. On page 2 we are told that "all Versailles" was in an uproar (10); there are five live-in servants in the household and three who come in to work. To look after a family of six, this is impressive, but hardly Versailles. It does not take long for readers to realize, moreover, that only the black chauffeur is a servant in the way P. G. Wodehouse or Kazuo Ishiguro would understand the term. The family is waited on by peasants recently arrived from the hinterland, and the nuance with which the word "palace" is pronounced will vary, when servants use it. Sadly, they might truly believe the house to be a "palace," since they have grown up in huts similar to those of medieval serfs, whom their parents resemble.

When, in the late 1950s, Julius's family moves to the "second palace" in the new suburb of Monterrico, its owners plan much of the decoration with the help of *House and Garden* (238). Both "palaces" also appear to owe a good deal to Hollywood; the bathrooms are said to be in "Beverly Hills" (12) and Julius's dining alcove in the kitchen is called "Disneyland" (13). The only real palace in the novel is a run-down eighteenth-century colonial building in the center of Lima, where Julius takes piano lessons. It has been converted into one- and two-room apartments, offices, workshops, trade schools, and so forth. The owners of such properties, including Julius's stepfather, are angry at not being able to evict the tenants so the buildings can be torn down and replaced by skyscrapers (428). Through factual description, foreign readers can, thematically, capture contradictions, even when the more important textual irony is not immediately evident.

In the course of the novel, Julius ages from five to eleven and experiences the death of his father from cancer and his sister from tuberculosis; two beloved elderly servants and the cook's baby also die. His surrogate mother—his nanny Vilma—leaves after his elder brother attempts to rape her. His older brothers treat him with incredible brutality, which nobody notices; his beautiful mother exists on caffeine, sleeping pills, and parties, while his stepfather sells out the country on the golf course. Julius is systematically stripped of his illusions and, when the novel ends, is heartbroken at discovering that Vilma has become a prostitute.

Luchting, who speaks of original sin, was the first to notice metafictionality in the text (19, 68–70) but does not draw attention to its parodic nature. The cook tells her story confusedly, in the form of a modernist or postmodern novel, such as *A World for Julius* itself (a postmodern novel of that form), and the cook tells us she "didn't give a shit for the chronology" (74–75). The first critics, who were Marxists, read the novel as ineffectual social criticism (Escajadillo, 144–46; Gutiérrez), while Luchting, in 1975, read it as a baroque treatise of the tension between life and death (42): the rich do not accept death and show bad faith, while the poor, and unspoiled children who identify with the poor, are in tune with the universe but out of place in the world Lima has become. All readings are justified by the story line, which is unmitigatedly tragic. Viewed thematically, it seems unlikely that the novel should be comic; nonetheless, it includes incidents that provoke laughter by thematic means and thus are perfectly translatable, though only the reader's interpretation can define such incidents as comic or not.

One such incident involves a school photograph in which a small boy, after hours of practice before a mirror, which are described at length, sets his face into what he believes to be a masterful expression, which in the picture makes him look like he's "about to fart" (384). The farcical incident involves no great subtlety of understanding, though at another level it parodies Sartre's theory of *le regard,* or lookism. The entire novel, in fact, can be read as parodying the stylistic experiments outlined by John Barth in essays on modernist and postmodern literature (68). It contains a circular plot, the loss of the inquit guideline, stream of consciousness passages (281–88, 318–32), intertextuality (221, 410, 582), prolepsis (20, 579), ludicity (170, 208, 466), glossolalia (352, 409, 411), and the validity of oneiric reality, which has the hero taking a double dose of his mother's sleeping pills to ensure double validity of his dreams (421-22). J. Ann Duncan was the first to point out that Bryce's novel contains techniques as innovative as any found in Butor, Sarraute, Robbe-Grillet, Borges, or Cortázar (130). The novel might be said to resemble *Finnegans Wake,* inasmuch as it acts as a sampler of literary experimentalism, but unlike Joyce's work, *A World for Julius* hides them in a very readable text. Duncan, who also mentions Bryce's humor, speaks of the lightheartedness of the text (120), with which it is difficult to agree, since the novel reveals poverty, neglect, and exploitation of others, as well as a situation in which a child is systematically deprived of everything he cares for. Bryce's novel, like Heller's *Catch-22,* tells a bitter story comically.

Bryce's comedy exists mainly at a textual level, where, Borges has shown, true literary effect is found (43-49), and the translator who makes the novel available in English is faced with the difficulty of conveying another culture through a male narrative voice that parodies different Lima conversation styles of both sexes and several classes, including his own, and most likely that of Lima readers too. There is truly no satisfactory way to render the Spanish of Bryce's narrative voice into British English. The upper- or upper-middle-class Lima Spanish of Bryce, and much that appears in Vargas Llosa's novels, can only be translated into American English. In England, class distinction still depends to a large extent on speech, which is not to say that in the United States and Peru it does not, but the rift between class usage is constituted differently in England than in the Americas. The average upper- or upper-middle-class educated Englishman does not *habitually* use foul language and bad grammar in order not to appear effete. The novels of Evelyn Waugh, Anthony Powell, and Julian Barnes abound with Englishmen who do not mind looking effete, and some even appear to work at doing so.

Bryce's narrator draws deliberate attention to certain ways of being. He laughs at language used at the golf club by bankers and businessmen who want to appear "manly" in front of the caddies and waiters (146), yet his own speech contains similar expletives not considered socially acceptable in the United States, at least, in the 1970s: for example, "Even Martin felt a regular asshole" (42). Julius's mentor is the black chauffeur Carlos, who has used foul language in front of the child all along, explaining, "I'm a sonofabitch, that's why" (103). In actual fact, Carlos is an extremely sympathetic, kindhearted man, but as a criollo he has to live up to certain expectations, and so he plays the part. The very naturalness with which obscenities are used by the narrator causes laughter, since at the time the action supposedly takes place, a veneer of correctness was required, which extended to the basic narrator in a written text. Typically, the women in *A World for Julius* rarely use foul language, although now some would probably use language more like that of the men. The one time Julius's mother tells a teacher to "fuck off," she is out of the country and cannot be heard by her own society (322).

I arrived at a narrative voice for my English version through several readings of *The Catcher in the Rye*. The nearest equivalent in English to Bryce's narrative voice would be that of an older Holden Caulfield; both are educated at private prep schools, have a reduced working vocabulary, and make grammatical mistakes in their mother tongue. They also speak an outdated slang from a similar period. Bryce's unidentified narrator hides his alienation by being sociable and by deliberately making his audience laugh.

The one possible redemptive force in Julius's world might be laughter. In the euphoria of a party where dancing grows increasingly wild, a young girl in blue, who does not appear again in the text, is described lovingly, laughing at the sheer joy of being alive. She calls to the little boy Julius, who is watching, to join her, and the reader is carried along as they race around the house: "'Come on, come on, don't be frightened!' She came so close she almost ran into them, . . . she was dying laughing, her eyes almost closed with merriment, . . . she was carried along, jumping, dancing, twirling, so pretty, right to the far end of the patio" (526–28). The United States Hispanicist Alan Trueblood has shown that this same sympathetic, shared laughter exists as the culminating force in *Don Quixote*. It is the laughter of good nature (73) ending in a bond of human affection (78)—a source of joy and an act of self-affirmation in the face of existence itself (79, Gallagan, 10)—the laughter known as "cervantene" to the eighteenth-century English humorists who disseminated it.

In my translation I hope to have found equivalents to the original Lima Spanish to make readers of English laugh, but I have no assurance this will occur. Any translation is a reaching out by the translator; in the case of the comic text, it is the will to share the gift of laughter.

Works Cited

Alas, Leopoldo. *La Regenta*. 3d ed. Mexico: Editorial Porrúa, 1981. Trans. John Rutherford, Harmondsworth: Penguin, 1984.

Barth, John. "The Literature of Replenishment: Postmodernist Fiction." *Atlantic* (January 1980), 65–71.

Bassnett-McGuire, Susan. *Translation Studies.* London: Metheun, 1980.

Bensoussan, Albert. "Alfredo Bryce Echenique, le principe d'innocence." *Co-textes* 9 (May 1985), 45–53.

Borges, Jorge Luis. "Palabrería para versos." *El tamaño de mi esperanza.* Buenos Aires: Editorial Proa, 1926, 43–49.

Bryce Echenique, Alfredo. *Un mundo para Julius.* Barcelona: Barral, Hispánica Nova, 1970. *A World for Julius.* Trans. Dick Gerdes. Austin: University of Texas Press, 1992.

Bühler, Karl. *Theory of Language: The Representational Function of Language.* Trans. Donald Fraser Goodwin. Philadelphia: John Benjamins, 1990.

Cueto, Juan. "Martes 24 de noviembre de 1987 'El humor.'" In *Alfredo Bryce Echenique: La Semana de Autor sobre Alfredo Bryce Echenique tuvo lugar en Madrid del 23 al 26 de noviembre de 1987, en el Insitututo de Cooperación Iberoamericana.* Ed. Fernando R. Lafuente. Madrid: Ediciones de Cultura Hispánica, 1991, 35–38.

de Man, Paul. *The Resistance to Theory.* Minneapolis: University of Minnesota Press, 1986.

Duncan, J(ennifer) Ann. "Language as Protagonist: Tradition and Innovation in Bryce Echenique's *Un mundo para Julius.*" *Forum for Modern Language Studies* 16:2 (1980), 120–35.

Eagleton, Terry. "Translation and Transformation." *Stand* 19:3 (1977), 72–77.

Escajadillo, Tomás Gustavo. "Bryce: elogios various y una objeción." *Revista de crítica literaria latinoamericana* 3:6 (1977), 137–48.

Fuentes, Carlos. "Carlos Fuentes: An Interview with John King." In *On Modern Latin American Fiction,* ed. John King. New York: Hill and Wang, 1987, 136–54.

Gallagan, Edward L. *The Comic Vision in Literature.* Athens: University of Georgia Press, 1984.

García Márquez, Gabriel. "The Solitude of Latin America." *Gabriel García Márquez and the Powers of Fiction.* Ed. Julio Ortega with Claudia Elliott. Austin: University of Texas Press, 1988, 87–91.

Gutiérrez, Miguel. "*Un mundo para Julius,* un fastuoso vacío." *Narración* [Lima] 2 (July 1971), 24–25, 29.

Harss, Luis, with Barbara Dohmann. *Los Nuestros.* Buenos Aires: Editorial Sudamericana, 1966.

Hart, Margaret. "Humor: Jokes for Translation." Paper presented at International Society for Humor Studies Conference: Humor 1994, 24 June 1994, Ithaca, NY.

Innis, Robert E. *Karl Bühler: Semiotic Foundations of Language Theory.* New York: Plenum, 1982.

Lefevere, André. Lecture at NEH Institute: Translation from the Bible to Benjamin, 2 July 1993, Binghamton, NY.

——. *Translating Literature: Practice and Theory in a Comparative Literature Context.* New York: MLA, 1992.

Lodge, David. *After Bakhtin: Essays on Fiction and Criticism.* London: Routledge, 1990.

López-Baralt, Mercedes. "Otra forma de complicidad entre el autor y sus lectores: Alfredo Bryce Echenique y *Un mundo para Julius.*" *Sin nombre* 7:1 (1976), 50–56.

Luchting, Wolfgang A. *Alfredo Bryce: Humores y malhumores.* Lima: Milla Batres, 1975.

Nash, Walter. *The Language of Humour.* New York: Longman, 1985.

Nida, Eugene A. "A Framework for the Analysis and Evaluation of Theories of Translation." In *Translation: Applications and Research,* ed. Richard W. Breslin. New York: Gardner Press, 1976, 47–91.

Nida, Eugene A., and Charles R. Taber. *The Theory and Practice of Translation.* Leiden: United Bible Societies (E. J. Brill), 1969.

Salinger, J. D. *The Catcher in the Rye.* New York: Signet Books, 1953.

Trueblood, Alan S. "La risa en el *Quijote* y la risa de Don Quijote." *Letter and Spirit in Hispanic Writers, Renaissance to Civil War: Selected Essays.* London: Tamesis Books, 1986, 65–82.

Vargas Llosa, Mario. *La verdad de las mentiras.* Barcelona: Seix Barral, 1990.

American Humor:
Bibliography

Teaching a Text-Based Humor Course: "You can't get there from here, stranger"

Donald Barlow Stauffer

Until recently, American humor was a poor relation of literary studies, either relegated to popular culture programs or folklore departments or sneaked in under some other rubric. But in the past two decades, humor generally and American humor in particular have come into their own as subjects for serious study. I find a certain irony in this, since, curiously, this is happening just when much literary study is itself becoming the subject for humor. Now that American humor has become legitimized, many of us are finding that courses in its rich tradition are particularly useful in helping to open students' eyes to the myriad cultural, social, and historical issues raised in the work of humorists from Ben Franklin to Garrison Keillor. But to do this requires texts—both the right texts and the available texts. While these two objectives are not irreconcilable, they are not easy to achieve, as I discovered when I first put together a course in American humor. In seeking *the* best text, I found, like the stranger who asked "Which way to Millenocket?" in *Bert and I*'s down east Maine humor, "You can't get there from here, stranger."

Arriving at even a preliminary list of writers and texts for a sophomore-level course is a daunting job, for everyone has their own notion of what humor is and their own ideas as to what should or should not be included in a course. Dorothy Parker once complained that every time she tried to describe the comic, she "had to lie down with a cold wet cloth on her head." I have often felt like lying down myself after trying to make my class respond to the verbal insanities of S. J. Perelman or, in an entirely different vein, to appreciate the understated musings and mutterings of James Thurber. The humor canon, it seems, is even more volatile than the straight-faced one, because the criteria—especially for recent work—are difficult to establish. The sheer bulk of humor, good and bad, threatens to overwhelm us all. In addition, time contributes to these difficulties in two ways: tastes change over time; and much humor is topical or time specific and therefore ephemeral. Yet even after making decisions in the light of these considerations

233

about what printed texts to use, I found that my task was made even more daunting by publishers, who do not appear to be aware of the need—or at least my need—for a good classroom text covering the huge field of American humor from its beginnings to the present.

But what about those elusive criteria for inclusion in an American humor course with a historical orientation? I should say up front that my own tastes are lopsided and possibly obsolete, since they were formed by many years of exposure to the *New Yorker*. The writers for that magazine were more than adequately represented in E. B. and Katharine White's 1941 *A Subtreasury of American Humor,* a book long out of print but the one that first introduced me to humor. Today, however, I find that book to be not as funny as I remembered it—especially when I try reading it through the eyes of nineteen-year-old undergraduates in the 1990s, most of whom have never read *anyone* on my reading list, with the possible exception of Mark Twain. What are such students to make of Will Cuppy, for example, or Franklin P. Adams, or Wolcott Gibbs's long profile of *Time,* written in Timestyle? The *Subtreasury* contains a lot of in-house jokes and parodies that are, or were, funny to *New Yorker* aficionados, but the undergraduate in Albany, as well as the lady in Dubuque, will be left cold by a lot of them. In their introduction the Whites quite openly, even proudly, acknowledge their *New Yorker* bias. It may have been true in 1941 that much of the best humor was to be found there, but some of it is now rather dated. I say this even though I still read Benchley, Perelman, Thurber, and White with pleasure—but I must say that Benchley has been surpassed by many later writers, and what looked like something new in his time now seems tame and sometimes cloyingly precious or cute or strained. And Dorothy Parker, whose reputation for her bons mots has survived, is today almost unreadable in print.

For this course I needed to go far beyond the Algonquin Hotel, using a framework much like that found in Walter Blair and Hamlin Hill's historical study, and then bringing it up to date with a number of recent writers. To begin at the beginning should mean starting with the Puritans, although obviously they were not much given to humor: it went against their grain. There are, indeed, humorous passages in several writings of the time, most notably, perhaps, Thomas Morton, who told his story of the attack on his colony of Merry Mount by the Plymouth colonists, satirizing them and famously labeling Miles Standish "Captain Shrimp." Both Samuel Sewall in his diary and Nathaniel Ward in *The Simple Cobler of Agawam* also had their humorous moments.

After 1700 the stern Puritan notions of what kind of writing was suitable for devout readers rapidly changed. The typically eighteenth-century genre of satire was already being practiced in Ebenezer Cook's *The Sotweed*

Factor and Hugh Henry Brackenridge's *Modern Chivalry*. Satire was also the dominant genre for humor during the Revolutionary War, as is evident in the poems of Philip Freneau and in a great number of broadsides and pamphlets. But I sacrificed inclusiveness to the demands of the fourteen-week semester and therefore chose to start the course with Ben Franklin and Washington Irving. From these I moved to the Southwestern humorists, then to Blair and Hill's "Phunny Phellows," then to Twain, and finally to folk humor. Along the way I included some satire, beginning with Poe, some women humorists and satirists, some writers of fables (Ambrose Bierce, George Ade, Josephine Daskam, and James Thurber), some nonsense writers (Leacock and Lardner), some *New Yorker* writers (Benchley, Thurber, Perelman), some Jewish humorists (Malamud, Roth, Leo Rosten, Dan Greenburg), and several more recent writers.

Most humor anthologies I have seen (with the exception of Blount) are virtually lily white: they contain few, if any, writings by blacks, Native Americans, or other ethnic minorities. Since black humor, or to be more precise, the humor of blacks, has played an important role in the tradition of American humor, I knew the class needed to read selections by and about blacks. I turned first to Langston Hughes's 1966 collection. Although this collection is rather disappointing, it includes his "Simple" stories, which are good; some folk pieces; some jazz jokes by Louis Armstrong, W. C. Handy, and others; and short pieces, poems, and jokes by Arna Bontemps, Dick Gregory, Godfrey Cambridge, LeRoi Jones, Richard Wright, Alice Childress, and so on.

I also found useful the encyclopedia of black humor by Redd Foxx and Norma Miller; this volume consists of a historically organized collection of essays covering humor and humorists from plantation shows to Richard Pryor, comedians of the seventies, and the black woman in comedy. Many black humorists were or are actually performers, probably in the tradition of their many predecessors in black minstrels, Broadway shows, and Negro touring companies: people like Moms Mabley, Bill Cosby, Redd Foxx, Dick Gregory, and Richard Pryor. These performers, of course, are responsible for a lot of the biting edge in the humor of blacks. One example is Dick Gregory's famous story about when he went into a restaurant in the Deep South and was told they didn't serve colored people. He answered, "That's okay, I don't eat colored people; just bring me a ham sandwich." Langston Hughes's Simple stories were not quite as aggressive but just as biting: "In heaven everybody is washed whiter than snow. . . . But in hell you stay your own natural color. So many Negroes has been going to hell for so many years it must look like Harlem down there, or Mississippi."

While I did not use any work by black performers, I felt it was important to include some secondary materials about the minstrelsy tradition and its place in American history. Foxx and Miller's book contains a very usable discussion of the tradition of black and white minstrelsy (a tradition explored more fully in connection with its social implications in Eric Lott's *Love and Theft: Blackface Minstrelsy and the American Working Class*). But the main black writer I used was Ishmael Reed, whose *The Terrible Twos* is full of wild and crazy satire that goes all over the place. Students, surprisingly, liked it in spite of its difficulties. Some said it was the best thing they read in the course.

Choosing contemporary humorists is another problem, because there are so many to choose from. Walking through a Barnes & Noble superstore, one finds about 500 linear feet of shelves devoted to humor. But the quality and style is inconsistent and often rather depressing. Too many books have titles like *Why Cats Paint, Shave the Whales,* or *The Working Mother's Guilt Guide.* Many are clearly commercial enterprises—like parodies of *The Bridges of Madison County* or Rush Limbaugh, the sayings of Newt Gingrich, and surefire titles like *Internet for Cats*—that are doomed to early oblivion. Another problem is that many contemporary humorists blur the lines between print and other media, such as cartoons, videotapes, and cassette tapes. Garrison Keillor, for example, needs to be heard as well as read. Woody Allen's early written work is good, but the bulk of his humor is on film. The work of many other performance-oriented humorists, to the extent it is still available, needs to be seen or heard as well as read: Bob and Ray (although their stuff reads quite well on the page), Steve Allen, Tom Lehrer, Bill Cosby, Richard Pryor, George Carlin, Lenny Bruce, Steve Martin, Gilda Radner, Groucho Marx, Jean Shepard (whose famous 1950s–1960s WOR radio monologues are completely lost). In the broader theoretical sense, of course, these are also texts, just as comic strips are. And many would agree that some of the best humor, dating from Krazy Kat and Walt Kelly, is to be found in the work of such cartoonists as Jules Feiffer, Herblock, Garry Trudeau, Bill Watterson, Jeff McNally, Gary Larson, and Berke Breathed (many of whom are, unfortunately, opting for early retirement). In spite of these intriguing and distracting issues, I chose to keep the texts for my course primarily literary and at the same time encourage students to explore the other forms in their papers and reports.

Yet it is clear from these few examples that a primarily text-based course in American humor will reflect the actuality of the recent past less and less as time goes on. Looking forward ten years into the next millennium, we can speculate that a humor course will have to go beyond the printed text to capture the quality of American humor. Since so many of the good humorists today are also performers or perform their own material (a tradition as American as Mark Twain), one would need to include videos and CDs of such people as David Letterman, Kate Clinton, George Carlin, Lenny Bruce, Roseanne Barr, Robin Williams, Billy Crystal, Spalding Gray, Jackie Mason, and Eddie Murphy. It would also be necessary to study the work of a new generation of newspaper cartoonists: Gary Larson, Scott Adams, Berke Breathed, Bill Watterson, Karen Johnson, Cathy Guisewitz, Jeff McNally, and others. Comedy clubs, comedy channels, new interest in using animation for satire that goes beyond the Saturday morning cartoon show (Beavis and Butt-head are a notorious example)—all may force us to enlarge our notion of text to become more widely inclusive of other media.

The Internet provides the most striking example—in the form of discussion lists, web sites, and hypertext links—of the sheer wealth of both humor and discussions about humor that is available. One can download all kinds of humor—some of it, quite frankly, bad. A quick search of user groups turned up twelve using the search word *humor* and ten using the search word *comedy,* including stand-up, slapstick, and improvisation. A search on the World Wide Web turned up 2,385 documents containing the word "humor," 554 with "American humor," 175 with "American television humor," 133 with "American cartoon humor," and 77 with "American literary humor." Of course, on closer examination many of these are neither useful nor interesting, but they reveal in a purely quantitative way the sheer amount of humor material that future scholars and teachers will have to sift through.

Once having decided on what writers to include, one might ask where to turn for texts. It is immediately obvious that American literature anthologies are not useful in a course such as this. As a matter of fact, three of the standard anthologies of American literature—the Harper, the Heath, and the Norton—are basically humorless, especially in their twentieth-century selections. None of the *New Yorker* writers, for example, appear in either the Heath or the Harper, although volume 2 of the Norton has selections by Thurber and, wonder of wonders, Dorothy Parker. But that is all: Mencken, Lardner, Rosten, DeVries, Roth, Heller, and Vonnegut do not appear. In fact, no other classic humorist of the twentieth century is represented in any of these collections. Hence, these three anthologies are pretty somber affairs, although all, of course, include Mark Twain, and one of George Washington Harris's "Sut Lovingood" stories. Contemporary writers—such as Art Buchwald, Neil Simon, Woody Allen, and Garrison Keillor—are nowhere to be found. Volume 2 of the Heath includes only Marietta Holley, Finley Peter Dunne, Ishmael Reed, and John Barth's "Lost in the Funhouse," while volume 2 of the Harper is limited to Eudora Welty's "Why I Live at the P. O." and selections from Nathaniel West's *Miss Lonelyhearts.*

Not surprisingly, the standard American literature anthologies cannot be adapted to an American humor course. But there are, in addition to many specialized collections of ethnic and women's humor (like the *Big Book of Jewish Humor* and Walker and Dresner's *Redressing the Balance*), a number of general humor collections in print. Any one of the following six anthologies could serve as a classroom text, depending on the tastes and aims of the individual instructor. The oldest is Kenneth Lynn's *The Comic Tradition in America,* first published in 1958. Next chronologically is Mordecai Richler's *The Best of Modern Humor,* published over a decade ago. Two others were published in 1990: William Novak and Moshe Waldoks's *The Big Book of New American Humor: The Best of the Past 25 Years* and Frank Muir's *Oxford Book of Humorous Prose.* A fifth is Russell Baker's 1993 *Book of American Humor,* and the most recent such work is *Roy Blount's Book of Southern Humor.* Another, more specialized anthology is the *Oxford Book of Comic Verse,* with entries by many Americans, including James Russell Lowell, Kenneth Koch, Donald Hall, X. J. Kennedy, Edward Gorey, and Langston Hughes.

Looking more closely at these, Novak and Waldoks's paperbound *Big Book of New American Humor* is focused on the recent past, as the subtitle tells us. Its 335 oversized pages contain cartoons, comic strips, TV routines, jokes, one-liners, and short sketches by a wide variety of people, including a long segment from the film script of *Annie Hall* and an entire page of light bulb jokes. This will give some idea of the eclectic nature of the collection, almost as eclectic as the shelves of Barnes & Noble. The only criterion for selection, the editors say, was that the work be "funny," a criterion that seems to have been rather broadly defined. This criterion was shaped, the editors boast, by the attitudes of *Mad* magazine, and although the editors tried to avoid tastelessness, they admit to lapses. The book is an interesting and entertaining potpourri of popular humor that includes writers like Peter DeVries, John Updike, Mel Brooks, Bruce Jay Friedman, Garry Trudeau, Jerry Seinfeld, and Dave Barry. It could well be used as a supplement or a resource for individual pieces, but on reflection I decided it would not do as a text for my course.

The Oxford Book of Humorous Prose is a quite different kind of book, as might be expected. Assembled by Frank Muir, a British TV personality and entertainer, it is 1,149 pages long. The full title—*The Oxford Book of Humorous Prose: From William Caxton to P. G. Wodehouse, a Conducted Tour by Frank Muir*—suggests the scope of the enterprise, although the book does focus primarily on the nineteenth and twentieth centuries and goes far beyond Wodehouse to include Erma Bombeck, Fran Lebowitz, Philip Roth, and Garrison Keillor, just to name some of the more recent American authors. One problem, of course, is that it contains primarily British writers. Still, it does have selections from many nineteenth-century Americans as well: Franklin's "Selection of a Mistress," Poe's "The Man That Was Used Up," Irving's "Rip," one Jack Downing letter by Seba Smith, a selection from Hooper's Simon Suggs, Harris's "Mrs. Yardley's Quilting," ten pieces by Twain, and brief snippets from many others, including Harte, Nasby, Ward, Shillaber, Billings, Ade, Bierce, Nye, J. C. Harris, and Dunne. Conceivably, one could justify using those selections in place of those in, say, Kenneth Lynn's nineteenth-century collection. I don't think I would, however, since most of the selections are too brief to give anything more than a mere taste of the writer.

The newest anthologies are *Russell Baker's Book of American Humor* and *Roy Blount's Book of Southern Humor*. Looking at Baker's collection now, after having taught the course, I find that his ideas about humor, and his selections, often reflect a bleak world view I do not share. But then I might just be one of the ten curmudgeons in the world who do not find Baker's own writings humorous. Here he is on parody and burlesque: "Deep down, all these pieces rest on foundations of malice, which is common in a great deal of humor." He continues, "there is more than a little misanthropy in almost every humorist, and an almost irresistible compulsion to express it cruelly." While I would agree that the basis of much humor is cruelty or pain, I do not believe that these ingredients are as widespread. Still, in spite of my reservations, I must point out that Baker's selections are wide and varied, covering much of the history of American humor. Unfortunately he arranges them not chronologically but under some idiosyncratic headings, such as "Shameless Frivolity," "The Human Muddle," "Geographical Sneers," and "A Gnashing of Humorists." One problem this creates is that anyone wishing to read the work of, say, Finley Peter Dunne (a Baker favorite) would need to look him up under three different headings; Benchley would also need to be pursued under three headings, and Thurber under four. Baker does include some thoughtful choices: Chester Himes, Zora Neale Hurston, Abraham Lincoln, Anita Loos, Erma Bombeck, Dave Barry, Fred Allen, but he has little interest in nineteenth-century Southwestern humor.

Roy Blount's Book of Southern Humor (1994) is a substantial recent addition to the field. Blount has put together a wide-ranging collection of Southern humorists (both terms loosely enough defined to include Garrison Keillor—the only Minnesotan in the book—and poets and musicians such as Louis Armstrong, A. R. Ammons, and Jelly Roll Morton). He generously includes three pieces by Mark Twain, and an equal number by himself. Further samples of Blount are the introduction and headnotes, which are gracefully and humorously written. The 600-plus page book is arranged, like

Baker's, under section headings: "My People, My People (How's Your Mama 'n' Them?)"; "Here Be Dragons, or How Come These Butterbeans Have an Alligator Taste?"; "Lying, and Other Arts of Communication"; "Black and White, and Other Political Stripes"; "Home on the Road"; and "Mind and Heart and Soul," but they do not seem so bewildering as Baker's. These sections are filled with some of the expected—Poe, Flannery O'Connor, Johnson J. Hooper, Joel Chandler Harris, A. B. Longstreet, Faulkner—as well as some interesting knowns and unknowns—Julian Bond, Molly Ivins, Lisa Alther, Alice Childress, and Donald Barthelme are among the former. This book alone contains enough material for a course and should certainly be used as a source book.

Of these six collections, I still find the best texts for my purposes to be those I settled on: Lynn's adequate and easily available *The Comic Tradition in America* for the eighteenth and nineteenth centuries, and Mordecai Richler's *The Best of Modern Humor* for the twentieth. While Richler also contains a few British and Canadian writers, it includes a lot of good, twentieth-century American humor. Its shortcoming is that it has only a single selection of important writers like Lardner, Benchley, and Perelman, and nothing by black humorists. However, Richler embraces the work of a rather wide range of American women, including Eudora Welty, Nora Ephron, Fran Lebowitz, Lisa Alther, and Veronica Geng. Richler is also good (as is Baker) about including political satirists: Dunne, Russell Baker himself (in a piece I *do* like—"Bomb Math"), and Buchwald.

All instructors know how difficult it is to structure a course around specific texts when so many books today soon go out of print. The individual collections of essays by Roy Blount, Jr., which quickly drop out of sight, are one such casualty. P. J. O'Rourke, the outrageously conservative humorist, is also relatively ephemeral, although his books seem to be reappearing after the 1994 election. But even Philip Roth's classic humorous novel *Portnoy's Complaint* was "not in stock" (a publishers' euphemism for keeping inventory levels down) and thus unavailable when I wanted to use it.

The three books I chose were Nathaniel West's *Miss Lonelyhearts,* Garrison Keillor's *Leaving Home,* and Ishmael Reed's *The Terrible Twos.* Why these books? West is an early example of black humor—so black, perhaps, that it was difficult for many students to see humor at all. Keillor continues the oral storytelling tradition of Twain and the Southwestern humorists into the twentieth century. Reed is one of our best comic writers, and he also happens to be black. His satire, black humor (in the non-ethnic sense), surrealism (à la West), and slapstick and outrageousness (à la Richard Pryor) strike a particularly contemporary note. All three of these humorists carry on typical American humor traits, particularly hyperbole.

Finally, I assembled a photocopied anthology of my own, mainly of black writers, women writers, and New Yorker writers, all of whom are inadequately represented in Richler. Kenneth Lynn's nineteenth-century anthology, although a model of its kind in many ways, is unfortunately an all-male preserve: Caroline Kirkland, Louisa May Alcott, Frances Whitcher, and Marietta Holley, for instance, are nowhere in sight. But women humorists are now well represented and more readily available in Nancy Walker and Rita Dresner's cleverly titled *Redressing the Balance*. This turned out to be an especially good source for my own homegrown anthology, since I was able to use a number of its selections, such as Alcott's "Transcendental Wild Oats," that wonderful satire of communal living at her father's Brook Farm. I paired this with a chapter from Lisa Alther's *Kinflicks,* which satirizes the communes of the 1960s. Also in this collection was a piece by Caroline Kirkland describing frontier life as experienced by women, which I coupled with a chapter in the same tradition from Betty MacDonald's twentieth-century treatment of farm life in *The Egg and I.* I also found two minor writers, Josephine Daskam Bacon and Carolyn Wells, and a piece by Marietta Holley, who is coming to be recognized as one of the best humorists of the nineteenth-century, male or female. As this narrative ultimately suggests, the final choices for the course reading list evolved out of a combination of prejudice, compromise, luck, and good intentions.

In addition, the list also was greatly improved by the vast literature of criticism as well as historical and bibliographical materials that has grown up around these texts. Of the many hundreds of studies and reference works, I have identified several as the most useful points of departure. Even though it is about ten years out of date, I would begin with M. Thomas Inge's "'One Priceless Universal Trait': American Humor," a very good short introductory survey of the field. His bibliographical essay discusses and evaluates reference works, critical anthologies, history and criticism, and humor in the media, ending with a four-page list of works cited.

American humor now has its own book-length research guide: Lawrence E. Mintz's *Humor in America: A Research Guide to Genres and Topics* (New York: Greenwood, 1988). Ten chapters, each written by an authority in the field, cover a wide variety of topics: literary humor, the comics, humor in periodicals, film comedy, broadcast humor, stand-up comedy, women's humor, racial and ethnic humor, political humor, folklore methodology, and American humor research.

A more recent and important research tool for humor in all of its aspects is Don L. F. Nilsen's *Humor Scholarship: A Research Bibliography* (Westport, CT: Greenwood Press, 1993). In ten chapters Nilsen lists works in a variety of categories, from Humor and the Individual, to National Styles of Humor, to Humor Theory and Epistemology. An appendix of humor resources lists humor journals and magazines, humor newsletters, humor organizations, and the like. Of particular interest is his thirty-five-page bibliography of American humor, but other sections should be consulted, for example, "Humor and the Media," "Jokes, Riddles, Hoaxes, and Stand-Up Comedy," "Humor and Ethnicity," and "Sex Roles."

Other useful reference works include Stephen Gale's *Encyclopedia of American Humorists,* a reference text of brief critical-bibliographical essays on approximately 150 major and minor literary humorists, and Stanley Trachtenberg's edited volume in the *Dictionary of Literary Biography* series: *American Humorists, 1800–1950.* This volume contains essays on individual writers, along with bibliographies and various historical surveys and appendices. Many other volumes of the Dictionary of Literary Biography contain articles about American humorists as well. David E. E. Sloane's *American Humor Magazines and Comic Periodicals* is a useful specialized work.

Two essay collections are noteworthy: Sarah Blacher Cohen's *Comic Relief: Humor in Contemporary American Literature,* with contributions on a wide variety of subjects; and June Sochen's *Women's Comic Visions,* a volume in the Wayne State Humor in Life and Letters Series, with chapters by various scholars on women writers and performers from the nineteenth century through Lucille Ball and Moms Mabley to Bette Midler, Whoopi Goldberg, and Kate Clinton.

As courses begin to point toward the twentyfirst century, my conclusion is that the American humor course still awaits its text.

Works Cited

Anthologies

Baker, Russell, ed. *Russell Baker's Book of American Humor.* New York: Norton, 1993.

Baym, Nina, et al., eds. *The Norton Anthology of American Literature.* 4th ed. 2 vols. New York and London: Norton, 1994.

Blair, Walter, and Hamlin Hill. *America's Humor: From Poor Richard to Doonesbury.* New York: Oxford University Press, 1978.

Blount, Roy, Jr., ed. *Roy Blount's Book of Southern Humor.* New York: Norton, 1994.

Foxx, Redd, and Norma Miller, eds. *The Redd Foxx Encyclopedia of Black Humor.* Pasadena: W. Ritchie Press, 1977.

Gross, John, ed. *The Oxford Book of Comic Verse.* New York: Oxford University Press, 1995.

Hughes, Langston. *The Book of Negro Humor*. New York: Dodd, Mead, 1966.

Kaufman, Gloria, and Mary Kay Blakely, eds. *Pulling Our Own Strings: Feminist Humor and Satire*. Bloomington: Indiana University Press, 1980.

Lauter, Paul, et al., eds. *The Heath Anthology of American Literature*. 2d ed. 2 vols. Lexington, MA: D. C. Heath, 1994.

Lynn, Kenneth S., ed. *The Comic Tradition in America: An Anthology of American Humor*. New York: Norton, 1968.

McQuade, Donald, ed. *The Harper American Literature*. 2d ed. 2 vols. New York: HarperCollins, 1993.

Muir, Frank, ed. *The Oxford Book of Humorous Prose: From William Caxton to P. G. Wodehouse, a Conducted Tour by Frank Muir*. New York: Oxford University Press, 1990 (a shorter paperbound version was published in 1992).

Novak, William, and Moshe Waldoks, eds. *The Big Book of Jewish Humor*. New York: Harper Perennial, 1981.

———. *The Big Book of New American Humor: The Best of the Past 25 Years*. New York: Harper Perennial, 1990.

Richler, Mordecai. *The Best of Modern Humor*. New York: Knopf, 1984.

Walker, Nancy, and Zita Dresner, eds. *Redressing the Balance: American Women's Humor from Colonial Times to the 1980's*. Oxford: University Press of Mississippi, 1988.

White, E. B., and Katharine S. White, eds. *A Subtreasury of American Humor*. New York: Coward McCann, 1941.

Single-author Works

Cohen, Sarah Blacher, ed. *Comic Relief: Humor in Contemporary American Literature*. Urbana: University of Illinois Press, 1978.

Gale, Stephen H., ed. *Encyclopedia of American Humorists*. New York: Garland, 1988.

Inge, M. Thomas. "'One Priceless Universal Trait': American Humor." *Studies in American Humor* 3 (1984), 61–73.

Lott, Eric. *Love and Theft: Blackface Minstrelsy and the American Working Class*. New York: Oxford University Press, 1993.

Middleton, Robert. "Humorous American Literature and the Film: A Bibliography." *Studies in American Humor* 4 (1985), 183–91.

Mintz, Lawrence E. *Humor in America: A Research Guide to Genres and Topics*. New York: Greenwood, 1988.

Morris, Linda A., ed. *American Women Humorists: Critical Essays*. New York: Garland, 1994.

244   Donald Barlow Stauffer

Nilsen, Don L. F. *Humor Scholarship: A Research Bibliography.* Westport, CT: Greenwood, 1993.

Sloane, David E. E., ed. *American Humor Magazines and Comic Periodicals.* Westport, CT: Greenwood, 1987.

Sochen, June, ed. *Women's Comic Visions.* Detroit: Wayne State University Press, 1991.

Tanner, James T. F. "Humor in American Poetry: A Selected Checklist of Recent Scholarship and Criticism." *Studies in American Humor* 6 (1988), 101–2.

Trachtenberg, Stanley, ed. *American Humorists, 1800–1950,* parts 1–2 (2 vols.). *Dictionary of Literary Biography,* vol. 11. Detroit: Gale Research, 1982.

Afterword

New Directions in American Humor:
An Afterword

David E. E. Sloane

"New Directions in American Humor" may seem a presumptuous title, but the field of American humor studies has indeed changed and continues to change dramatically in the 1990s. This domain is enlarging rapidly, and at the turn of the new century, humor studies will have advanced dramatically beyond the territory and preconceptions surveyed and staked out in Walter Blair's landmark study *Native American Humor,* published in 1937.[1] Due to the work of younger scholars, popular culture as an emerging phenomenon now comes to the forefront of humor studies as never before.[2] Feminist inquiries have broadened the confining emphasis on the old Southwest and the frontier as the regions defining "American" humor and have plunged the field into the larger, domestic realm.[3] Regions other than the folksy frontier and writers other than those young professionals of the nineteenth-century Southwest—such as Longstreet, Hooper, and Harris—now come in for a share of modern analysis. Ethnic humor now appears in a variety of subgenres, including Native American, Chicano, African-American, and others supplementing the traditional ethnic jokes that pandered to American nativism in the nineteenth and early-to-middle twentieth century. This book has attempted to contribute to that task. In fact, so much seems to be in flux that some readers may be reminded of a story from a 1930s college humor magazine: A young student runs up to a famous ichthyologist as he crosses the MIT campus in Cambridge and engages him in spirited conversation. When the student leaves, the professor's colleague turns to him with wonder and asks, "Why, Jones, that young student was obviously much taken with you and the subject, yet you seemed not even to know his name!?" Professor Jones turns to his colleague and snaps, "Professor Smith, every time I remember the name of a student, I forget a fish." Happily, it is not necessary to remember each strand of inquiry presented in the volume presented here but only to recognize how they represent the kinds of studies marking new directions for twenty-first-century American humor and other studies. The job is a complex one, and researchers will find a wide array of motivations for taking it on.

In the 1950s, *Bert and I* immortalized one down east Maine story from the state fair that had a local character winning a ride in a hot-air balloon. The balloon took off and was soon out over the ocean and then back over land. The riders released air and drifted closer to earth, where they soon spied a farmer tilling his field. "Hey, farmer, where are we?" yelled the descending balloonists. "You're in a balloon, you durn fools!" came back the reply.[4] American humor as a genre study is located in about the same position. First there is the issue of humor high and low. We humor scholars would like to think of humor as attempting some social good, but does "low" humor do that? Do "Polish jokes" improve the lives and self-perceptions of Poles? Do the figures sometimes seen on suburban front lawns of the feet, legs, and enlarged posterior of a (presumably) bent-over woman gardener ennoble and enlighten us as we commute to work? Do they represent a nascent social statement—or, more important perhaps, are they powerful Freudian representations of the as-yet-untamed id of the modern aging suburbanite? Humor theory has not fully come to grips with such issues, although various paradigms have been tried since the first definitions of comedy were made in Greco-Roman theatrical terms. The classic theories of Freud, Meredith, Bergson, and Hobbes are at this time under extensive reconsideration, yet these theories do not add dimensions to studies such as those undertaken by the scholars represented in this book.

The humorist's lot is a hard one, particularly when she or he is "not funny," as feminists responded to female-insensitive housewife and secretary jokes, which were a staple of earlier humor. We are now in an era where a standard, and never-challenged, comment of males to each other during the 1930s to the 1950s ("When rape is inevitable, relax and enjoy it") threatened the job of Indiana University's basketball coach Bobby Knight—even though basketball is king in the region where he is located.[5] Press attacks on a racist joke in 1976 were the only way of purging Secretary of Agriculture Earl L. Butz, although many believed his abysmal policies were the real reason for his dismissal.[6] Knight and Butz have been justly criticized for their insensitivity, but others have experienced varying degrees of acceptance or rejection for far less. Even Mark Twain was identified by Brander Matthews in his 1896 essay "The Penalty of Humor" as a visionary idealist rated below his true power and importance and suffering from the label "humorist." Readers of the two volumes of expatriate African American Ollie Harrington's essays and cartoons—*Dark Laughter* and *Why I Left America,* recently shepherded into print by M. Thomas Inge—will see reconfirmed why racism is not funny, even when it is treated as funny.[7] Needless to say, the bias of scholars and libraries also tends to downplay the truly negative propagandistic uses of humor as flagrant racial, sexual, and social slander. Nevertheless, such uses are common; every American war generates reams of such humor, be it directed at Hitler, Hirohito, or Hussein. Humor expressing the uglier side of prejudice, jealousy, hatred, and the deeper, darker emotions of the human soul may well continue to be neglected as a subject of study.

English critics of the 1860s began the effort to define American humor as a genre. American humor had already been identified along the lines of that represented in the Yankee Jonathan type recently analyzed by Cameron Nickels, Daniel Royot, and Winifred Morgan, and early British critics saw much American humor as typified by "lawless exaggeration."[8] Niagara Falls, both sublime and awesome, could be seen as a totem for that approach to nature and the world generally, and it is little wonder that Doesticks, Twain, and a variety of other literary comedians made their way to the Falls anticipating comic copy in their abrasion by its commercial exploitation. The beauty of the Falls must necessarily be tainted when the observer is confronted by an alcoholic Irishman dressed in Indian tribal clothes to hawk souvenirs. The downplayed down east humor, however, is not disallowed by this definition; it merely appears as its reverse, in exaggerated Maine reserve. The Massachusetts farmer who argued that the railroad might be fast some places, but it was just as slow in the station as anything else, is a fitting Eastern counterclaim to the stranger's taunt to Jim Smiley, "I don't see no points about that frog that's better'n any other frog."

The real sticking point for a unified theory of American humor is that humor functions at so many different levels that no monist theory is likely to work without so many exceptions that it ends up full of holes. I have identified at least five levels of humor that can function in any given joke and are not necessarily present, absent, or mutually involved in a comic situation. These five categories are:

- language process as a lineal act
- synaptic relational interpretations of language
- conceptual responses
- cultural reinterpretations
- unidentified psychological components

First, the processing of language that occurs when one reads or listens to a text *is* a lineal act. It is hard to read multiple texts at the same time, and processing tends to move in a line, in English at least, from left to right across a page. For students investigating the impact of pronominal phrases, I offer the sentence "The pen of my aunt on the table under the lamp in the hallway by the door to the back stairs of our apartment leaks." The postponed verb at the end of the string of constituents often brings a laugh. Why? Merely the phrase by phrase suspension built into the sentence structure creates a tension that is released by the fulfilled expectation. Is it anticlimax? I don't think so conceptually, but it may be that the humor comes from suddenly halted structural repetition or even from the sound value of the final word "leaks." In any event, most sentences and relations are processed linearly—for example, "John is eager; Mary is cautious," accompanied by meaning variants using the linking conjunction, "John is eager, but Mary is cautious," "John is eager, and Mary is cautious," "John is eager, so Mary is cautious," "John is eager, for Mary is cautious." Students find the idea amusing (although not a rip-roaring thigh-slapper), but the humor comes from merely processing along a line of subject-predicate, subject-predicate. The conceptual relation between the two sentences follows after basic lineal processing and juxtaposition word by word, phrase by phrase, and finally idea by idea. So, on one level, information must be processed merely to bring the words within the processing brain through visual or aural channels. Why is Winston Churchill's "A preposition at the end of a sentence is something up with which I will not put" be funny? It is our most magnificent example of structural inversion linked with its own context.

Second, however, and even more important, it appears that language is processed not only literally and correctly as to its meanings but also unliterally and incorrectly, based on a range of associations lying solely within the nervous system of the recipient and not, or at least not necessarily, in the language itself. Some widely known comic sequences show that large numbers of people are in fact conditioned to respond in such ways, although relatively little is understood about this behavior. In one comic bit broadcast over a comedy TV channel a few years ago, an interviewer asks the interviewee to quickly repeat, one at a time, each of three words—"Hop," "mop," "pop"—and then as rapidly as possible answer a brief simple question: "What do you do at a green light?" "Stop!" is the usual answer; the interviewer chooses either a deadpan or disgusted look and says, "No, you go!" Hardy victims can be blasted with a second round, "Host, post, most, what do you put in a toaster?": "Toast." The response is, "No, bread."

The mechanics of the sequence rely on the carrying power of rhyme over language processing. Nonnative speakers, who process for content much more heavily than they race across the surface of the cumulative sound pattern each word accumulates, fall for the gag far less frequently. Its power—which I use repeatedly in teaching courses on language implications—suggests that a variety of synaptic relationships figure in our processing of language and that they are at least unconscious if not subconscious. The Chomskyan linguistic argument for deep language structures underlying normal language expression corresponds to this modest litmus; to the theories of the transformationalists, who argue for such processing patterns and capabilities, may also be added the position of the stratificationalists and other corresponding paradigms. The problem for humor students is that part of our response to humor, irony, implication, allusion, nonsense rhyme, and a host of other technically identifiable minor forms of language humor may lie in relationships buried within the experiencer that are hard to externalize without seeming absurd. And indeed, perhaps this is why explanations of jokes appear so lame. As Kenneth Burke points out regarding literature generally, we must beware of the "tyranny of the informational."

Third, if the first level of humor is identified by a logo consisting of arrows pointing along a line, and the second identified as a synaptic branching, the third should probably be identified as a treelike diagram, similar to a management chart or genealogical family tree. This diagram represents the choices between and the merging of two opposites, or the choice between several possibilities. This is illustrated by a Vermont humorist's story that begins with a fellow who was visiting the state asylum to see his friend. This friend was a paranoid schizophrenic, which was bad in that he thought everyone was trying to kill him but good at least in that he did not feel entirely alone. As the two men walked around the grounds, a nurse trailed after them to make sure nothing set the patient off. When a bird, flying over, deposited a load of bird poop on the patient's head, the nurse grabbed his arm and said, "Don't move an inch; I'll run right into the building and get some toilet paper and take care of everything." As she ran off, the patient turned to his friend and said, "Now there goes a durn fool; by the time she gets back with that toilet paper, that bird'll be miles from here."[9] The story is wonderful. Choice making lies everywhere, first in the good news/bad news remark about the illness and then in the body of the story itself, where the divergent expectations are polar opposites. The humor here is not just lineal, nor is it synaptic; it is, rather, clearly informational humor based on the irony of the interpretations by the dramatic "character" who does the responding.

Fourth, cultural reinterpretations of events and experiences are the most obviously identifiable components of American humor in stories and anecdotes with obviously American settings, dialects, artifacts, and historical events. The ideograph that represents this best would be a circle representing the joke, with various circles coming off of it: each dependent circle would represent some part of the social context of the joke and contributes its social meaning and humor to the experiencer. Translations of American humor into foreign language have this particular problem to confront at every level, from the choice of individual words up to the layout of incidents and relationships. One illustration of social context as the basis of humor at the level of a one-liner occurs in a Petroleum Vesuvius Nasby letter to Mark Twain. Nasby declined to continue giving his lecture attacking slavery and the Confederacy, observing, "that lemon, our African brother, juicy as he was in his day, has been squeezed dry."[10] In this case, the more dimensions that are known, the funnier the remark gets. Nasby in persona was a rebel postmaster from "Confedrit X Roads, Kentucky." The irony of the "lemon" metaphor doubles and triples. The situation in 1869 was furthermore mixed, although Nasby's own particular goals for the freedman seemed to him to have been accomplished, or was this a marketing comment and evidence of resigned futility? Nasby was an uncompromising hater of slavery and therefore not skeptical toward the African brother or sister, although here he is being suggestively ironic about his own profit-making motivation to work that vein of public platform lecturing for profit.

Artemus Ward, Twain, and other literary comedians, even those opposing slavery and disunion, tended to be cool toward fiery abolitionism. Book after book of nineteenth-century literary comedy falls obviously into the category of socially critical humor. Twain's *The Innocents Abroad, Roughing It, Life on the Mississippi, The Gilded Age,* the three works that identified him as an American and a regionalist—all use social context as their mode of humor. *The Innocents Abroad,* published in 1869, remained Twain's best seller for years because of its application of a comic American vandal viewpoint to European artifacts usually approached with sanctimonious reverence. It was a viewpoint Artemus Ward had already adumbrated in his *Artemus Ward in London* letters (1867), these letters based in turn on P. T. Barnum's stance as an unabashed American showman—a role that infuriated English commentators. Ward's "London" letters, before becoming a book in 1867, were first admired in *Punch* in 1866 as American humor. One features an episode where a pragmatic London innkeeper jumps up at a seance and asks (regarding the spirit of Cromwell), "Is he dead?" Twain, in *The Innocents Abroad,* made it his theme for "the boys" when they viewed Egyptian mummies, Capuchin friars' bones, and finally Christopher Columbus's handwriting, but for Twain it becomes an American's joke expressing an American viewpoint, even though it began with Ward in England. Parson Brownlow's Civil War statement in *Parson Brownlow's Book*—that he intended to fight against secession until Hell froze over and then go on fighting on the ice—might be another example; this example contains an additional "balloon" beyond the lineal expansion, for the exaggeration displays depth of sentiment, as does Gertrude Stein's "A rose is a rose is a rose." (Stein, incidentally, clearly uses the first two levels of structural linguistic tactics to get to levels three, four, and five.)

A recent, and convincing, article on Mark Twain's "Whittier Dinner Speech" disputed the evidence of Twain's own recollection of the event and "contextualized" the burlesque that comprised the speech as a representation of conflicting Western and Eastern American cultural values, not merely a Westerner's naively awkward affront to Eastern gentility.[11] In this case, the superficial values of the speech parallel critically perceived deeper values. To some extent this may be modern theoretical critics' double-talk, but the ideas seemed to be discussed on multiple levels in the article, thus justifying the approach. Once the discussion gets this complex, however, one begins to sense how any monist theory is likely to fail. Marietta Holley's various volumes of humor, stories, and travel narratives, for instance, have proved almost unrecoverable because they are so oriented toward events of her historical moment.

Fifth, unidentified psychological components seem endemic to much humor, and certainly to sexual humor. In the case of sexual humor, one could say that the id, as assessed in writings like George Groddeck's *The Book of the It*, for example, is not accessible to much critical analysis. Feminist humor—"a woman without a man is like a fish without a bicycle"—can be gender humor but not sexual humor, or vice versa, as in the following crack between female musicians in one late-night joke fest: "What's better than roses on your piano? Tulips on your organ." Sexist jokes acceptable in the days of *Captain Billy's Whiz Bang* and the *Calgary Eye Opener*—where every secretary sat on her boss's lap or gave her boyfriend Hans a black eye and walked home, and where the only proper way to install an office secretary was to screw her on the desk—freeze audiences now. In various structured joke-telling sessions I have viewed over many years, one fact stands out. There is an inviolable Gresham's Law of sexual humor. Once sexual jokes enter into a joke-telling session, almost all other forms of humor are forced out. In part, this law may apply because sexual humor is indeed, as the material just cited suggests, an aggressive tool, venting tension or antagonism. Other eras have featured racy humor, but to what audiences was the humor exposed, and what psychometric dimensions would we apply to analyze its effect on the receiver?

To some extent this is also true of certain kinds of social humor. I think it unlikely that Twain's *Those Extraordinary Twins*, appearing as the second half of *Pudd'nhead Wilson* in the first and many subsequent editions, could get by any politically sensitive audience in these days of mandatory

wheelchair ramps and handicap-accessible bathrooms. The story is an intellectual exercise in humor relating to deformity and disadvantage. Some jokes
seem tasteless now unless understood as what they in fact are—an intellectual
exercise in constructing the grotesquerie they embody in words. Our response is as much visceral as intellectual. The visceral will always make up
a strong component of humor, and no less of American humor. Is there,
however, a secretive gynocentric estrogenic internality in women's humor
that sets it against an equally testosteronic external male humor? Why did
the pediatrician crack penis jokes with me after the birth and circumcision
of my son? None of the nurse-midwives cracked vagina jokes with my wife
after the birth of our daughters.

I have identified five levels of humor that one could address before
venturing very far into conventional theories. It is truly a chaos theorist's
playground. We know American humor is a dissenting reconstruction of
environment. All American tall tales do this work. Twain is a reformist and
reinventor from his earliest screeds to his last, late, dark manuscripts. Modern black humor, Jewish humor, and stand-up comedy all fit within this
fantasist's realm. Such humor caricatures the bigot. At its best it is the expression of positive democratic ideology: the assertion of the naïf that his
naïveté can be stronger than reality; idealism in the face of negativism and
fatalism. We see in it the egalitarian inner moral cognitions of the people
Walt Whitman called the Americans of all nations, and their optimism,
whether thought or felt, thrives as American humor.

Many sources of analysis of modern American humor and culture
remain underexplored: for instance, the great radio broadcasts of Jean Shep-
herd over WOR in the 1950s and 1960s, possibly unmatched as comic fantasy in modern American humor, existed well before Garrison Keillor attempted to raise the medium to an art form; and folkloric humor such as
that recorded in Paul Dickson's *The Official Explanations* and *The Official
Rules,* both published in paperback and hardcover editions by two publishers
in the 1980s but now, sadly, out of print. (Fitting here is a comment made
by a World War II pilot flying over the Pacific to radio contacts in Hawaii:
"We're lost, but we're making record time.") A variety of volumes by Alan
Dundes, Richard Dorson, B. A. Botkin, and Vance Randolph represent folk
sources, and an equally wide variety of works can be found representing
more consciously literary sources as well.

The most instructive way to illustrate the complexity of what is
being proposed here is to set in ideographic form the five different means
by which a response to a comic moment might occur:

1. Processing a sentence.

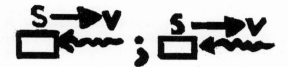

2. Synaptically connecting words and meanings.

3. Placing the given idea in juxtaposition with conflicting ideas.

4. Relating the social concept to other social ideologies, biases, and beliefs.

5. Allowing for nonverbal psycho-sexual impulses.

Using this schema as a tool for analysis brings into focus both the unlikelihood of a flat monist interpretation of a joke, comic sequence, or extended comic narrative, and the purpose of this book. Jokes by themselves and humor generally function at numerous complex, interrelated levels. A wide variety of inquiries are called for. Unlike the situation in many volumes of collected essays, the chapters presented here are not oriented toward a single agenda; rather, they suggest varied ways the humor specialist might work. Needless to say, exceptions and alternative directions exist, and it might be instructive to name some before launching into a brief summary of what the scholarship offered in this volume accomplishes. First, plenty of room remains for studies of major comic authors. Twain studies especially remain wide open for a variety of textual and contextual studies, partly because of the glacial revelation of new material involved in the Mark Twain Project's extended publishing schedule but also because of the shifting social and racial climate in America.[12] On the occasion of Twayne's publication, a few years ago, of the complete edition of Washington Irving's works, scholars at the national convention of the Modern Language Association held what amounted to a wake over the seemingly moribund canon of this genteel white male. Directly thereafter came the publication of Jeffrey Rubin-Dworsky's *Adrift in the Old World: The Psychological Pilgrimage of Washington Irving* (Chicago: University of Chicago Press, 1989), a volume that presented a new biographical-cultural slant on Irving. Such occurrences remind us that the case on Irving, and a wide array of American popular humorists, is far from closed. "Rip Van Winkle" today is not only an intriguing story but a media experience by America's foremost modern manipulator of animated comic visual art: Walt Disney.

Humor moves up and down scales of acceptance, sometimes considered high literature and sometimes low, as Steven Gale suggests. Considerable room for reinterpretation exists. Nor will those contextualizers now working on a redemption of nineteenth-century sentimental literature for serious study be any more likely to abandon Irving than the Fireside Poets who, although now out of favor, dominated American poetry for a century and reigned supreme in the Northeast and Midwest as recently as the 1950s. Longfellow's "Hiawatha" was parodied mercilessly in 1856 and is still parodied today. What power awakens this parodic instinct, and what is its meaning? I am hesitant to identify other writers as at commensurate level with Twain and Irving, although someday Woody Allen's dramatic comedy may approach that estimation. This is not to imply disrespect to other comic writers. Twain and Irving rightfully stand alone, and it is appropriate that some of the scholars whose work appears in this volume take Twain as a reference point in discussing other writers. How will Mike Judge's canon, predominantly oral and visual for the medium of television, be equated with Garrison Keillor's, predominantly oral and written, and oriented toward radio and print; or with *New Yorker* humor, a *milieu* by itself?

A vast array of writers and techniques continue to be studied heavily. These include the "southwestern humorists." G. W. Harris's Sut Lovingood (a collection of essays on Harris and the Lovingood papers was published in 1996 by The University of Alabama Press), J. J. Hooper's Simon Suggs (a new edition appeared as recently as 1993, also from The University of Alabama Press), and other Southwesterners of varying levels of quality offer ongoing problems of interpretation, and new writers are being added to the tradition.[13] Among Northeastern humorists, Paulding and a host of lesser writers remain untouched, and Northeastern satiric journals published before and after the Civil War are barely even opened as a reference, in spite of their lively humor.[14] P. T. Barnum has garnered some attention: a detailed biography by A. H. Saxon and a collection of his letters appeared recently, and a fine book by Neil Harris is now two decades old. However, George Burnham, P. T. Barnum's competitor, is unexplored as a practitioner of the Northeastern leg-pull; and others, both female—now increasingly studied by feminist critics developing the female legacy—and male, could be cited.[15]

One incident suggests how perspectives change. In 1981 Carl Bode edited for the Penguin American Library an edition of Barnum's *Struggles*, which, astonishingly, deleted Barnum's important speech to the Connecticut legislature in 1867 demanding equal rights, education, and the vote for African-American males in Connecticut. The speech is a masterpiece of humor and ethics in the Northeastern perspective and includes a racial viewpoint apparently not seen as important in 1981. To most students of literature, Barnum does not even appear to be a humorist.

Similar discontinuity is obvious in the study of humor periodicals. The *New Yorker* continues to be studied, but not *Ballyhoo*—which permanently changed the face of American comic magazines in the 1930s—*Jim Jam Jems,* or *Capt. Billy's Whiz Bang,* which challenged the nation's social and sexual mores in the 1910s and 1920s but overcame various legal challenges to die of inaction and attrition. At the onset of the twenty-first century, new forces broaden this study, reaching out to film, radio, television, and now the computer and the Internet. The opening essays in this collection focused on a specific phenomenon of low humor: television's *Beavis and Butt-head,* controversial to the point of being blamed for inciting criminal acts.

Studies of major authors—such as Poe and Wharton—who are not normally given extended consideration as humorists per se help make clear that humor is an important genre in the writings of many major American authors. These studies may also serve as reminders that humor occupies an exceptionally important place in American culture as distinct from a number of other world cultures, although by no means all. Emily Dickinson, F. Scott Fitzgerald, Faulkner, Hemingway (as an ironist), James, Melville, Hawthorne, and later writers all use humor to sufficient extent that these authors could be subjects of generic studies; Barth, Bellow, Malamud, Roth, Updike, and onward, comfortably fit in the humorist realm. American scholarship may not as yet be ready for "Theodore Dreiser's Humor: Irony as Fantasy," but even the most serious American writers sometimes tilt in that direction.

One of the most salient observations made at the American Literature Association–sponsored 1994 Cancun Conference on American Humor and Mark Twain Studies was by Alita Kelley, who works primarily translating comic writers from Spanish to English. Kelley noted that Cervantes is seldom talked of in Spanish scholarship as a humorist and that his humor is treated more as an embarrassing indiscretion than as a central focus of exploration. Kelley's observation about a major non-American writer relates also to the discussion of humor's importance interculturally. We know, for example, from James Papp's study of translations of *Adventures of Huckleberry Finn* into Slovak that black and poor white dialect speech from American novels may read far differently when rendered as classical Slovak contrasting Gypsy dialect.[16] American humor may travel far differently than we presume; few if any full-scale studies have been devoted to this subject, vital as it is to our projection of American ideals to other nations. In Gujarat, India, formal adults, noticing someone who smiles as much as a typical friendly American, will ask one another, "Why is he grinning like a monkey?" Indeed, Ronald Reagan started one of his most important presidential addresses with a joke.

Humor occupies a central place in American discourse. Both major and minor authors become potentially valuable in understanding the "American" way of thinking—past, present, and future. By the next century, studies of humor will be substantially broadened—using the academic analyst's tools—beyond the belletristic. The success of this enterprise will tell us much about our national beliefs.

Notes

1. For example, the major studies of American humor published in the period 1930–1970 revolved heavily around the various schools of frontier humor. Walter Blair's *Native American Humor* (1937), to which all later studies are indebted, is the first significant work of interest. This volume is updated by Walter Blair and Hamlin Hill's *America's Humor, From Poor Richard to Doonesbury* (1978). Blair's *Horse Sense in American Humor* (1942)

is worth mentioning, as are his other works. Also worthwhile are Jennette Tandy's *Crackerbox Philosophers in American Humor and Satire* (1925) and Constance Rourke's seminal *American Humor: A Study of the National Character* (1931). To this list might be added, among many others not named, two later important surveys: Jesse Bier's *The Rise and Fall of American Humor* (1968) and Nancy Walker and Zita Dresner's *Redressing the Balance: American Women's Literary Humor from Colonial Times to the 1980s* (1988).

2. Commercial publication of American humor is strong and varied, encompassing not only major American houses, including Norton, Random House, and Holt, but also a variety of smaller presses like Robert Wechsler's Catbird Press. Among for-profit publishers, Garland Press, Greenwood Press, and Gale have all found significant markets for humor studies, such as Stanley Trachtenberg's two-volume *American Humorists, 1800–1950* (1982), made up of biographical articles. University presses, including those of the universities of Alabama, Georgia, and Texas, along with Wayne State University and the University of Mississippi, are finding significant publishing opportunities, both in neglected texts by unrecognized humorists and in cultural resources. In fact, the latter two presses each publish a series of works on humor. The subject matter even encompasses American business—for example, Alan Dundes and Carl Pagter's collection of current business ephemera, *When You're Up to Your Ass in Alligators . . . More Urban Folklore from the Paperwork Empire* (1987), one of several collections by Dundes along these lines.

3. So many collections of Southwestern humorists have appeared over the years that a comprehensive listing might not be useful here, but five general studies and collections deserve mention: Hennig Cohen and William Dillingham's *The Humor of the Old Southwest* (1975), M. Thomas Inge's *The Frontier Humorists* (1975), Wade Hall's *The Smiling Phoenix* (1965), Franklin Meine's *Tall Tales of the Southwest* (1937), and Arthur Palmer Hudson's *Humor of the Old Deep South* (1936). It should be understood that this necessarily truncates a long and distinguished list that includes other collections and anthologies, as well as individual works. *Roy Blount's Book of Southern Humor* (1994) suggests that the tradition continues as a moneymaking publishing venture, with African Americans and literary humorists now admitted to full parity with frontier dwellers.

4. Robert Bryan and Marshall Dodge, *Bert and I—and Other Stories from Down East* (recorded at Yale and distributed by Records, Inc., Boston, 1958).

5. Knight used the phrase on an NBC talk show in 1988 and then tried to get the comment expunged from the interview. He later explained that he meant the word "rape" to mean merely something over which you

have no control. Although the context suggests his explanation truthfully reflected his intent, it hardly satisfied critics, and in fact indicates his lack of sensitivity to the topic of rape itself. Clayton Williams uttered the same words in 1990 at a time when he had a double-digit lead in the Texas gubernatorial primary race against Ann Richards. Richards won and Williams's statement and another much like it are credited as a significant component of his defeat.

6. Butz, Secretary of Agriculture under both Nixon and Ford, "joked" to John W. Dean III in the back of a plane headed to California that all "coloreds" wanted was. . . . On second thought, you will have to find it for yourself in *Facts on File*, but it is certainly one of the most condensed statements of racial stereotypes in the annals of American bigotry—personal, sexual, and scatalogical, all in the space of about eleven words.

7. Both books were published by the University of Mississippi Press under the editorship of and with introductions by M. Thomas Inge in 1993.

8. Cameron Nickels, *New England Humor: From the Revolutionary War to the Civil War* (1993); Daniel Royot, *L'humour americain, des puritains aux yankees* (1980); Winifred Morgan, *An American Icon: Brother Jonathan and American Identity* (1980). The emphasis on lawless exaggeration as a defining medium for American humor was urged strongly by the *North British Review* 33 (November 1860), 247–60, but was pushed heavily by other British analysts of the decade, and thereafter, with "lawless" sometimes referring not to exaggeration as an intensifying adjective but rather having its own meaning, relating to corrupt Yankee ethics.

9. Alan Foley, *Vermont Wit, Humor, Wisdom* (Northfield, VT: Green Mountain Records, 1980), GMR-1054, recording.

10. Locke wrote this to Twain on 14 July 1869, commenting on the passage of the fifteenth amendment, which satisfied Nasby's long and uncompromising demand for equal rights for black and white Americans. This comment is reprinted with further text in *Mark Twain's Letters: Volume 3, 1869*, edited by Victor Fischer and Michael B. Frank (1992), 258, n. 6. Further useful information on Nasby in this volume expands the context even more. Those wishing to fill in the background of Nasby's involvement as an American humorist with American culture and Mark Twain should consult John M. Harrison's *The Man Who Made Nasby, David Ross Locke* (1969) and David E. E. Sloane's *Mark Twain as a Literary Comedian* (1979).

11. Harold K. Bush, Jr., in his article "The Mythic Struggle Between East and West: Mark Twain's Speech at Whittier's 70th Birthday Celebration and W. D. Howells' *A Chance Acquaintance*," *American Literary Realism, 1870–1910* 27:2 (winter 1995), 53–73, advances this argument.

12. See, for example, the annual *American Literary Scholarship* analytic bibliography from Duke University Press, or David E. E. Sloane and Michael Kiskis, "Prospects for the Study of Mark Twain," in *Prospects for American Literary Study*, ed. Richard Koplay (Syracuse: Syracuse University Press, 1997).

13. David Parker's *Alias Bill Arp* (1991); Jake Mitchell and Robert Wilton Burton's *De Remnant Truth: The Tales of Jake Mitchell and Robert Wilton Barr* (1991); Johnson Jones Hooper's *Adventures of Captain Simon Suggs* (1993); and *Sut Lovingood's Nat'ral Born Yarnspinner: Essays on George Washington Harris* (1996), edited by M. Thomas Inge and James Caron, are only some of the texts that show this area to be lively in the 1990s.

14. David E. E. Sloane, *American Humor Magazines and Comic Periodicals* (Westport, CT: Greenwood Press, 1986) lists over two hundred American humor magazines and newspapers on a timeline that stretches from 1765 to 1985. Many the publications, even though frequently available in various microprint and microfilm editions, remain unstudied, either in terms of their own value or as a context for other writers and editors from a particular period.

15. I intended *The Literary Humor of the Urban Northeast, 1830–1890* (1982) to be a major broadside in the battle to identify Northeastern humor as a school, but in retrospect it seems to have been scarcely a popgun shot. It remains to be seen if regions other than the entrenched Southwest will gain a similar identifiable entity for the purpose of "humor studies." The books by Nickels, Royot, and Morgan at least support the Yankee-Knickerbocker phase of the Northeastern regionalist position.

16. James R. Papp, "Mark Twain as a Slovak: The Problem of Translation," Mark Twain Suite Reading, National Convention of the Modern Language Association, 28 December 1994.

Works Cited

American Literary Scholarship/Annual. Durham, NC: Duke University Press, annual since 1963.

Bier, Jesse. *The Rise and Fall of American Humor.* New York: Holt, Rinehart and Winston, 1968.

Blair, Walter. *Native American Humor.* New York: American Book Company, 1937.

———. *Horse Sense in American Humor.* Chicago: University of Chicago Press, 1942.

Blair, Walter, and Hamlin Hill. *America's Humor: From Poor Richard to Doonesbury.* New York: Oxford University Press, 1978.

Blount, Roy, Jr. *Roy Blount's Book of Southern Humor.* New York: W. W. Norton, 1994.

Bryan, Robert, and Marshall Dodge. *Bert and I—and Other Stories from Down East.* Boston: Records, 1958.

Bush, Harold K., Jr. "The Mythic Struggle Between East and West: Mark Twain's Speech at Whittier's 70th Birthday Celebration and W. D. Howells' *A Chance Acquaintance.*" *American Literary Realism, 1870–1910* 27:2 (winter 1995), 53–73.

Caron, James E., and M. Thomas Inge. *Sut Lovingood's Nat'ral Born Yarn-spinner: Essays on George Washington Harris.* Tuscaloosa: University of Alabama Press, 1996.

Cohen, Hennig, and William Dillingham. *The Humor of the Old Southwest.* Athens: Georgia University Press, 1975.

Dundes, Alan, and Carl Pagter. *When You're Up to Your Ass in Alligators . . . More Urban Folklore from the Paperwork Empire.* Detroit: Wayne State University Press, 1987.

Foley, Alan. *Vermont Wit, Humor, Wisdom.* Northfield, VT: Green Mountain Records, 1980. Recording.

Hall, Wade. *The Smiling Phoenix.* Gainesville: University of Florida Press, 1965.

Harrington, Oliver. *Dark Laughter,* edited and with an introduction by M. Thomas Inge. Jackson: University Press of Mississippi, 1993.

———. *Why I Left America,* edited and with an introduction by M. Thomas Inge. Jackson: University Press of Mississippi, 1993.

Harrison, John M. *The Man Who Made Nasby, David Ross Locke.* Chapel Hill: University of North Carolina Press, 1969.

Hooper, Johnson Jones. *Adventures of Captain Simon Suggs,* edited and with an introduction by Johanna Nicol Shields. 1845. Tuscaloosa: University of Alabama Press, 1993.

Hudson, Arthur Palmer. *Humor of the Old Deep South.* New York: Macmillan, 1936.

Inge, M. Thomas. *The Frontier Humorists.* Hamden, CT: Archon Books, 1975.

Meine, Franklin. *Tall Tales of the Southwest: An Anthology of Southern and Southwestern Humor: 1830–1860.* New York: Alfred A. Knopf, Inc., 1937.

Mitchell, Jake, and Robert Wilton Burton. *De Remnant Truth: The Tales of Jake Mitchell and Robert Wilton Burton.* Tuscaloosa: University of Alabama Press, 1991.

Morgan, Winifred. *An American Icon: Brother Jonathan and American Identity.* Newark: University of Delaware Press, 1980.

Nickels, Cameron. *New England Humor: From the Revolutionary War to the Civil War.* Knoxville: University of Tennessee Press, 1993.

North British Review 33 (November 1860), 247–60.

Papp, James R. "Mark Twain as a Slovak: The Problem of Translation." Mark Twain Suite Reading, National Convention of the Modern Language Association, 28 December 1994.

Parker, David B. *Alias Bill Arp: Charles Henry Smith and the South's "Goodly Heritage."* Athens: University of Georgia Press, 1991.

Rourke, Constance. *American Humor: A Study of the National Character.* New York: Harcourt, Brace, 1931.

Royot, Daniel. *L'humour americain, des puritains aux yankees.* Lyons, France: Presses Universitaires de Lyon, 1980.

Rubin-Dworsky, Jeffrey. *Adrift in the Old World: The Psychological Pilgrimage of Washington Irving.* Chicago: University of Chicago Press, 1989.

Sloane, David E. E. *American Humor Magazines and Comic Periodicals.* Westport, CT: Greenwood, 1986.

———. *The Literary Humor of the Urban Northeast, 1830–1890.* Baton Rouge: Louisiana State University Press, 1982.

———. *Mark Twain as a Literary Comedian.* Baton Rouge: Louisiana State University Press, 1979.

Sloane, David E. E., and Michael Kiskis. "Prospects for the Study of Mark Twain." In *Prospects for American Literary Study,* ed. Richard Koplay. Syracuse, NY: Syracuse University Press, 1997.

Tandy, Jennette. *Crackerbox Philosophers in American Humor and Satire.* New York: Columbia University Press, 1925.

Trachtenberg, Stanley, ed. *American Humorists, 1800–1950, Part I* [and *Part II*]. 2 vols. *Dictionary of Literary Biography,* vol. 11. Detroit: Gale Research, 1982.

Twain, Mark. *Mark Twain's Letters: Volume 3, 1869.* Ed. Victor Fischer and Michael B. Frank. Berkeley: University of California Press, 1992.

Walker, Nancy, and Zita Dresner. *Redressing the Balance: American Women's Literary Humor from Colonial Times to the 1980s.* Jackson: University Press of Mississippi, 1988.

Contributors

Lawrence I. Berkove is professor of English and director of the American Studies Program at the University of Michigan at Dearborn. Within his specialized field of American literature of the late nineteenth and early twentieth centuries, he has published extensively, most particularly on Twain, Bierce, and Dan De Quille, and other Comstock authors.

Louis J. Budd is James B. Duke Professor Emeritus at Duke University. He is the author of *Mark Twain: Social Philosopher* (1962) and *Our Mark Twain: The Making of His Public Personality* (1983), as well as hundreds of other articles, papers, and collections of Twain materials that illuminate present-day Twain scholarship.

Gregg Camfield is assistant professor of English at the University of the Pacific, specializing in American literature as well as humor studies. His publications include *Sentimental Twain: Samuel Clemens in the Maze of Moral Philosophy* (1994) and *Necessary Madness: The Humor of Domesticity in Nineteenth-Century American Literature* (1997). He is currently writing *The Oxford Reader's Companion to Mark Twain*.

Steven H. Gale is the University Endowed Chair in the Humanities at Kentucky State University. He has published fifteen books and over one hundred articles in international scholarly journals. His monographs include three volumes on S. J. Perelman, the *Encyclopedia of American Humorists* (1988), and the *Encyclopedia of British Humorists* (1996), as well as works on Harold Pinter, drama, film, and African folktales, and creative pieces. The founding president of the Harold Pinter Society, Gale is also the founding coeditor of the *Pinter Review: Annual Essays* and the general editor of Garland's "Studies in Humor" series.

Don Graham is J. Frank Dobie Regents Professor of American and English Literature at the University of Texas in Austin. His books include *The Fiction of Frank Norris: The Aesthetic Contest* (1979), *Cowboys and Cadillacs: How Hollywood Looks at Texas* (1983), *Texas: A Literary Portrait* (1985), and *No Name on the Bullet: A Biography of Audie Murphy* (1989). *Texas on My Mind: Selected Essays* will be published by TCU Press in 1998. Graham is currently at work on a study of the Australian writer Michael Wilding.

Thomas Grant is a professor of English at the University of Hartford. He has authored a book on the comedies of George Chapman, many articles on American humorists and comic magazines, and articles on American drama and Western film.

Alita Kelley, since 1992 assistant professor of Spanish and French at Pennsylvania State University in Delaware County, has been a commercial and literary translator for over twenty years. Her own poetry and some of her other writings also appear under the name C. A. de Lomellini.

Holger Kersten is assistant professor in the English department at the University of Kiel, Germany. His Ph.D. thesis was published in German as "From Hannibal to Heidelberg: Mark Twain and the Germans" (1993). He has published articles on Mark Twain and Stephen Crane and is working on a project dealing with humorous dialect texts in American literature.

Karen L. Kilcup is associate professor of American literature at the University of North Carolina at Greensboro and was recently named Dorothy M. Healy Visiting Professor of American Studies at Westbrook College. She is the author and editor of many publications on nineteenth- and early-twentieth-century American literature, including "'I like a woman to be a woman': Theorizing Gender in the Humor of Stowe and Greene," "Reading Trickster; or, Theoretical Reservations and a Seneca Tale," and *Nineteenth-Century American Women Writers: An Anthology* (1996).

David G. Lott is assistant professor of English composition and literature at Montgomery College, in Maryland. He has reviewed, presented, or published work on American sports journalism for the American Literature Association, the American Culture Association, the Sport Literature Association, and the Center for U.S. Studies at Essex University, in the United Kingdom.

James R. Papp is Assistant Director of English Programs at the Modern Language Association. He was formerly a visiting fellow at the Hungarian Institute of Educational Research in Budapest after teaching British and American studies for three years at Comenius University, in Bratislava. He received his Ph.D. from UCLA in 1992, studying cognitive, rhetorical, and sociopolitical approaches to parody.

David E. E. Sloane, professor of English at the University of New Haven, is past president of the Mark Twain Circle and the American Humor Studies Association. He received his doctorate from Duke University in 1970 and has published *Mark Twain as a Literary Comedian* (1979), *The Literary Humor of the Urban Northeast, 1830–1890* (1982), *American Humor Magazines and Comic Periodicals* (1987), *Adventures of Huckleberry Finn: American Comic Vision* (1988), and *Mark Twain's Humor: Critical Essays* (1992), among other books and articles on humor, literature, applied linguistics, and business writing.

Judy Sneller is associate professor of English at the South Dakota School of Mines and Technology, Rapid City, South Dakota, where she teaches technical communications and American Literature. She has published several essays on women's humor, with special attention to New Orleans writers Ruth McEnery Stuart, Mollie Moore Davis, and Grace King.

Donald Barlow Stauffer is an emeritus professor at the State University of New York at Albany. He is the author of *A Short History of American Poetry* and numerous essays on Poe and Whitman. He has taught at Beijing University, Seoul National University (Fulbright)—as a Fulbright scholar—and the University of Würzburg.

Douglas Sun is an assistant professor of English at the California State University at Los Angeles. He received his Ph.D. from the University of Chicago and has published articles and delivered lectures on James Thurber, Tom Wolfe, and George Plimpton.

David Tomlinson is a professor of English at the United States Naval Academy in Annapolis, Maryland, where he has taught since 1970. He has served as chair of the academy's English department and as president of the Maryland Association of Departments of English.

Siva Vaidhyanathan is a doctoral candidate and assistant instructor in American studies at the University of Texas at Austin, where he teaches courses in Asian-American studies. He has researched African-American humorists from Booker T. Washington to George Schuyler to Richard Pryor. He is working on a cultural history of intellectual property from Mark Twain to 2 Live Crew.

Nancy A. Walker is professor of English at Vanderbilt University. She has published widely on American women's humor, including the book *A Very Serious Thing: Women's Humor and American Culture* (1988). Her most recent book is *The Disobedient Writer: Women and the Narrative Tradition* (1995). She is currently editing a collection of essays on American humor and working on a study of American women's magazines of the 1940s and 1950s.

Michele S. Ware is visiting assistant professor of English at Wake Forest University, where she teaches American literature. She is currently working on a manuscript about aesthetics and artists in Edith Wharton's short fiction. Her scholarly interests include the American short story and American women's political poetry.

Index